FOR COD & COUNTRY

BARTON SEAVER

STERLING EPICURE
New York

STERLING EPICURE
New York

An Imprint of Sterling Publishing
387 Park Avenue South
New York, NY 10016

4 6 8 10 9 7 5 3

Published by Sterling Publishing Co., Inc.
387 Park Avenue South, New York, NY 10016
© 2011 by Barton Seaver
Distributed in Canada by Sterling Publishing
C/o Canadian Manda Group, 165 Dufferin Street
Toronto, Ontario, Canada M6K 3H6
Distributed in the United Kingdom by GMC Distribution Services
Castle Place, 166 High Street, Lewes, East Sussex, England BN7 1XU
Distributed in Australia by Capricorn Link (Australia) Pty. Ltd.
P.O. Box 704, Windsor, NSW 2756, Australia

Sterling ISBN 978-1-4027-7775-2
Sodexo edition ISBN 978-1-4549-0603-2

All images © Katie Stoops
Image on p. 42 courtesy of MSC/J. Simpson

For information about custom editions, special sales, premium and
corporate purchases, please contact Sterling Special Sales Department
at 800-805-5489 or specialsales@sterlingpublishing.com.

Dedicated to my dad and Chef Corky Clark, the two best fish cooks I know.

A special thanks to Rick Moonen, for setting the sustainable stage for chefs all over the globe, and to David Scribner, for giving me a glimpse into his crazy world.

Contents

Delicious Is the New Environmentalism

"In our quest for food we begin to find our place within the systems of the world." —John Hersey wrote that in his fantastic book *Blues.* I have always loved that quote because it accurately acknowledges that we are not sovereign over our resources but rather a part of the world that supports us. We *are* because the world supports us.

We have forgotten that, and we are paying the consequences. We have taken too much sea life from the oceans, eaten too many of the creatures that make up the intricate network of life. We have even taken and needlessly wasted creatures we did not want in the form of bycatch. In the process of wasting our resources, we have destroyed jobs. We have let whole communities fail and disappear, as is the case in New England and the Chesapeake. We have ravaged the oceans in search of food and are now discovering that our place in the world's systems is in jeopardy.

This is a heavy way to start a book about cooking fish. Fish are living and contributing members of an ecosystem. When a fish meets a person, it becomes seafood. Yet we are so indignant in our approach to the ocean that we fail to understand that fish are valuable as fish, not just as seafood.

But we do have a chance to eat our way back to healthy oceans. A lot has been made of the term "sustainable seafood," which I am happy to see has gained such traction in the marketplace. But the idea

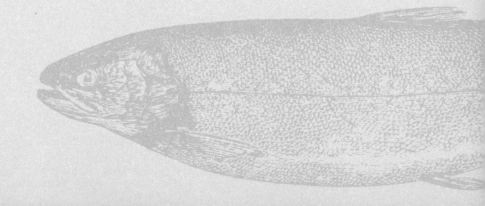

behind sustaining our resources is a little misguided. We have depleted them to the point where we have to restore them before they can be ably maintained. What we think of as a healthy fishery is often a mere shadow of what it historically was. We operate with an understanding of a natural world that has already been heavily affected by humans.

So why eat seafood at all, you might ask? Because if we don't, then we will lose a vital and necessary part of our diet. We would put even more hardworking communities out of work. We would lose control over the fisheries that we do have a chance to manage well. We would lose our chance to encourage the restoration of ecosystems. The compelling narrative of conservation is a story of responsible consumption.

The answer is to support the best fisheries we have access to and to provide incentive to those lagging behind to get better. The answer is to eat smaller portions of seafood—and *many* more vegetables.

Celebrate seafood for what it is, and understand that it was once sea life. There are delicious options you can serve your family that actually help to restore ecosystems. Enjoy the recipes that follow. Do some research into the impact our food choices have on the oceans. And eat with joy so that we may continue to partake in the bounty of the seas. You can save the world by eating an oyster, so get to it.

That's right, environmentalism on the half shell with a bottle of Tabasco® and a six-pack of beer. Count me in!

How I Cook

I started cooking when I was a little boy. Both of my parents had busy schedules and hustled about trying to make it all work. They were great parents, but, more important to this story, they were great cooks, too—and intrepid ones.

My mom largely took care of the slow-cooked dishes that filled the house with their aromas. One of her dishes that I remember best is stuffed grape leaves. She would prepare the filling, then spend hours rolling each little delicious package and layering them into the largest pot we had. Sometimes she would cajole me or my brother into helping. My mom also would make vats of curry, one of which once spilled in the trunk of our Volvo station wagon, forever etching the story, and the smell, into our family history. Thanksgiving and other holidays were an opportunity to make everything from scratch. My brother and I still talk about the fruitcake my mother made every year. She would set the fruit to macerate in brandy in October, then bake the cakes just in time for the holidays . . . not that anyone in our family actually ate them.

My father would often cook weeknight suppers in his work clothes, his tie off. We had a collection of aprons that he kept behind the door. My favorite was a gray one that made him look like a train conductor. To me, Dad was the short-order cook of the family, churning out nutritious and delicious meals in no time. But he had his adventurous side as well. Tortillas were made from scratch for taco night. My brother and I were always hounding him to make one of his famous stir-fry wok concoctions. Dad would very occasionally have a Glenfiddich Scotch while he cooked, and those were the meals I remember liking the most. I never asked whether he poured the drink because he'd had a good day or a bad one. But on those days when he was sipping a Scotch, Dad seemed to use cooking to remember what life was supposed to be all about. He would kick back and enjoy the process and then, at the table, the results.

My first contribution to the table was the salad dressing. I can't quite imagine why they put up with my creations, which were just wrong. I had this idea in my head that a salad was a term that meant "lettuce swimming in vinegar." To this potent bath, I would add further punishment in the form of soy sauce, mustard powder, and a smattering of every dried herb we had. I think my dad was waiting me out, or waiting till we ran out of vinegar, which never happened.

What I remember the most about my dad's cooking, and what my friends remember too, was his ability to cook seafood. We would host gatherings at which Dad cooked soft-shell crabs that made everyone swoon. It was always one of the best meals of the year, as it usually included the summer's first corn and tomatoes. We would also hand churn peach ice cream in the backyard for dessert. Sounds like a fairy tale, but it's what happened when Dad turned his full attention to a meal. Then there was a night off the coast of Long Island when I found a spot for flounder and kept hauling them in. Dad was busy in the small galley kitchen of the boat, filleting and sautéing as fast as he could. The results were simple and stunning. And my lasting memory of that meal (fish + lemon + butter + heat = delicious) is the reason I do what I do today.

> And my lasting memory of that meal,
> fish+lemon+butter+heat = delicious,
> is the reason I do what I do today.

There were the trips to the fish market and clamming adventures and pick-your-own-fruit farm weekends that always resulted in pie for the next day's breakfast. In fact, it was while driving south on I-95, after I decided that college wasn't the right fit for me, that Dad asked if I had ever considered cooking professionally.

Understand Your Ingredients

Fast-forward not too many years after that to the cold fish kitchen at the Culinary Institute of America. Chef Corky Clark was berating our class for not having been able to answer a question on the previous night's homework: "Why do you add the paprika to the butter in the goulash?" It amazed me that this chef, this puzzlingly raving man, cared so much that it hadn't occurred to any of us that paprika's flavor was fat soluble and needed to be introduced through the butter. I decided that afternoon that I wanted to work for him. I had met lots of people in my life who thought they knew better or thought they were always right. **Here was a man who *did* know better— he knew more than anybody.**

It wasn't the paprika that was so important to Chef Clark. It was something larger—and smaller—at the same time. It was the importance of starting at the beginning. Of looking at every ingredient, understanding its properties, its

nature, its flavor, and what purpose it might have on the plate. While I worked for him, Chef Clark must have brought in every species of fish that was available on the East Coast, and then some. I saw well over a hundred species, and every other day we would look at whatever came off the docks, then fillet it, sauté it, cure it, or smoke it. By doing this, I learned how to appreciate the myriad ways in which seafood presents itself. I learned that every salmon tastes different. Not just king salmon versus sockeye salmon, but this king salmon versus the one next to it. The important lesson I learned from Chef Clark is that if you don't start at the beginning then you will never know what you are working with. He instilled in me the drive to get back to the source and to approach ingredients at their most basic level.

The Flavor of Fresh

In my first job as an executive chef, I began purchasing locally produced vegetables and meat from a couple of small farms that were already supplying several other chefs in Washington, D.C. The flavors were a revelation. The carrots were sweeter, the lettuce crisper and full of life. The dishes in which those ingredients were used really stood out, but not because of my efforts. **When you have great ingredients, the easiest and best thing to do is to let them shine.** I began to realize that, more often than not, I was complicating dishes, using too many ingredients or combinations that were forced. I began to develop confidence in the products I was buying. And I began to develop confidence in myself.

Being a chef is no easy task. Aside from the ridiculous hours, it is a profession in which you are judged from a uniquely subjective viewpoint, and on every dish. I, like most young chefs, initially thought that the best ingredient on the plate was me, that through my manipulation and effort, I was going to make plates that wowed. But as I tasted the produce that was being brought to my kitchen, I began to understand that the flavor of an unadorned, summer-ripe tomato would never be bested, not even by my greatest efforts. That's when I learned to step back a little, to take myself off the plate. And by doing so, cooking became easier. I then understood that my role was to taste the ingredients, come up with intelligent and supportive pairings, and do only what was necessary to get those flavors to the plate.

As a result, my food has gotten a lot simpler. It has fewer ingredients, and a happy by-product is that it's easier to manage and to execute correctly on a busy night. I've developed techniques to coax the most flavor out of the few ingredients I use. I now really apply what Chef Clark taught me. In short, my food has gotten better. I am comfortable with what I serve. It feels right to me, homey but still sufficiently sophisticated for a restaurant audience. After years of slow-simmered veal stocks, of immersion in the latest techniques of avant-garde cuisine, of outright misguided ego, I am cooking food that I know—the food I grew up with. These are the flavors I have known since childhood. In short, I am cooking an updated version of my dad's cuisine. But even with training and some good advice along the way, I still like a good punch of vinegar in my salads.

Brining

A long time ago, I was introduced to the idea of brining a chicken before roasting it. The stark and shocking difference that it made to the quality of the meat was an eye-opening moment for me as a cook. I have since brined every piece of chicken I cook, and I have taken this technique further, to include presalting or brining nearly every protein—yes, that includes seafood—that passes through my kitchen. Brining is very important to all the recipes in this book and it is one of the things that sets apart my fish cooking from others. See page 249 for details.

It's More Than a Meal

I expect a lot from food. I expect it to yield good health and joy and to be a cause for bringing together family and building an understanding of our place in a wider community. I also expect to have fun—both when I cook and when I sit down to eat. **Cooking, as my dad well knew, is a way to make life better.** It should be stress free. I try to reflect that in my own style of cooking.

What do I look for in a meal? For health, I start with wholesome ingredients. For joy, I use tasty ingredients like butter and salt, but in moderation. For family, I work hard to make my recipes easy to prepare. Dinner shouldn't be a train wreck of competing interests and you should be able to sit down at the table ready to enjoy the company of those you love most. For community, we start at the beginning, just as Chef Clark taught. Think not only of how an ingredient might affect you, but consider also the often far-flung connections that food creates for the global community.

Butter Is the Devil

Okay, now that I have your attention, I'd like to retract that statement. I agree that we need to reduce fat in our diet, but demonizing it isn't the answer. Our ubiquitous use and unknowing consumption of fat are the problems. We have become so accustomed to its almost invisible presence that **we don't recognize how great an ingredient it can be when brought front and center and used with confidence.** I use fat in many of my recipes, but I use it conspicuously, topping a fillet with a finishing pat of anchovy butter, for example. The butter, as it slowly melts from the heat of the fillet, gives off a fragrant aroma that is at once nutty and sweet, plus there's the wonderful visual appeal. That's what I call sexy fat. The same goes for olive oil drizzled over char-

grilled kale so that all the fruity and grassy aromas of the gently warmed oil waft off the plate. **To me that is a good use of calories.**

And consider this. If a small amount of butter makes broccoli taste good to you and your kids, and it gets that broccoli into your mouths, then that fat is probably a healthful use of calories. Food is meant to be enjoyed, but it should also sustain us. What I'm saying is, find the balance. Spend some money on a great-tasting olive oil. Buy a high-quality butter from a local dairy that makes you sigh with happiness when you taste it. Then use small amounts of each to great effect in the dishes you prepare.

Salt to Taste . . . A Brief Love Story

"Salt to taste" is one of those ideas that need some explaining. Chefs are in love with salt. We brine things to flavor and moisten them. We come up with flavored salts to accent our dishes. We fall prey to what we call "sexy salts," such as the big, beautiful flakes of Maldon sea salt or the hyper-colored red Hawaiian sea salt or Himalayan pink rock salt. We are not afraid to add salt, but we also understand that it's all about balance. For some dishes, we want the salt itself to come forward, but in most cases salt's role is to enhance the other flavors in the preparation.

Home cooks seem to have a love/hate relationship with salt. They either love it too much and add so much that every dish is distinctly salty or they don't use it at all. The latter case could be because they or someone in the family needs to moderate sodium intake for health reasons or because they've heard so much negative information about sodium. But I have a feeling that it is simply because they've never learned how to use salt appropriately.

A lot of recipes call for salt "to taste." This phrase acknowledges the fact that people's tastes are different. What is salty to one is underseasoned to another. In my recipes, when I say salt "to taste," I mean salt the dish to the point that it tastes great to you—not until it tastes salty. But I would ask that you push yourself to experiment. Try this: keep seasoning a small part of a dish until it tastes too salty, measuring the amount of salt you add as you go. This is best done with something like mashed potatoes, where you can separate off a portion to play around with and then mix it back into the pot. You will probably be surprised at how much salt you can add before it tastes salty. You will also notice how the flavor of the dish gets better as you add that salt.

So I say to those of you who are stingy with the salt shaker, use more salt. If you're eating real food, meaning fresh vegetables, fish, meat, and poultry that haven't been processed, then the amount you're consuming is far less than what you'd get in most snacks, chips, and other products.

When I cook I use kosher salt for nearly every application. I highly recommend using this variety as it has a significant volume, making it easy to train your fingers to feel how much salt you are adding to a dish. **If you use the same salt over and over again you will begin to develop a physical memory that will take a lot of the guesswork out of seasoning.**

Black Pepper

I love black pepper, but it has its place, and it doesn't belong in every dish. I had trouble getting my cooks to realize this, so for a time I simply banned black pepper from the kitchen until everyone could be retrained on how to use it.

Here's the pitch: Salt and pepper are seemingly best friends, and they are often applied to foods at the same time. But pepper doesn't possess the same chemical properties as salt. Because of its make-up, salt has the capacity to enhance and magnify the flavors of other ingredients. It also has the ability to draw out sweetness. **Pepper, on the other hand, makes things taste more like, well, pepper.** If pepper belongs in the mix of flavors in a dish, then by all means use it. But I urge you to think about what you are doing before you add this very potent and somewhat overpowering component. Does the delicate flavor of sablefish benefit from a showering of freshly ground pepper? Does peppery fresh arugula really need more bite in the form of peppercorns? Pepper is often best added at the end of a dish, grinding the peppercorns directly over the food so as to make the most of its fruity aroma. My recommendation is to taste a dish first, add a small amount of pepper, then decide whether it needs more.

As for white pepper, it's just plain overpowering to my taste. I never use it under any circumstance.

Citrus and Seafood

Citrus is an absolute blessing. It might be, other than salt, the easiest way to make your food delicious. Acid, like salt, helps to punctuate flavors and enliven the palate. Think about eating something fatty. It gets boring pretty quickly because the flavor is one-dimensional. Food that has been punched up with acid, whether citrus, vinegar, or wine, on the other hand, has a lot more lasting appeal. Lemons in particular seem to be just the thing for almost any seafood dish. I like to use acid throughout the cooking process, but even a few drops squeezed over the top as the dish goes to the table really amplify the flavor. My favorite is Meyer lemon, a cross between a mandarin orange and a lemon. It has a thin skin and a sweet, juicy flesh that is aromatic and can fill a room with its gin-like floral scent. Usually available in stores from fall through early spring, Meyer lemons are culinary magic. I often bring a basket of them as a gift when we are invited to dinner at a friend's house.

Cutting Citrus into Segments

This is a technique I use throughout the book; it eliminates the membrane, which can make citrus chewy. Cut the fruit over a bowl to catch the juices.

1. Using a paring knife, slice off both the top and the bottom of the fruit to expose the flesh.

2. Slice off the peel, cutting down the side and following the curve of the fruit.

3. When the bitter-tasting white pith has been entirely removed, cut between each of the membranes to release the individual segments.

❶ Smoked paprika   ❷ Cinnamon sticks   ❸ Ground mace

Herbs and Spices

Dried herbs and spices are among the best ways to add big flavor to a dish without adding fat. Below is a list of my favorites for cooking seafood, some of which may surprise you. Please remember that spices don't last forever. After a few months (sooner, if they've been exposed to heat or sunlight), most ground herbs and spices lose their punch and should be replaced. Buy the smallest containers you can find, unless you know you'll be using a particular spice on a regular basis.

Cilantro is a popular herb, and you will see that I use it in many recipes. I like to keep it whole, just as with parsley. I think that so much of the joy in cilantro is in that initial bite—the cool aromas fill the senses and really punctuate and draw out the sweetness of whatever it is prepared with. If you chop it, just give it a quick once over with a super sharp knife so that most of the aroma is maintained. **When herbs are chopped to a powder then all of the oils, aromas, and flavors are lost to the cutting board and it just becomes something green.** I pair cilantro with nearly any style of cuisine, so don't feel as though it has a place only in guacamole. It can be one of the most rewarding herbs to use.

Cinnamon is an underappreciated and, I would say, underutilized spice. It has a depth and range of flavor that complements both savory and sweet dishes. My friend Joshua is obsessed with the combination of cinnamon and tomatoes, and I love it with the flavors of lemon and olive oil. I use a pinch of cinnamon in one of my dry rubs, as it brings out the warmth in smoky flavors when grilling.

I have recently discovered Mexican cinnamon (called *canela* in Spanish, it's actually from Ceylon). **It's highly spicy, as in heat, with a very pronounced flavor.** I never understood why cinnamon candies were spicy hot until I tried this variety. It is best used freshly grated over a dish just as it comes to the table. I like to use a Microplane® or a nutmeg grater for this purpose.

Coriander is the seed of the cilantro plant; it shares some of cilantro's flavor qualities but is at the same time unique. I love the bright, clean taste of the seeds, which, like fennel seeds, play very well with others. In fact, I like to use coriander and fennel together, as they have complementary roles. **Coriander really punctuates other flavors and provides interesting depth.** I like to use it with milder tasting fish such as halibut and sablefish. Some people complain that coriander—and fresh cilantro—can taste soapy (this seems to be a genetically determined tendency), but chances are, if you like one, you will like the other.

Dill is a favorite staple of northern European cuisines, and it certainly has its place in seafood cookery. It is the perfect herb to pair with salmon and trout but goes well in many applications. I like it tossed into mixed greens to give an everyday salad a burst of flavor. **It does wonders for tomatoes as it really draws out the cool acidic bite,** especially with heirloom varieties such as Cherokee purple or the super sweet sun gold cherry tomatoes.

Fennel seed is one of those spices that a lot of people think they don't like. But if you ask them whether they like Italian sausage, well, absolutely. Surprise, surprise, fennel seed is one of the primary flavor notes in Italian sausage. **It can be a very effective layering spice, as it tends to blend in and rarely overpowers; it plays well with others.** I like it ground, but the flavor is stronger if it's used whole. Ground is best in vinaigrettes or quick-cooked sauces, where you want a smooth texture.

To toast fennel seeds, place them in a dry pan over medium heat and cook, tossing, until their aroma is strong, about two minutes.

To grind fennel seeds, place them in a mortar and, using the pestle, grind to a fine powder. Or you can use a coffee grinder; just make sure it is clean first. Also, think twice before using your everyday coffee grinder because your coffee will taste off for a few days. For that reason, I have a coffee grinder that I use exclusively for spices.

Mace is the lacy outer covering of the nutmeg seed. It has a scent and flavor similar to nutmeg but I don't consider it a "baking spice" because it has a slightly more savory character. **I like to use mace when I smoke seafood—** it combines with those flavors in a way that is just sublime. I also use it in spice mixes. You can buy whole mace (called blade mace) to grind fresh as you need it, or ground mace, which I've found to be a fine product.

Nutmeg is like cinnamon, in that most people don't think of it as a savory spice, but rather as a garnish for warm autumn or winter drinks such as mulled cider. But in those same months, I love to grate a little nutmeg over the top of a dish. It adds a spectacular dimension and an enticing aroma. **Try it on summer and autumn squash—it's a wonderful pairing.** If you've never used whole nutmeg, you're in for a treat. You can grate it using a special grater, a Microplane, or the smallest holes on a box grater. Previously ground nutmeg bears no relation to the intense fragrance and flavor of freshly grated nutmeg.

Oregano has two completely different identities. When it's fresh, I find it brash and often overpowering. Dried, it can provide a great layer of flavor when simmered in soups or added to roasted vegetables. **It needs to be used with care, as it can easily become a dominant flavor.** I use it in both the dried leaf form as well as the powdered version, depending on the dish. The best oregano is dried on the stalk and is available bundled into very delicate bouquets in Mediterranean specialty foods stores.

Parsley gets a slightly larger role in my kitchen than in most chefs'. With all of its delicious flavor, potent aroma, and pleasing texture, chefs usually just chop it to bits (literally) and lose any of the real value in using it. But **I love to keep the leaves whole, adding them to salads and tossing them into vegetables just before serving.** The flavors keep better and it really adds a nice touch to a dish. I always use flat leaf, or Italian, parsley, as I think that it has a more balanced flavor than the curly variety.

Red chile flakes are a great way to bring depth and complexity to a dish without adding a whole lot of heat. Using fresh chiles can be a risky enterprise, as you never know how spicy any particular chile (even from one jalapeño to the next, for instance) will be. A slight bit of heat can really punctuate a dish in ways that enliven the palate and keep the dish bright and interesting. Chile flakes sprinkled on a slice of pizza provide just a hint of spice and keep you wanting more. **I like to grind the chile flakes to embolden the complex flavors without going overboard on the heat.** This can be done as needed in small batches with a mortar and pestle.

Smoked paprika from Spain is one of my favorite pantry items. It possesses the deep, rich flavor of the pepper and a wonderful smoky essence that is beautiful. It's available in three levels of heat—sweet, bittersweet, and hot. I prefer sweet, which isn't actually sweet; it's mild. **Paprika is fat soluble, so when it is added to a dish, it is best when combined with a fat such as olive oil or butter in order to really bring out its flavor.** I use smoked paprika in place of bacon in some dishes, yielding a preparation that is lighter but still complex in flavor. And in spice mixtures, it provides a nice foundation for other spices to play off. I find I also turn to it frequently during the winter, when I can't get outside to grill.

Thyme is one of the best herbs to grow, as you often only need one sprig to add its deep rich flavor to a dish. Thyme, along with rosemary, is what I call a hard herb. I tend to use soft herbs— parsley, dill, cilantro—as they are added in at the very end of a preparation and give vibrancy and life to a dish. Hard herbs, though, are best when added at the beginning of the cooking process. **I like to sauté thyme in with the butter when I cook vegetables, or toss the leaves into the cavity of a fish before I roast it.** The tiny leaves are perfectly edible, but the woody stems must always be removed before the dish is served.

Opposite: Dried oregano

Pantry Items

There are a few ingredients that I almost always reach for when cooking. They are all of high quality and have robust flavors that contribute to the overall character of my dishes. Think of your pantry like a salad. It should be a mix of great ingredients, all of which complement each other while having unique characters of their own.

Capers

These are a great little treasure to have around, though I often see jars of them languishing unloved at the back of refrigerators. Capers are the buds of a bush that's native to the Mediterranean. Capers are sold in a variety of sizes, ranging from tiny little ones to big over-the-top two-bite caper berries, which are the fruit of the caper bush.

Most capers are sold brined, submerged in a salty, slightly acidic bath. These need to be washed before using them. I'll soak them for a few hours in water to cover to remove some of the salt. Capers are also available packed in salt. **These have a cleaner, more "flowery" flavor than brined capers.** They should be soaked in water before use, at least for a few hours, if not overnight. Whichever type you use, capers add a nice little flavor punch to a dish—as a last-minute addition, they yield big results.

Extra-Virgin Olive Oil

This is one of the staples of my kitchen. I often have a couple varieties around, each for a different purpose. I cook with canola oil when searing a fillet, but whenever the oil will be a part of the dish—as when sautéing a vegetable like zucchini, whose juices combine with the oil—I always use a good quality extra-virgin olive oil. For cooking, I buy it by the gallon and use it with abandon. You should be able to find an oil you like for about twenty-five dollars a gallon, and it will keep in a cool dark place for months. **The secret is to look in ethnic stores, where they don't see olive oil as a luxury but as an essential kitchen staple.** Another economical source is price clubs, which carry multiple brands.

For salad dressings, I like to use an extra-virgin olive oil with a more pronounced flavor. Oils with a peppery bite are great for this purpose. I also have a couple of top-quality/top-dollar bottles around that I drizzle over dishes. For simply grilled seafood served with lemon, a final shot of a great olive oil can add a huge dose of personality.

Olive oils can be as complex as wines, so it pays to experiment and find a few different brands or types that you really like. Most gourmet stores will have a few bottles open for tasting, but do not think that the varieties sold in grocery stores can't match up. **Sure, the single-acre, family-owned, generations-old, varietal-specific, hand-crushed, priest-blessed, sacrificial blood of Olympus olive oil on sale at fancy kitchen stores for $119 is great.** In fact, it can be really, really great. But for most of us, the grocery store brand can be just as satisfying an investment. You simply have to taste and decide.

Wherever you buy your olive oil, it should be well balanced and not too strongly flavored. Grassy olive oils are best for bread dipping. **Peppery ones work well for salads and vegetables that have some sweetness.** Freshly pressed oils can be worthwhile, but tricky, as they can have slightly volatile and powerful flavors. Fruity low-acid oils are my choice for drizzling over grilled seafood.

Nuts Nuts are probably the most consistent ingredient in my cooking other than salt. They are adaptable to different flavors and add so much personality and texture to a dish. I always try to have pistachios, almonds, pecans, walnuts, and pine nuts on hand. I make sauces from them, add them to vegetable braises and roasts, and use them for added texture and substance in salads. I also like to use nut oils as a finishing touch of flavor for steamed or boiled vegetables.

If you have the opportunity to taste nuts before purchasing them (say, in the bulk foods aisle of the supermarket), by all means do. They should be sweet and aromatic; if they exhibit any bitterness at all, don't buy them—they are not fresh.

Quinoa is actually the seed of a leafy green vegetable plant, rather than a cereal grain, and is one of my favorite pantry ingredients. It is highly nutritious and one of the few plant-based complete proteins, containing all the essential amino acids the body can't produce in nutritionally significant amounts. It's also high in iron and other minerals. In our house we eat it a couple times a week, sometimes as a side dish, sometimes as the foundation for a meatless meal. I like to cook quinoa pilaf style (see Pecan Quinoa Pilaf, page 243), briefly sautéing it in butter or olive oil in order to enhance its already nutty flavor.

Quinoa has a natural bitter coating that needs to be removed before cooking. Be sure to wash it under cold running water, rubbing the grains with your fingers, then rinse it until the water runs clear, about 3 minutes.

Opposite: Raw quinoa

Toasting Nuts

I like to toast nuts, either dry in the oven or submerged in oil and cooked slowly on the stovetop. Both methods develop an incredible depth of flavor in the nuts. To toast nuts in the oven, scatter them evenly on a baking sheet large enough to hold them in a single layer. Bake in a preheated 325-degree oven for 5 to 8 minutes, depending on their size. The nuts should develop a sweet and potent aroma. They do not necessarily need to change color; all you are trying to do is to enliven the natural oils within. Only dry toast what you are going to use in the next couple of days, as the nuts go rancid much more quickly once they're cooked.

For the stovetop method, use olive oil, and cook a few cups' worth—the oil will take on the flavor of the nut and is a great medium for sautéing fresh vegetables (nuts will keep, refrigerated, for several weeks).

Equipping the Fish Kitchen

I have just a few tools that I rely on to get me through the preparation of any meal. This is by no means an exhaustive list of everything in my kitchen, but here are all the things that I keep at the ready when I cook.

Heatproof spatula This is the perfect kitchen tool. I use it to stir in pots, to flip seafood, to spoon out mayonnaise—whatever I need it for. And it is nonporous, so after a quick wipe with a towel it's clean enough to put right back to use.

Knives Kitchen knives are among those things that are all too tempting for the new cook. And I have seen too many stores willing to sell you things you just don't need. In truth, the most important thing about a knife for the home cook is not which chef endorses it, how it feels in your hand, or even what high-tech, Star Trek–type material it's made from. For a restaurant prep cook who is going to blow through fifty cases of vegetables in the next few hours, well then, yes, the grip does matter. But you are most likely going to be cutting no more than a few onions and a couple of cloves of garlic at a time, so buy a knife appropriate to your actual use.

In my kitchen, I use just three knives, although I have a lot more left over from my overzealous early years. I mostly use a six-inch chef's knife. It is great for chopping and slicing and is small enough to give good control for delicate filleting operations. A paring knife and a long, thin-bladed slicing knife are the other two that I could not do without. Although nearly everything can be accomplished with the chef's knife, it is much easier to slice large roasts and paper-thin raw fish ribbons with the elegant slicing knife. Paring knives can't be beat for small tasks like coring tomatoes, peeling apples, and other such detailed utilitarian operations.

Once you settle on what type of knife you need, ask yourself this: "Can I sharpen this knife effectively?" Experience has taught me to use easy-to-sharpen, hard-rubber-handled knives that cost no more than forty dollars. Knives break. Knives end up in the garbage disposal. Knives open Christmas packages and those damn plastic encasements that other knives are packaged in. In short, a knife is a tool meant to be used as a tool. It is not meant as an opportunity to genuflect to generations of culinarians before you. It is not your soul connection to the late James Beard, nor will it channel the spirit of Julia into your cooking.

Spend the money on a sharpening stone and invest some time on a class, offered at most specialty kitchen stores such as Williams-Sonoma, or on YouTube, to learn how to sharpen that forty-dollar knife and it will be with you for a long, long time. Well, depending on how many plastic packages you open with it.

Microplane This is one of the best kitchen gadgets around. Sure, you could do without one, but it makes easy work of zesting, grating, and chopping small ingredients like garlic.

Tongs I use tongs for everything, as an extension of my hands, to help keep everything clean while I cook. They are especially useful on the grill. I have heard that some chefs are not keen on handling seafood with tongs, but to my mind, they are the gentlest way to manipulate any food. Just remember to clean them after touching raw fish.

Towels Get yourself some really cheap bar mops, as they are called in kitchen stores. These heavyweight square towels are not so big that they droop out of your hand onto the burner to catch fire. Nor are they too small to wipe your hands on or to remove a pan from the oven. Use only one towel per meal, become very familiar with it, and know where it is at all times. This will make you a more efficient cook.

A giant cutting board Having a mental picture of the meal you are about to cook and the process by which it will happen greatly increases your chance of success. Having one big board that you can organize yourself on is a great step in this direction.

Instant-read meat thermometer I don't use this very often, but when I need it, there is simply no alternative. I often call for cooking at low temperatures in this book, so it might be useful to have a device that can tell you when the poaching liquid has reached 170 degrees, for example.

Cookware I am lucky in that I have a kitchen well equipped with Le Creuset pans. They are simply the best pans that I have ever worked with. Although expensive, they will last forever if taken care of properly, so they are a worthwhile investment.

A Cook's Quick Guide to Fish

I've included in this chapter a primer on pretty much everything you need to know about the fish in this book—from sustainability to selection.

Seafood as a Seasonal Food

Many of the delicacies of the world's oceans, rivers, and lakes have a specific season in which they are most accessible, best flavored, or available at all. Some of the most famous, like Copper River salmon in Alaska or shad roe on the East Coast, are a cause for celebration every year when they return to the market because their availability is so limited. Like strawberries and asparagus, they herald the coming of a new season.

Admittedly, it can be difficult to detect this seasonality. Canned products, quick-frozen products, and farm-raised seafood allow us to enjoy shrimp, salmon, crab, and much more year round. But nothing can compare to the taste of super-fresh fish or shellfish, in season, at the height of its flavor. A just-harvested clam eaten outdoors, with the smell of a gentle salt breeze in the air, or the rich vitality of a salmon recently plucked from a stream is an experience that is of a particular place and time. However, if you are not on the seashore, the freshest (and still seasonal) fish might be in the frozen aisle. More on that later.

Being aware of the seasonality of seafood is also important because it helps to connect us to where that fish or oyster or crab came from and how it was caught or harvested. Understanding that your shrimp are (or were, as I was writing this book) coming from the Gulf of Mexico or that your salmon is from the icy waters of Alaska establishes a geographic and communal connection. If your seafood remains a generic, anonymous product that seems simply to come from a warehouse somewhere, it is easier to overlook the damage that industrial fishing has inflicted on the ocean. If you choose to enjoy seafood seasonally and with knowledge of its origin and harvest, you can support fishermen who are acting responsibly, which will help us to create more sustainable and profitable fisheries—although it is not quite that simple.

In an effort to get you to think this way, I've arranged the recipes in this book by season, with sections of vegetable recipes to accompany your meals at the end of each chapter. Many of the fish in these chapters are farm-raised seafood or are canned and smoked products that are available year round, so I correlate the recipe to the vegetables used to set the stage. The period of time a particular fish may be in season can extend across our seasons, so don't be surprised to see halibut, for instance, in spring, summer, and fall. Those recipes will differ and reflect the time of year, though, in the vegetables I pair with the fish, as well as the cooking method I use. In the chapter A Separate Season, I highlight seafood that is available year round—sustainable farm-raised fish and shellfish, as well as canned seafood products.

To Catch a Fish

Fish are caught using a variety of methods, some of which are environmentally sound, while others are capable of bringing about the wholesale destruction of our oceans. It is important to learn a little about how a fish ends up on your plate so that you can make informed choices. First, it helps to understand the terms used to describe fisheries.

Fishery This refers to all the actions, people, and places involved in catching fish. It is important to understand that fishery does not exist without our effort. We all too often believe a fishery is a resource created for our sustenance. Rather, the word describes the effort put forth by humans to remove sea life from the oceans in order to make them available for consumption.

Bycatch This is all the other sea life that comes up in a net or on a line that was not targeted by the fishermen. **Bycatch has been a major problem with many of the world's fisheries,** as unwanted and unsalable sea life has been needlessly destroyed in order to bring seafood to market.

Pole caught This is what most people think of when they think about going fishing: a fisherman with his or her fishing pole. This is a very sustainable way to catch fish, as there is very little bycatch. A baited or rigged line is thrown into the water with the intent of catching a certain species. **Targeting the species by the season and the type of bait used allows for strict selection of what is removed from the water.** Pole-caught fish is usually of the highest quality, as it is caught near to shore and arrives at market quickly.

Purse seine This is a circular net used to trap a school of fish, such as sardines; squid and some salmon are also caught this way. **It is considered an environmentally sound method of harvest with little bycatch because the nets are deployed only when the school of fish is identified.**

Trolling This is when multiple baited hooks are towed behind a boat. It is in effect the same as pole caught. **Any bycatch is removed from the hooks and returned to the water immediately.** Like pole-caught seafood, fish caught using this method are usually of very high quality, as trolling is done close to shore and the product arrives at market quickly.

Trapping A baited cage is placed on the water's bottom (think lobster traps). This is a highly sustainable method, as bycatch is returned to the water alive.

Gillnetting A nearly invisible net is strung across a span of water. As fish swim through it they get caught in the net by their gills. **There can be some incidental bycatch, as everything of a certain size will get stuck in the net.** But these nets are usually strung in areas where a certain type of fish is abundant, leading to low bycatch.

Long line This method deploys a series of baited hooks strung on a long line that is set at different depths, depending on the desired catch. **Bycatch can be a major issue with this type of fishing, in particular marine birds and turtles.** While some fishermen use long line safely, you should generally avoid fish that has been caught this way.

Trawling A large net is dragged behind a boat and then hauled onboard. This method is responsible for the worst damage to the oceans. It catches absolutely everything in its path, including juvenile fish, turtles, old leather boots, you name it. Trawls are deployed at various depths in the ocean with varying impact. Midwater trawls are still indiscriminate, but are better than bottom trawls, which can rake the sea floor clean of life, as well as disfigure rocky bottoms. **Think of it this way: trawling over rocks and coral is the marine equivalent of hunting deer in the woods with a bulldozer.** Some major advances have been made in trawling technology, but it still remains one of the most destructive fishing methods.

Dredging This is when a cage is dragged along the sea floor to catch bottom-dwellers. **Often used to harvest scallops, clams, and oysters, this method results in bycatch as well as habitat destruction.** Dredges that operate in water with sandy bottoms are not as destructive as those used over rocky terrain.

Sustainability Through Portion Size

The easiest and most important thing we can do to help the oceans is to moderate our consumption of sea life. I call for moderate portion sizes in this book, five ounces for a single serving. To my mind, part of being environmentally responsible is eating in balance, which means a just-big-enough serving of protein and an abundance of vegetables. We need to understand the direct connection between our food consumption and the pressure put on our environment to produce that food. By moderating our intake of ocean-based protein, we take pressure off the fish populations and our wallets. For too long our average portions of protein have been too big. This has a deleterious effect on our bodies as well as the environment. In our house the vegetables come first, and the protein is the side dish. So, I encourage you to make good use of the vegetable and side dishes in this book.

Aquaculture: The Cases For and Against Farm-Raised Seafood

Aquaculture is not a new idea. Humans have been farming marine resources for thousands of years. However, the high-intensity farms that we now rely on *are* a new phenomenon.

Aquaculture allows us to create vast amounts of cheap protein in a small area. The problem is, just as with high-density cattle and chicken farms, the production of that protein may carry a significant environmental cost. Sea creatures are not supposed to be raised in the conditions that many farms usually employ, and so require an unhealthy amount of antibiotics to keep them healthy. Many of the farmed species that we find most delicious also require large amounts of wild fish as feed input in order to raise these carnivorous fish. There is also a high concentration of waste associated with aquaculture, mostly fecal matter, which can foul the surrounding environment.

But when done properly, marine farming can really be a benefit, and can even help restore health to an ecosystem. Vegetarian species such as catfish and tilapia require very little input. Farm-raised oysters and clams can actually help clean their environment. Even some carnivorous species can be raised so that the production benefits far exceed the environmental cost.

The aquaculture industry still has a long way to go, but there is hope on the horizon, and we can all support their progress with our wallets. There are great people who are making a big difference in how our seas will be farmed. It is up to us to find the products being offered by this new guard and to reward them for their work. Groups like the Monterey Bay Aquarium and Blue Ocean Institute are beginning to acknowledge some of the hopeful new ideas that are coming to market and are ranking these new products according to their progressive methods. Companies like CleanFish provide sales and marketing support to qualifying sustainable artisan producers.

So ask questions at your fish counter and get to know the people behind your farmed fish. If you do your homework, you will find good options, from both an environmental and enjoyment perspective.

The Seafood in This Book

I have chosen to include recipes showcasing a wide variety of fish and shellfish, most of which are readily available at fish counters around the country, though you'll find a couple of my East Coast favorites, like bluefish. Although typically not found at market, some seafood such as fresh sardines, mackerel, pink salmon, and sablefish are all widely available through national distributors to any retailer who wants them. You may need to encourage your local fish store or the fish counter at your supermarket to start carrying them.

All the fish I use in this book are delicious and can be sustainably sourced. I hope you notice that I include many recipes for smaller fish and many for shellfish. We now generally prefer to eat larger fish. However, this is in contrast with our historical consumption of seafood. **A study of recipes in cookbooks published over more than a century confirms that we used to eat smaller fish but have shifted our preferences to larger predatory species.** Some large species we have always eaten, like cod and salmon. But our diets used to be rich in inshore species such as herring, sardines, clams, and oysters. In some cases, the shift occurred because we depleted the inshore fisheries and because technology allowed us to pursue larger fish farther from shore. I would encourage you to go back

to the older ways and eat low on the food chain. Choose the smaller, less costly species, which are also quicker to replenish themselves—this makes both economic and environmental sense. Go on and enjoy some striped bass, tuna, and salmon, but do so rarely and in moderation. **Try something new (and small), and use this book to help lessen our impact on the oceans by diversifying the species we take from them.**

When it comes to being environmentally sustainable, not all the species represented here are a matter of black or white. Mahimahi, for example, is currently sustaining a healthy population. However, while some mahimahi is pole caught, which has limited environmental impact, it is also caught using long-lining, which can result in the incidental bycatch of turtles and seabirds. The problem is that, on the plate, you can't see or taste the difference between these two methods. **Your only defense is to patronize a well-informed fishmonger who cares about where his or her fish comes from.**

So, use this book as a guide to dinner. And use websites like the Monterey Bay Aquarium and Blue Ocean as a guide to sustainability (see Sustainable Sources and Web Links, page 272).

Ask your fishmonger questions and look for information on the specific seafood that you are thinking of serving.

Seafood Substitutions

There are a lot of delicious fish that have no place on our dinner plates because of overfishing or the environmentally destructive way in which they are caught. That's not to say you won't find them at your fish counter, but to my mind it's no longer environmentally responsible to consume them. Below is a list of fish favorites you won't find in this book, with sustainable substitutes in the hopes that you might try a different fish and find a new favorite. Some of the species listed below, such as cod, are making a comeback. There are very small pockets of fishermen who are really making some strides toward creating a sustainable cod fishery, and I believe that they should be supported. But their product is a very small portion of the catch and it is hard to find. See the links section on page 272 for information about how to support this new generation of cod fishermen. So, while I do not recommend eating Atlantic cod today, I hope that one day soon it will again be a healthy fishery and a viable option for our dinner.

Atlantic cod Substitute Pacific cod.

Bluefin tuna Try wahoo or pole-caught albacore and yellowfin tuna.

Chilean sea bass Try sablefish, Pacific halibut, or farm-raised sturgeon.

Flounder Some flounder are better than others in terms of being caught in an environmentally responsible way, but try farm-raised barramundi in its place.

Grouper Try barramundi, U.S. farm-raised cobia, sablefish, U.S. tilapia, or amberjack.

Monkfish Try mahimahi, Pacific cod, sablefish, or catfish.

Octopus Substitute squid (especially if you are a fan of the Spanish soccer team!).

Orange roughy Try U.S. tilapia, catfish, or Pacific halibut.

Shark Use amberjack or farm-raised sturgeon.

Skate Use scallops, U.S. tilapia, or barramundi.

Snapper Again, some snapper are caught in a sustainable manner; others not. Purchase snapper fished off the Carolinas or try barramundi.

Amberjack There's growing commercial interest in amberjack, but it's not usually found beyond the Atlantic and Gulf coast, where it is appreciated by sport fisherman. I include it in the book because you will find it in the market from time to time. **It is the perfect cross between the meatiness of steaklike swordfish and the snowy, flaky richness of grouper.** Because it is a very dense-fleshed fish, it needs to cook slowly so that it does not dry out. Amberjack is great on the grill, but don't sear it over a hot fire; instead, let it slow roast via indirect heat on the cool side of the grill.

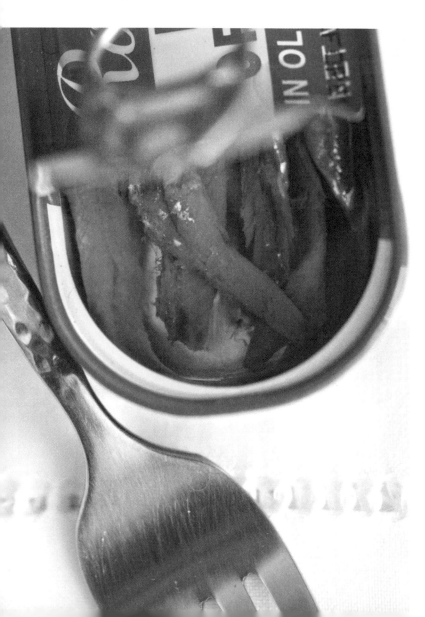

Anchovy Most often seen in canned form, these little guys hold a place of honor in nearly every cuisine. The vast majority of anchovies are culled from the cool waters off Peru. Unfortunately, most of the anchovies caught are turned into feed for aquaculture, pigs, and chicken or into agricultural fertilizer.

Anchovies are not faring so well right now in terms of sustainability. I include recipes for them—actually, a lot of recipes—because we should eat more of them in order to create a sustainable market. They are considered a trash fish meant for industrial uses, but if we appreciated them more, then they would command a higher price, thereby increasing the possibility that we would fish them less and achieve a greater efficiency of use. **It makes little sense to me to take a perfectly tasty anchovy and feed it to a chicken.** I would rather eat the anchovy, and it is more environmentally friendly too.

I fell in love with anchovies while living in Spain, where they are ubiquitous in the cuisine. A number of different species show up in the market and are sold as anchovies, but they all have the same basic flavor. Experiment with different brands of the canned product to find one you really like. Anchovies are available as oil-packed fillets as well as salt-packed whole fish. I love the salted variety. They require a little work to fillet, but they are worth the trouble—a little meatier and a little more developed in their flavor. I don't mean to say they are "fishier"; rather, the taste is bolder.

To use a salt-packed anchovy, soak the whole fish in water for about 20 minutes. After soaking, the meat can be easily removed by running a finger down the backbone to separate one fillet and then the other. The bones will remain on the spine. Use the fillets just as you would oil-packed ones.

I usually save the oil from oil-packed fillets to use in vinaigrettes or to drizzle over the dish when it is plated. **Anchovies are pretty cheap and keep for a while, so I stock up and always have a couple of tins on hand.** The salted variety usually comes in one-kilogram tins, so it is an investment. The salt keeps them preserved, and if you use them with any frequency they will be fine stored for many months in a plastic bag in the refrigerator.

Recently, a product called white anchovies (sold in small trays) has become widely available in the United States. These anchovies have been vinegar cured and have a bright, clean flavor completely unlike canned. Try them laid over crisp salad greens or as a twist to a classic Caesar salad.

Filleting Salt-packed Anchovies Filleting these small fish can at first seem intimidating, but in five easy steps you will have delicious and ready-to-use fillets.

❶ Soak needed amount of anchovies in cool water. ❷ Cut along the backbone to separate the fillets.
❸ Gently peel the fillets away from the bone. ❹ Remove and discard the backbone and tail. ❺ Fillets are ready to use.

Arctic Char

Although it is available as a wild-caught species, the vast majority of Arctic char comes from sustainable farming methods. The wild product is fantastic and full of flavor, but is also very expensive and infrequently seen at markets. The farmed product is high in omega-3s and is nearly always available. It is farmed in the pristine waters of Iceland, stays fresh a long time, and is usually quite reasonably priced. The great chef Rick Moonen calls it "salmon lite" because, like salmon, it has the same pink-colored flesh, but it is quite a bit softer in its flavor. **It's a fish you want to cook and enjoy with the skin on, as it crisps nicely, adding to the overall appeal of the dish.** I love to cook Arctic char whole, either roasting or grilling it, and, in general, it fits nicely into a roasting pan or on the grill. Char can dry out pretty quickly, though, so I recommend low-heat methods for cooking the delicate fillets.

Barramundi

This newcomer to the market is a welcome one. It is a freshwater fish native to Australia, but a company called Australis has developed a way to farm it in a highly sustainable manner in western Massachusetts. **Still relatively unknown to the American consumer, this fish has become the darling of chefs looking for a sustainable replacement for high-priced and not always sustainable red snapper.** Barramundi has a firm flesh and a sweet, delicate flavor. Its skin is clean and thin, which allows it to crisp nicely. Because of its flaky texture, it can be difficult to grill, but it is well worth a try.

Frozen barramundi fillets are just now becoming available in supermarkets. Look for it and try it—it's a great product.

Bluefish

I love bluefish. It has a rich, seductive flavor that pairs perfectly with strong flavors like basil and smoke. It's also a fish that's next to impossible to find fresh anywhere but on the East and Gulf coasts; because of its high oil content, it spoils very quickly once out of the water. However, there is nothing sweeter or better to eat than fresh bluefish, particularly when it's grilled. **Bluefish taste best when they are running close to shore in the summertime, feeding on the schools of herring and menhaden that they follow up the coasts.** Bluefish is a recovering species, having been overfished by both commercial and sport fishermen, and their numbers have only recently become abundant again. Bluefish can be quite high in toxins such as mercury and PCBs, so, when eating blues, try to find smaller fish, which will not have as much mercury buildup in the flesh. Also, some of the toxins are in the darkly colored flesh just beneath the skin. You can easily remove this portion when the fish is cooked.

Catfish This sweet-fleshed fish is a staple across the United States and a religion in the South. In my opinion, we should all be eating catfish at least two or three times a month. It's available farmed or wild-caught all over the country and is almost always fresh to market within a couple of days, if not hours. **Catfish is wonderful fried, but it's also a great fish to smoke and then use in soups or stews.** I like to make gumbo with it, and I've also found it to be a good twist to substitute it for clams in a traditional chowder recipe. The best thing about catfish is that it is cheap and can be served often without breaking the bank. When buying catfish, look for a domestically produced product. Catfish farms in the United States are well managed, and the catfish are farmed in a very clean and environmentally healthy way.

Clams They come in all shapes and sizes and colors, but **I have never met a clam that I did not love.** Clams range from the simply grotesque and gigantic geoduck of the Pacific Northwest (they can weigh as much as fourteen pounds—search out an image of one on the internet, but make sure there are no kids around, as you might have some explaining to do if they see it) to the steamers of New England culinary fame. In between are the quahogs, sold under different names representing their size. These are your littlenecks (the smallest), cherrystones, and chowder clams (the largest). Quahog is the clam you see most often in stores and on raw-bar menus. I am in love with the soft-shell razor clam, which has a shell shaped just like an old straight razor. Not often seen in markets and sometimes used for bait, these are a coastal delicacy; if you can find them, by all means dig in. Small hard-shell clams like mahogany, cockle, and Manila clams are perfect for pastas and soups. They have a clean, bright flavor but are expensive, so they are best used as a garnish to a dish.

I fell in love with clams as a fourth-grader, when my father took us on a trip to the Bay of Fundy in Nova Scotia. We went clamming one afternoon and were miserable at it. We were way out in the mud, and the clams were burrowing faster than we could dig. We looked around and saw all the locals digging much closer to shore in the drier sand, so we gave it a shot. The clams came up by the dozen with every scoop of the shovel. Backbreaking as the work still was, the effort was worth it—it was some of the best food I have ever eaten.

For the most part, clams are a farmed product. Their presence is great for the environment as they filter the water and help restore wild populations of clams. Clams are shipped live and stay fresh for a long time out of the water, but the majority of them are delivered within just a day or two to market.

Opposite: Arctic Char. Above: Littleneck clams

Cobia This species, popular in the Gulf of Mexico as a recreational fish, is also known as black kingfish or lemon fish, and it has a great texture and plate presence. **It is a meaty, firm fish with a lot of richness to it.** While it is currently not widely available outside of the Gulf states, there is significant growth in the U.S. farmed cobia industry. When farmed in the United States, it can be a clean and fast-growing species that has little environmental impact. I include a recipe for cobia because it is coming to a fish counter near you, and that is a good thing.

Crab *The Deadliest Catch* on the Discovery Channel has connected Americans with the sometimes-brutal reality of the fishing industry that provides for our tables. While the show certainly plays up the drama, the fact remains that fishing is a tough business and fishermen deserve a lot of credit for the risks they take.

Crab is found along every coast, from the rock and Jonah crabs of Maine, to the blue crabs of the Chesapeake and Gulf of Mexico, to the stone crabs of Florida, to the Dungeness and king crabs of the cold Pacific waters. **While each species has its own unique taste, they are all relatively similar in that they share a sweetness and a prized meaty texture.**

I would not be worth the local taxes I have paid if I didn't say that Chesapeake blue crab is by far the greatest of all crab offerings. Baltimore and the surrounding Bay communities have a rich tradition and a fierce pride centered on the generations-old crab fishery. Unfortunately, the crab populations, and the crabbers, are not doing well. The Chesapeake Bay has reached a point of near complete environmental disaster due to overfishing, pollution, and disease. What was once the most productive estuarine environment in the world has been reduced to vast dead zones where literally nothing can survive. Communities are disappearing, the generations of skill and tradition along with them. **The iconic dish of the Chesapeake, the crab cake, is now more often than not made from crabmeat imported from Asia.** Other major crab fisheries are faring much better, and crabs are caught in ways that avoid the incidental bycatch of unwanted species.

Crab is often sold live at market (soft-shell crab is always sold live), which is a guarantee of freshness. The northern crab species (king and snow) are most often sold in frozen leg clusters. When buying these, look for even icing in the packaging, as this is a sign that they have not been subjected to thawing and refreezing.

Crab is also sold as crabmeat. There are fresh and pasteurized versions, both of which can be good-quality products. I prefer the just-picked meat but have had great success using the canned product as well, so find a brand that you like and stick with it. Crabmeat is available in many forms, from the meaty jumbo lump morsels to the always-full-of-cartilage claw meat. I like the lump and backfin meat the best; they deliver the most flavor for the dollar.

Halibut While still being fished in Canadian waters, Atlantic halibut is having a rough time in U.S. waters, the victim of overfishing. Pacific halibut, I'm glad to say, is alive, well, and sustainably managed. If you can't verify that you're buying Pacific halibut, I would advise you to choose a different fish entirely, as the Canadian stocks of Atlantic halibut are currently being overfished.

Pacific halibut's super-thick fillets are fun to work with because they cook slowly and therefore can be infused with great depth of flavor, whether through a long, slow poach or a slow-roast method. **The snowy white flesh has beautiful, big flakes with a very subtle flavor—be careful not to overpower it with other ingredients.**

Pacific halibut season opens in March and lasts through the fall.

Herring Herring are very similar to sardines—in fact, they are members of the same family. Oftentimes small herring are canned and sold as sardines, so chances are you might have had one without knowing it. I separate them out because herring have a legendary history and have been an important foodstuff for many cultures. The fish run in giant schools off both the Atlantic and Pacific coasts and are a primary source of food for many of the fish species served in restaurants. Larger herring, those that won't fit in a can, were traditionally pickled or smoked in order to preserve them for leaner months. These days we don't so much preserve them out of need, but rather in memory of a cuisine from days gone by. **Pickled herring are quite delicious and make a great appetizer or canapé (see Cured Herring on Endive with Chive Aioli, page 50).** Herring roe is also a staple of many cuisines, and if you are so inclined and lucky enough to find it, fresh herring roe makes a great meal simply sautéed with garlic and onions in butter and served over toast.

Herring are not faring so well, due to industrialized fishing that catches them only for processing into fishmeal, supplements, and fertilizer. As with anchovies, reestablishing herring as a favored foodstuff could help put an end to the indiscriminate capture now ravaging populations.

Lobster More Americans propose to their beloved over a dinner of lobster than any other food. **It is the pinnacle of luxury because it's the pinnacle of deliciousness.** The problem is that it often is the pinnacle of expensive too.

Lobster should always be purchased live to ensure its quality. Never ever buy those cooked lobsters they have at the grocery store for super cheap. Know why they're being sold cooked? Because they died. And you don't ever want to eat a lobster that got cooked after dying of unknown causes. Lobster meat, though, is a different story. It is processed from fresh-cooked or raw, just-out-of-the-water lobsters and can be a very high-quality product. For

example, Clearwater, a company in Canada, packages fantastic lobster meat products, among other things.

Lobsters have tons of flavor throughout their body that is not often used fully. **The shells make great stock for a soup base.** And the roe, or the dark green stuff inside, makes a tasty flavored butter you can use to top other grilled seafood. Don't use the light green liver, as it is full of toxins and should be discarded.

My favorite way to prepare lobster is to grill it (see the directions on page 125).

How to Pre-cook a Lobster for the Grill

Lobster is admittedly a little intimidating. Follow the steps below to easily prepare lobsters for cooking on the grill, in a sauté pan or under the broiler.

Bring a large pot of salted water to a boil. Put the lobsters in the water head first. Be sure to do this! If you put them in tail first, they will snap it back as they hit the water and could give you a big splash of boiling water right to the face. Cook the lobsters for about two minutes, then remove.

Remove the claws from each lobster and put them back in the pot with the heat off to sit in the hot water for another 5 minutes, as the claws need more time to cook than the delicate tails.

Cut each lobster in half lengthwise by placing the tip of a large knife where the body meets the tail. Pierce through the body and then rock the knife toward you to cut through the body. Repeat the same action in the opposite direction to finish cutting in half.

Inside of the head there is a small sack that has bits of broken shell and stuff that you don't want to eat. Remove this gently with your fingers. Also remove the light green tomalley; though very tasty, it's a storehouse of environmental toxins and should be avoided. Everything else stays, particularly, if you're lucky enough to get a female lobster, the dark green roe (it'll turn fiery red when cooked, hence the other name it's known by, the coral).

Remove the claws from the water and crack the shells. You can remove the meat entirely from the shell or leave on the claw tips to make it easier to eat.

Mackerel Found along the Gulf Coast up through maritime Canada, the mackerel family of fish provides one of the greatest culinary opportunities. Mackerel all share a delicious firm flesh that is well suited to big flavors. Smoke is one of the best matches to mackerel, as the oily, rich flesh absorbs the flavor and rewards the eater with a moist and meaty bite. Canned mackerel makes an appearance in this book too. It can be a high-quality product that makes for an easy and healthful meal. Mackerel is super high in heart-healthy omega-3s and can be prepared in any number of ways. The season for mackerel is pretty much year round. **They are among the prettiest of fish; their bright, smooth silver skin showing off their colorful markings and oily sheen.** Mackerel are long, sleek, and fast looking: If a young boy sitting in class were to doodle a warrior breed of fish sent to conquer an imaginary water world, mackerel would certainly be the reigning tribe.

There are numerous species of mackerel, and I recommend eating only the smaller Spanish and Boston mackerel varieties. King mackerel is very high in toxins and should be avoided altogether.

Mahimahi Caught on both coasts, mahimahi supports an important sport fishery as well as a commercial one. They are big and boldly-colored fish with a unique shape, kind of like a bullet with a flat head. When just out of the water, they shimmer with a rainbow of colors that is a sight to be seen. The flesh of these beauties is a grayish pink color. You never want to serve mahi with the skin on—it is super tough. **I like to grill mahi, as it is great with a little smoke to it and because the fish tends to be at its freshest during the summer grilling months anyway.** See page 22 for a brief discussion on the difficulty of sourcing sustainable mahi.

Mahi does not freeze well, so avoid any fillet that looks washed out and gray. Most likely it has been refreshed from frozen, or it's just old and you don't want it anyway.

Mussels No doubt about it: You need to eat more mussels. They taste great; they're good for you (mussels are high in iron, vitamin B12, and omega-3 fatty acids); and they're great for the environment (as filter feeders, mussels remove excess nutrients from the water they live in, thus improving its quality).

The vast majority of mussels that we buy are farmed. These farms produce a product that is consistent, so you always know what you are going to get. Different brands have different characteristics, though—mostly subtle variations of size and flavor due to the water in which they are farmed. **Look for mussels grown in high tidal flow areas like Maine or Prince Edward Island. This means that more water passes through the farm and the mussels living there, which makes them plump and full of flavor.**

Mussels can be enjoyed in so many different ways. Smoked, marinated, steamed—they are almost limitless in their flavor versatility. If a flavor combination sounds good, it probably will be delicious when paired with mussels. Beer and roasted garlic, white wine and herbs, red wine and herbs, tomato sauce and whatever else you can think of. This is probably the most versatile seafood that is available.

Oysters Eating farmed oysters is our patriotic duty. They are not just sustainable, they actually help to restore depleted ecosystems. Unlike some farm-raised seafood, whose escape can wreak devastating effects on their wild brethren, oysters freely cast their spawn into the surrounding waters, helping to replenish populations, and are among the most important foundations of coastal habitats. Like mussels and clams, oysters are filter-feeders, filtering water through their bodies and removing tiny bits of nutrients.

This helps to keep the waters clean, which then enables sunlight to reach the seafloor, thus spurring plant growth, which then enables the young of many ocean species to hide from predators, which leads to a healthy ecosystem. When filter feeders are not in the system, either because we got too greedy and ate them all up or because they were killed by an environmental disaster (like an oil spill or disease), then the waters get murky and everything falls apart. **Oysters are what is known as a keystone species, a species that holds together the whole intricate framework of the environment.**

Farmed oysters also provide a great opportunity for watermen to make a living. In many areas where oysters are a traditional source of income, farming the seas is about all that is left. These communities would otherwise disappear, their residents moving away to find other jobs. But oysters keep these families working and build hope for the future. So, I tell you again, save the world and eat an oyster. Redemption on the half shell, with lemon and Tabasco!

Shucking Oysters Shucking oysters for cooking and eating raw is not complicated but does take some practice. The best shuckers in the world are a true marvel to watch. But with just a well placed knife and a little patience, the pulsing briny world of the oyster can be revealed by the home cook with the same results.

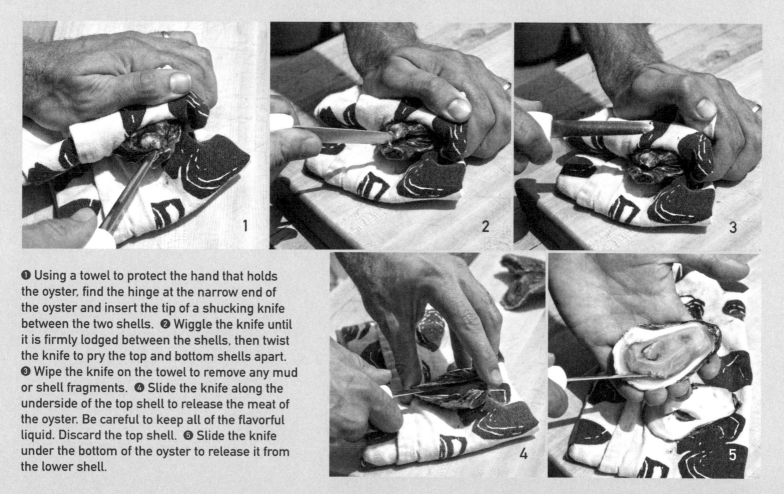

❶ Using a towel to protect the hand that holds the oyster, find the hinge at the narrow end of the oyster and insert the tip of a shucking knife between the two shells. ❷ Wiggle the knife until it is firmly lodged between the shells, then twist the knife to pry the top and bottom shells apart. ❸ Wipe the knife on the towel to remove any mud or shell fragments. ❹ Slide the knife along the underside of the top shell to release the meat of the oyster. Be careful to keep all of the flavorful liquid. Discard the top shell. ❺ Slide the knife under the bottom of the oyster to release it from the lower shell.

Pacific Cod Pacific cod has the same large flake and dense texture as Atlantic cod, which was almost fished out of existence. Atlantic cod still remain a cautionary tale of environmental irresponsibility. Pacific cod has some concerns associated with its fishery but, by and large, is a well-managed and abundant resource. Pacific cod is great at the table and freezes well.

Below: Trout roe

Roe Fish roe is a simple way to put on the ritz at a meal. Pair it with some bubbly wine, and you've got a classy show on your hands. Caviar can be bought off the internet (see Sustainable Sources and Web Links, page 272) and in some specialty stores, especially around the holidays. You can find salmon roe (sometimes sold as red caviar) and trout roe at reasonable prices, and while they might not match the finest caviars in finesse, they certainly make for a fun appetizer. All roe is sold salted. I like to remove this salt by rebrining the eggs (see Trout Roe with Cava and Brioche Toasts page 218) which also increases their flavor and culls out broken or otherwise damaged eggs. Also look for the capelin roe, often used as a garnish at sushi restaurants. It is usually sold dyed and flavored with ingredients like wasabi or beet juice. It has great texture, is pretty affordable, and can be used just as you would regular caviar or roe. I particularly like it on bagels in the morning.

The mack daddy of roe, though, is caviar, harvested from the wild sturgeon in the Caspian Sea. This population of fish has been so severely depleted that they are now an endangered species. Beluga, Osetra, and Sevruga caviars from Azerbaijan and Iran are incredibly expensive, when they're available. Several operations in the States, however, are producing sustainable sturgeon and packaging its roe, allowing you to enjoy caviar with a good conscience.

Sablefish You must try this fantastic fish, also known as black cod. It has a rich texture, almost silken, with a pleasant sweetness and mild flavor. It is very similar to the overfished Chilean sea bass, so if you have any favorite recipes for sea bass, try sablefish instead. It is caught in the cold waters of the North Pacific and is just now becoming popular with chefs and home cooks. Sablefish freezes very well, so it is available year round. It shares the same season as halibut—look for it fresh from spring through fall.

Sablefish is expensive, so make a celebration of it with a more elaborate dish such as slow-roasted Sablefish with Lentils and Pomegranate–Red Wine Butter (page 185).

All sablefish are wild caught. The fisheries of Alaska and British Columbia are well managed and use environmentally sound fishing practices. This is not the case with the West Coast fisheries (California to Washington), which still engage in bottom trawling and long-line fishing, with significant rates of bycatch. Ask your fishmonger where your sablefish is coming from and support fisheries that are doing the right thing.

Salmon

Okay, I'm going to say it: salmon is boring. Not because it tastes boring, but rather because I, and most chefs, are bored with it. **Unfortunately, salmon is a victim of its own deliciousness.** It has a rich texture and a unique flavor that makes it a crowd pleaser and a restaurant staple (more on that later).

The salmon fisheries of the West Coast, such as Copper River, are now legendary. These fish are a wonder to behold as they swim back into the river systems of the Pacific Northwest. They are a keystone species: even the trees in the great woods depend on the salmon for nutrient enrichment through the droppings of the birds that eat the fish. It is a humbling experience to realize how integrated this system is; the Native American communities depend on and honor the salmon's role in this great system as well.

Salmon can be a burden for chefs because it has to be on every menu. Customers demand it, so it has ascended to the realms of the almighty chicken as a go-to selection.

Farmed salmon: In general, farmed Atlantic salmon tends to be bland and, from an environmental point of view, unsustainable. There are, however, some producers making great-quality product as well as breaking ground, or making waves, with new technologies that reduce some of the negative environmental impact of salmon farms. Farmed salmon is a prime example of how we have gotten ahead of ourselves with our food production. High-density net pens wreak havoc on local ecosystems, endangering the indigenous salmon by allowing diseases and parasites carried by farm-raised fish to spread Further, these farms can also threaten the overall health of the ecosystem through a buildup of waste product. There are other issues surrounding farmed salmon. To learn more, go to **www.farmedanddangerous.org.** But don't stop there, also visit **www.cleanfish.com** to search out some of the great progressive farms that are making change happen, like Loch Duart in Scotland.

Wild salmon: Fresh wild salmon is available as the different types of salmon come into season. Wild Alaskan salmon is very well managed; in fact, it is a model fishery, showing how we can succeed in responsibly feeding ourselves. The first salmon runs begin in the late spring and continue through the fall. As they begin their return to the rivers of their birth to spawn, these fish are fat and full of flavor, having gorged themselves to bulk up for the long journey home, during which they do not eat. Wild salmon is also available frozen.

When it comes to taste, fresh wild salmon is the way to go, no doubt, and Alaskan salmon is the best choice. **There are five types commonly available: king salmon is the richest, sockeye the gamiest, coho the most balanced in flavor, pink the lightest in flavor, and keta the most similar to good-quality farmed Atlantic salmon.**

Pink salmon: One of my personal missions is to get more folks eating pink salmon. It is the most plentiful of all of the salmon species in Alaska, and it is also the cheapest. Traditionally it has been fodder for the canned salmon processors and for cat food companies, but only because consumers have not had access to fresh fillets. **The fillets are delicious, and even more appealing because they're so inexpensive.** Canned pink salmon is also very good, and I've included a few recipes that make use of it. Experiment with brands until you find one that suits your taste.

Sardines The poster fish for what people think of as "gross." **I, on the other hand, think sardines are among the most delicious little guys swimming in the sea.** And sardines are a superfood, packed with omega-3 fatty acids, iron, and B vitamins. Also, because sardines are short-lived, they don't accumulate pollutants in their bodies.

As far as I'm concerned, fresh sardines were made for the grill. While hard to find, they are well worth the effort needed to scale and gut them, if your fishmonger won't do it for you. (Don't bother to bone them; it's far easier to remove the bones once they're cooked.) Look for fish with clean, unbruised, and unbroken skin (they're delicate and often get damaged in transport). Fresh sardines should be bright and shiny and smell sweetly of the sea.

Canned sardines seem to be making a comeback. The legendary sardine canneries of Monterey Bay are long gone, but there are lots of new brands attempting to elevate the canned sardine to new heights of deliciousness, and rightly so. They come in a variety of preparations, including smoked, bathed in mustard, or packed in tomato sauce. **The smoked boneless, skinless fillets, either packed in water or oil, are easy to eat and make a simple meal with the addition of a little Tabasco.** Sardines are also available salt-packed; these should be treated the same way as salt-packed anchovies (page 24–25).

From a sustainability point of view, sardines are an excellent choice, harvested from well-managed fisheries using eco-friendly fishing methods.

Scallops Scallops are among the most popular shellfish on the market. They have a rich, sweet flavor comparable only to lobster.

Sea scallops: Sea scallops are sold in a variety of sizes, with the largest ones commanding a very high price. Sometimes sea scallops are further labeled as diver scallops, meaning a diver hand picked them from the seafloor. **Beware of labels claiming "diver caught," as there are very few of these available in the general market.** I prefer not to use sea scallops (and haven't included any recipes for them), as they are mostly caught by dredge, which disturbs the seafloor. However, most dredged scallops come from sandy bottoms, where the impact of using a dredge is not nearly as long lasting or severe as it is along rocky bottoms. I am not against using sea scallops, and if you can find true "divers," then by all means snap them up. They can be substituted for much of the seafood in this book, especially in the sablefish and halibut recipes.

Bay scallops: Wild bay scallops are caught using the same methods as sea scallops, with the same environmental impact. Bay scallops, however, are also farmed and are sometimes sold live in the shell. They can be a fine treat, as the shells are beautiful and the scallops couldn't be fresher. In this case, I recommend serving them raw so that you get as much of that pristine flavor as possible. When they are sold shucked, they make for a great addition to any preparation. **Often it is too difficult to make an entrée portion of these little guys without overcooking them, so I like to add them to other dishes such as salads for an interesting twist.** Look for frozen bay scallops out of Argentina that are certified by the Marine Stewardship Council—they're wonderful.

Wet-pack versus dry-pack scallops: Depending on their treatment after leaving the water, scallops can be sublime or they can be dreck. It depends on whether they were treated with a water-retention chemical called STP (sodium tripolyphosphate), the same chemical used to treat ham. Scallops that have received this treatment should, by law, be labeled as such, but this isn't always the case. If you're not certain whether the scallops at the fish counter have been treated, take a good look at them. **An untreated, or dry-pack, scallop will be shiny, firm, and tacky to the touch.** A treated scallop will look opaque, ooze liquid, and feel slippery. If you're still uncertain, ask the fishmonger whether the scallops are wet (treated with STP) or dry-pack (untreated). If they've been treated, don't bother with them; they're not worth buying at any price. They'll exude all that extra water when they hit the pan, so they're impossible to sear. Also, from my point of view, wet-pack scallops taste like they've been sauced in deodorant.

Shrimp Shrimp are a dilemma for me. Much of the shrimp sold at fish counters is farm-raised, and most comes from largely unregulated farms in Southeast Asia and South America that have a significant negative impact on the surrounding environment. U.S. shrimp farming is much more highly regulated, but my issue with American farm-raised shrimp is that only a few top-quality producers manage to raise shrimp that taste good.

Fresh, never frozen, wild-caught shrimp are my shrimp of choice. You can't match the flavor. **But from a sustainability point of view, where that shrimp was caught matters.** Shrimp fisheries in the United States are the best regulated (and produce the best-tasting shrimp) in the world, though there are still issues of bycatch that remain to be addressed.

My choice, when I'm preparing a shrimp dish, are northern, or Maine, shrimp. They are available fresh or frozen, already shelled (look them over for any remaining shell pieces, though). Also try wild-caught shrimp from the Carolinas and Florida, especially when sold fresh. I have always loved Gulf shrimp, but the state of the shrimp fisheries in the Gulf of Mexico is unknown at the time of the writing of this book, as a result of the BP oil spill. It's just another cautionary tale of the fragility of our marine environment.

Squid Okay, squid do not grow in tiny rings in a breadcrumb sea. That said, they are an inexpensive and particularly healthy seafood choice, being low in fat and high in protein. I love to cook squid on the grill, especially when **I find fresh whole squid at the market—the skin chars beautifully and absorbs lots of great smoke flavor.** Any fishmonger selling whole squid should be happy to clean it for you, so ask for it to be prepared with the skin on—tubes and tents. This means that you want the bodies (tubes) whole and the tents (tentacles) intact.

Unfortunately, because squid spoils very quickly, you're more likely to find it frozen, already cleaned. But this is also a tasty product.

Striped Bass Sometimes proclaimed to be the king of fish, striped bass certainly is one of the species that first comes to mind for East Coast fish lovers. It is a great success story, too, of how we can work to restore fisheries to productive levels. Striped bass had reached dangerously low population levels in the 1980s, and an unprecedented multistate cooperative effort brought them back. It is now one of the major fisheries on the East Coast, both commercial and sport.

Striped bass makes for great eating, although it can contain high levels of PCBs, an environmental toxin, and should be consumed in moderation. It is almost always served with its beautiful skin on, but I like to remove the skin and the dark-colored flesh underneath as that is where the toxins mostly build up. **These fish can grow to epic size, and fillets can be up to two inches thick.** It has grayish-beige flesh that cooks up to a pretty white. The flake is fairly meaty, with a firm texture. Great on the grill or sautéed, striped bass is available most of the year.

Farm-raised striped bass is also available—these fish are actually a hybrid, a cross between wild striped bass and freshwater white bass. Use farmed striped bass as a replacement for snapper or when wild striped bass is unavailable. It doesn't have the same robust flavor and texture, but it's still a tasty fish. Also, farmed bass has no toxin concerns, so use it in place of wild for young children and pregnant moms.

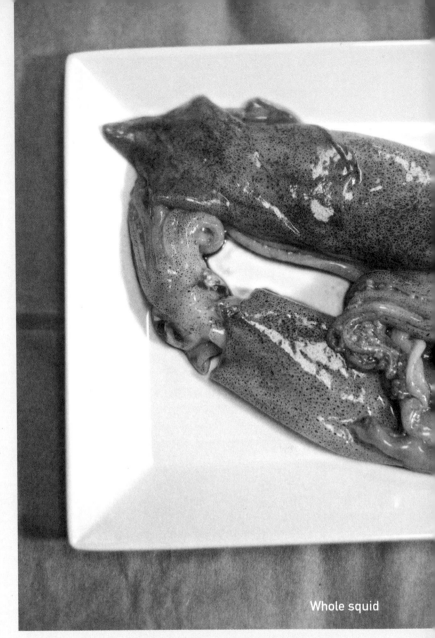

Whole squid

Sturgeon Sturgeon are a very slow-growing, long-lived fish of prehistoric pedigree—and they look the part, with thick, armored plates running the length of their bodies and super-thick skin. **Having survived in plentitude for millions of years, wild sturgeon were almost exterminated because of our love of caviar.** The sturgeon populations in the Caspian Sea that are the source for wild-caught caviar are today at dangerously low levels.

The good news is that sturgeon fisheries in the Pacific Northwest are recovering, and sustainable farm-raised sturgeon and sturgeon roe are now being produced there as well. The flesh is a pale off-white, flecked with an egg-yolk yellow fat that is very rich. Sturgeon should be cooked slowly to allow the fat to keep the meat moist. My favorite way to prepare it is to hot smoke it. Also, because the flesh can be a little rubbery, once it's cooked, serve it thinly sliced.

Tilapia Entirely farm-raised, tilapia is one of the most frequently consumed fish in the United States. But be careful what you buy, as the fish produced outside of the U.S. can have high environmental impact. So when buying this fish, always look for a domestically raised product, as U.S. farming operations are very clean. It is perfect for the home cook because it's always available and inexpensive; it's sold as a fillet, stays fresh for a long time, and has a mild flavor. All of which is a nice way of saying that eating tilapia is the most benign culinary experience a diner can have eating seafood. And many people are looking for exactly that. **I've included a number of recipes for tilapia that dial up the flavor interest factor.** It is one of the best environmental choices that we can make when shopping for dinner!

Trout Trout is always available. It's delicious, and it's one of the most versatile fish on the market. I love cooking trout whole, as it makes for such a great plate presentation. But it is also available as boneless fillets, which are very easy to prepare.

Most of the trout sold in this country comes from farms in the Western states, but there is a large cottage industry of small trout farmers as well, making fresh trout available in nearly every market. **My favorite producer is Sunburst Trout Farms in North Carolina. The Eason family has been at it on this property for more than eighty years, and their trout is simply the very best, with striking pink flesh.**

Try looking for a producer in your area. You can't beat driving over to a local farm and having your fish pulled directly from the water for freshness!

Smoked trout (which is also available from a lot of small, local producers) makes for an easy and luxurious garnish for soups and salads. If you like, you can try smoking your own (see page 252).

Tuna, Albacore Albacore is a lighter style than we are typically familiar with when eating fresh tuna. Much of the albacore that is caught goes into canned tuna, but there is a small amount available as tuna steaks through well-managed pole caught fisheries along the Pacific Coast. Look for these light pink loins, which have many of the same texture and taste characteristics of the more familiar bluefin and yellowfin tuna. Albacore is dense and meaty, with a rich, silky texture. Use it wherever fresh tuna is called for, but be aware that it is not as fatty as other types, so it needs to be served medium rare.

You might notice that I do not include any recipes for bluefin or yellowfin tuna in this book. Although yellowfin is listed as a sustainable fish by some guides, I choose not to serve it very often. Here's why: Eating tuna is like cutting down a redwood tree to build a campfire. Sure, it makes a nice fire, but you could get by just fine by cutting down a smaller tree. **Tuna and other apex predators such as sharks and swordfish are, in effect, the trees of the ocean.** Biomass is created through photosynthesis in plankton. Plankton are eaten by sardines. Sardines by mackerel. Mackerel by tunas. So the tuna is really the great aggregator of energy in the sea. All that plankton and all that energy gets stored in the flesh of the tuna, just as hundreds of years of sunlight is stored in that redwood. So when we eat tuna, or swordfish, we are eating the most inefficient protein on earth. The environmental cost is so high that it just doesn't warrant our sustained use of the product. Now, I think it is okay to eat some tuna, but rarely and with great celebration of what it is that lies on your plate.

And bluefin is just a disaster. There are so few of them left in the seas that we should not touch them at all, for any reason.

Wahoo Wahoo is the largest member of the mackerel family. As for its culinary characteristics, wahoo is rich and flaky, with beautiful white flesh, like mahimahi. **And like tuna, its flesh has lovely concentric rings and an oily sheen.** Wahoo also cooks like tuna, in that it is best served medium rare and sliced thin so that there is a textural difference between the seared outer surface and the silken rare interior. I sometimes see this fish served as "white tuna" in sushi restaurants, which, while not entirely correct, is not entirely off as a descriptor. I've included a recipe that uses wahoo raw, as **I love the way its cool flavor warms to match simple pairings such as fresh herbs.**

Wahoo is caught off every U.S. coast but is not always easy to find near shore. It is largely a recreational catch, but it supports a small commercial market as a bycatch of other fisheries. There is not a whole lot known about the population of wahoo, but there is a precautionary management plan in place to ensure that it is watched over. Wahoo does not freeze well, so always look for a fresh, never-been-frozen product.

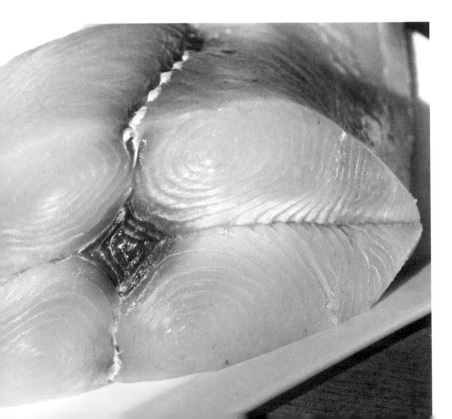

A Note to Midwesterners

To be perfectly honest, I am not too familiar with many of the fish available in the markets in the Midwest. I have seen and eaten pike, perch, carp, catfish, smelt, bass, and various trout. While there are some recipes that include some of these names, most of these recipes can easily trade out one fish for another, **so here is a list of species commonly available and the substitutions that I would make for them.**

Bluegill is a delicious fish. It is one of my favorites, but I can't ever find it. You can use it in place of bluefish, striped bass, mackerel, and other well-flavored species.

Carp is not really in my repertoire, but if it is available and to your liking, then use it in place of the more expensive halibut, sablefish, or even the slightly meatier mahimahi.

Pike can be used in many recipes for meatier fillets in place of bluefish and striped bass. Generally it is a good stand-in for species such as snapper, as it has a nice skin and firm, flaky texture.

Sunfish is, in my opinion, a great stand-in for flounder. You can also use it in recipes calling for tilapia.

Whitefish can be a great substitute for such white-fleshed fish as halibut, sablefish, and Pacific cod. It can also be used to replace some of the skin-on varieties such as barramundi and the much more highly flavored bluefish.

Other commonly available species like **channel catfish, smelts, and trout** are all represented in these recipes.

Left: Wahoo loin

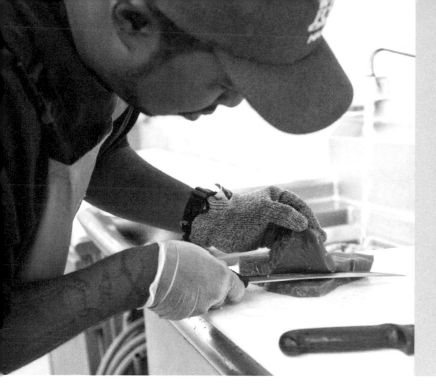

Omega-3s

Scientific studies have shown great benefits of a diet rich in omega-3 fatty acids ranging from reduced rates of coronary heart disease in adults to beneficial brain development impacts in children. We get these acids from both plants and seafood, although there is a great difference in the amount found in these ingredients. Fatty fish such as salmon and mackerel tend to have the highest concentrations of omega-3s, but they are also found in walnuts, leafy green vegetables and some cooking oils. Some small fish such as anchovies, sardines and herring deliver high levels of omega-3 thus giving me yet one more reason why they top my list of favorite seafoods. As we learn more about the benefits of omega-3 it is important to realize that even small portions of our favorite seafoods can deliver big benefits.

Mercury and Other Toxins in Seafood

While health professionals and the media tout the benefits of a diet rich in seafood, there are also some major concerns with toxins. These environmental toxins are the result of years of industrial input into our oceans. They accumulate in small fish, which in turn are eaten by larger fish, and so on. **The toxins travel up the food chain, eventually being absorbed into the flesh of the species that we find so tasty.** By consuming these fish, we absorb the toxins, and this can be a very bad thing indeed. However, not eating seafood can also be a bad thing, so it's important to understand the risks, and the benefits, of our dietary choices.

Some of the fish I like most have high levels of mercury, while others have high levels of a compound known as PCB; some are high in both. These include bluefish, wild striped bass, and, to a lesser extent, mackerel. While I include recipes for these fish, they should be enjoyed only occasionally. Both the EPA and FDA have information available on their websites about

fish and mercury. The Natural Resources Defense Council also has an online guide that conveniently lays out the facts and guidelines for seafood consumption (see Sustainable Sources and Web Links, page 272).

Being careful about what you eat is a good idea always, especially if you are pregnant or nursing. Many of the recipes that include seafood with elevated levels of toxins can easily be adapted to use other types of seafood.

Ways to Minimize Toxin Intake In terms of PCBs, one effective way to reduce your intake is to cut away the dark tissue just beneath the skin of a fillet. This is where PCBs tend to aggregate in the flesh. This by no means negates the PCB buildup, but it can help to reduce the amount you ingest when you enjoy your once-every-so-often striped bass fillet.

The easiest way to reduce your intake of all toxins is to eat smaller species of fish. Not as long-lived as larger species, they have less time to absorb the toxins. So not only are smaller species generally better for the environment, they are also better for you.

How to Shop for Fish

Most of the seafood bought in the United States is in the form of fillets. This eliminates most of the best ways to determine the freshness of the fish, but it also eliminates a lot of the work.

Even with fillets, there are still ways to suss out quality.

1. Check out the general cleanliness of the fish area. If it is grimy and smells like fish and the attendant has on a dirty apron, go for the canned sardines. If the store looks pleasant and bright and has a clean aroma with a presentable staff, then you have your first green light.

2. Look for fish fillets that are shiny and glistening in the light. If the fillets are pale and dull, pass them by.

3. Once you have decided on the best-looking species, ask to smell a piece. If the staff refuses, it is not a sign of poor quality but rather that they follow the health code. A bummer that you can't smell it, but another green light that they know better than to let you. The next best thing to do is to ask some questions. When was the fish brought into the store? When was it thawed? The answer you are looking for is "as recently as possible."

In the case of prepackaged fish, smell the container. Look at the overall quality of the display. Are the packages dry and clean to the touch? Also look at the package date—the seafood should be no older than a day or two at most.

And here is the best advice: introduce yourself to the person tending the counter. Once you are on a first-name basis, you are more likely to get something that you will be happy with and that they'll be proud to sell to you.

The Marine Stewardship Council

The Marine Stewardship Council (MSC) is one of the best things to happen to the sustainable seafood marketplace. It is an organization that operates the world's leading certification program for sustainable wild capture fisheries. When a product is labeled as coming from an MSC-certified fishery, you know, unquestionably, that it is coming from the right source.

One of the biggest problems facing the seafood industry is that seafood is so hard to trace through the distribution system. A salmon fillet coming from an environmentally unfriendly fishery looks just like one coming from a fishery that is doing everything right. The MSC program includes a very rigorous chain of custody auditing so that you can be sure of what you are buying. As a consumer, you can use their guarantee of origin as a way to reward fisheries that are making sustainability happen. It is something that you can tell your fishmonger, too—that you prefer to buy seafood that has been certified to the MSC standard.

So, when you are in the store, look for the logo that guarantees your purchase is supporting the right fisheries in the right places.

Frozen Seafood

Don't avoid frozen fish! In fact, seek it out. Technology has advanced and in almost all cases (except for certain fish that don't freeze well) buying frozen seafood can be as good as buying fresh. The only downside is that you cannot inspect its quality until you have already purchased it. **However, frozen seafood offers some of the best value at the fish counter.** Many fishing vessels and processors are equipped with state-of-the-art technology that allows them to quick-freeze seafood to subzero temperatures within hours of hauling it out of the water, thus ensuring top-quality product at the peak of freshness.

Stores can buy frozen seafood in bulk, knowing that they have a longer period to sell it, and often the savings will be passed on to the customer. If you buy the fish still frozen, there's also no rush for you to use it. You can put it in the freezer and move it to the refrigerator to thaw the day you want to cook it.

Frozen seafood also does not need to be shipped with the haste required for fresh fish. **This means it can be shipped by more environmentally friendly means, such as by container ship or by train, rather than by plane.**

Thawing To thaw frozen seafood, take it out of its wrapping and place it on a plate or in a shallow bowl (in the case of shrimp, for instance). Cover it with a moist paper towel and set it in the refrigerator. It should take six to eight hours to thaw. In the case of frozen whole fish, it's best to put it in the refrigerator the night before.

Buying thawed fish When buying seafood labeled as previously frozen in a store, check to see that the fillets are even in color. Any bleaching is an indication that the fillets were thawed in water, which leaches out flavor. Also ask when the fillets were thawed. Anything thawed more than a day before should be passed over.

Consuming Raw Seafood

Raw fish is something that you have to be careful about. From parasites to toxins, it is a risk to eat anything raw, but especially seafood. I have been made very sick by food that I have eaten, and yet still I eat raw seafood. There is something so beguiling about the silken texture of a slice of fatty raw king salmon that I keep coming back. The same goes with slurping a raw oyster straight from the shell. **Is it worth the risk? That is something you have to decide for yourself.** I've included a handful of dishes based on raw seafood; if you are going to prepare them, you need to have great confidence in your fishmonger. The recipe will not make the seafood safe. The recipe can't even make the seafood delicious. Only pristine, fresh, fresh, fresh seafood can make these recipes worth trying. So if you can't praise your seafood as the most brilliant that you have ever seen, then cook it.

I am very particular about which fish I serve raw. I especially dislike the texture of raw shrimp and other crustaceans and, in fact these sea creatures can be very dangerous when not cooked. I also avoid bottom-dwelling fish such as catfish.

Pairing Wine with Seafood

There is a lot of differing opinion on what to drink with seafood. Part of the problem is that seafood is the most diverse of all of the proteins. How can you consider salmon in the same boat as, say, clams? These are totally different flavors. Some of the straight rules that some folks try to apply, such as Sauvignon Blanc as a good pairing with everything, well, these rules broadly work, but mostly you should follow this one rule:

Drink what you like, eat what you like.

If you really enjoy the wine and you really like the recipe, then chances are you are going to have a good experience—even if it is a light, delicate flavor such as fresh raw shellfish paired with a robust California Cabernet. While I don't recommend this pairing, if it's what you dig, then go ahead. You are not drinking wine to impress anybody, just enjoy yourself.

Often, the flavors in a dish that you want to focus on are the accompanying ingredients to the protein. For example, with a dish such as Bluefish with Charred Green Beans and Almond Aioli (page 105), try to pair the wine with the almonds. It is a strong flavor and a consistent presence in each bite, so try a nutty Fiano di Avellino from the Campania region of Italy. Or with a dish that uses fresh tarragon as a finishing herb, look for a crisp unoaked Chardonnay, which has the tarragon-like zing of green apples.

Most of all, though, have fun with the wine selection. **If you have a great relationship with a particular wine merchant, get his or her opinion and ask for something a little different.** Most wine folks are happy to point you in a direction that will suit your needs and also give you a bit of entertainment. The best way to become knowledgeable about wine is to try something new and learn about that one wine and region. It is tough to sit yourself down in front of a giant book and task yourself with memorizing the whole thing before you go shopping. If you are stressed about wine, have a glass of wine. If you are stressed about what wine to serve with dinner, pick the wine first and make a dish that tastes like the wine.

A Note on Beer A crisp, clean, refreshing beer is often what we reach for first with seafood, especially shellfish such as oysters and shrimp. **The staggering variety of flavors that are offered in beers can create some really great pairings with seafood dishes.** So consider this option as well, especially if you are hosting a more informal gathering where beer is the natural choice.

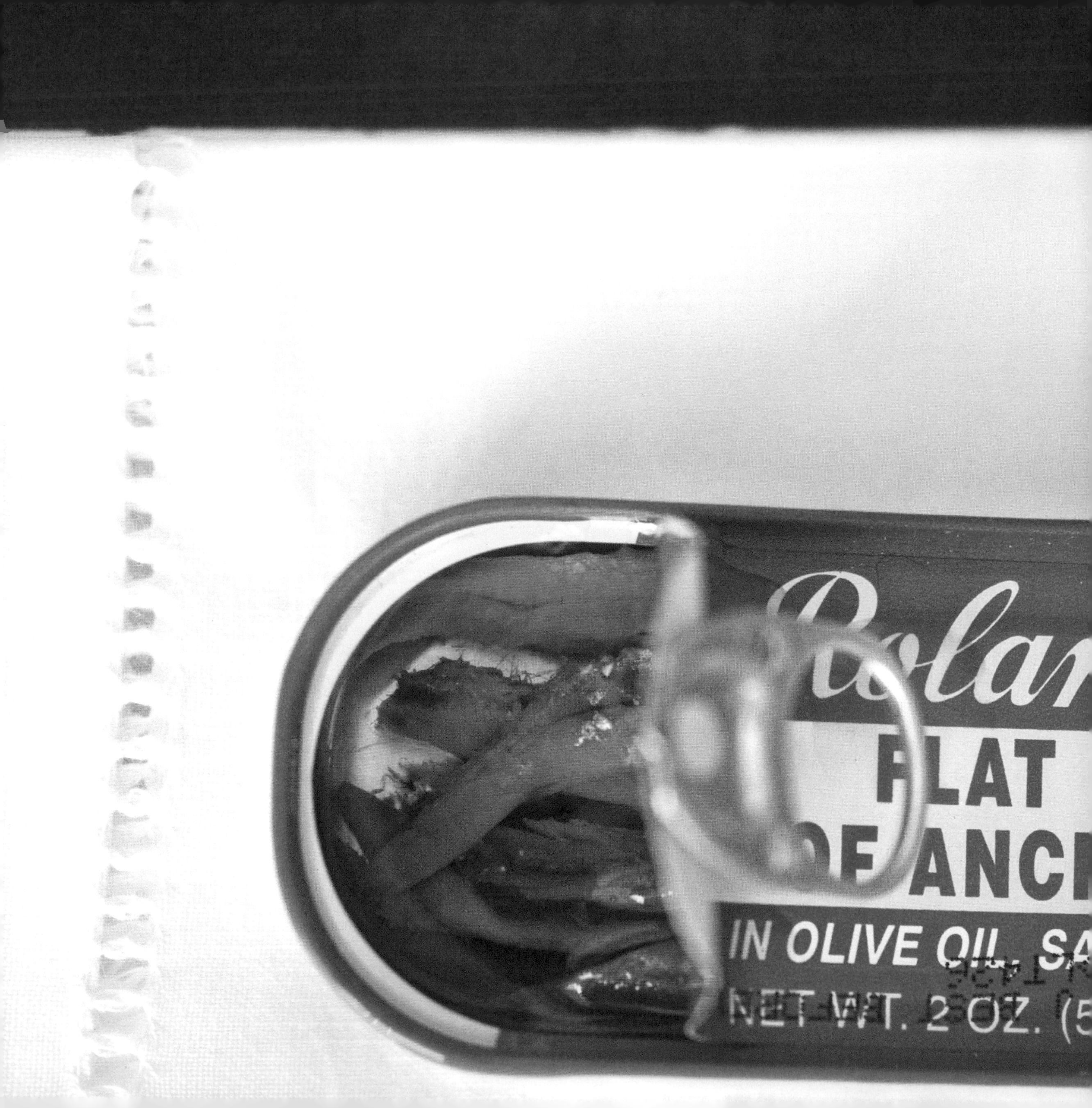
FLAT
IN OLIVE OIL
NET WT. 2 OZ.

SPPRING

Spring is often hailed as the greatest season. I beg to differ. I like spring, don't get me wrong, but I like consistency, and you don't get much of that with spring. In the kitchen, this season brings more of a swing in ingredients than any other time of year. As it begins, you don't have much left in the vegetable larder but turnips and leftover rutabagas. Unfortunately, people change their attitudes a lot faster than plants grow. A little nice weather and the ladies are out in their sundresses, men are running around in short-sleeves, and everyone wants to eat juicy, ripe tomatoes. But by the end of spring the gardens are starting to produce: baby salad greens, asparagus, sugar snap peas, and the first strawberries.

It's a little different with the seafood. In spring, the small fish begin to make their way up the coasts, and the bigger ones follow. Late spring in Alaska marks the return of the noble salmon to the large river systems. Halibut, sablefish, crabs, and mackerel, among others, all begin to stir the waters once again.

I like to cook comfort foods for the still-cool nights. But as the days lengthen, my plates begin to show the colors of an ever-changing palette of fresh ingredients.

A little nice weather and the ladies are out in their sundresses, men are running around in short-sleeves, and everyone wants to eat juicy, ripe tomatoes.

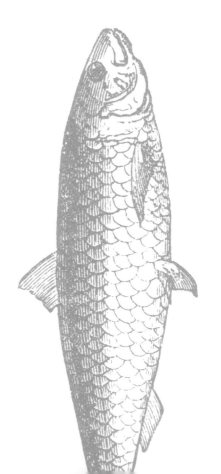

Cured Herring on Endive
with Chive Aioli

I was inspired to include this recipe while watching a herring run on the shores of Martha's Vineyard. The vast schools of fish were making their way up the shore and into the creeks to spawn. They were being chased by a few hungry striped bass, and all the while I kept thinking about having herring for breakfast. This recipe takes a couple of days, so plan ahead. The fish will keep in the oil for up to a week, so make extra if you want. You can also make this recipe using store-bought pickled herring, skipping the curing process. If you do, look for white wine–marinated herring, or another favorite preparation (though I would advise you not to choose herring packed in sour cream).

Kosher salt

1/2 tablespoon sugar

3/4 pound skin-on herring fillets

1/2 cup extra-virgin olive oil

1 large egg yolk

1/2 teaspoon red wine vinegar

1/4 bunch fresh chives, very thinly sliced, about two tablespoons

2 Belgian endives, leaves separated

For the herring, mix 1 tablespoon salt and the sugar. Layer the fillets in a small baking dish and sprinkle with half of the mixture. Flip the fillets over and sprinkle with the rest of the mixture. Wrap tightly with plastic wrap and refrigerate for 24 hours.

Very gently dip the herring in cold water to remove the salty film, but do not wash thoroughly. Slice the fillets into 1-inch strips, pack into a small dish, and cover with the olive oil. Cover with plastic wrap and return them to the fridge for another 24 hours.

When you are ready to serve, strain off and reserve the olive oil.

For the aioli, in a small bowl, whisk together the egg yolk, vinegar, and a pinch of salt. In a slow, steady stream, whisking all the while, add the reserved olive oil from the herring. Continue to whisk until the aioli thickens. Stir in the chives.

Place a piece of herring in each endive leaf and top with a small spoonful of aioli. Serve immediately.

Serves 4 as an appetizer

Mackerel Crudo with Almond Oil and Raisins

Mackerel is one of my favorite fish, and it's fantastic raw, with a robust flavor that stands up to a savory-sweet topping of raisins and almonds. Make sure your fish is absolutely fresh for this—please read Consuming Raw Seafood (page 43).

2 tablespoons water

1 tablespoon golden raisins

1 tablespoon sherry vinegar

2 tablespoons slivered almonds, chopped

2 tablespoons extra-virgin olive oil

12-ounces skin-on Spanish or Boston (not king) mackerel fillet

Kosher salt

Baby mint leaves picked from heart of sprigs

Combine the water, raisins, and vinegar in a small microwave-safe bowl and heat on high power for 1 minute. Allow the raisins to sit so they absorb the liquid. This is best done overnight for the most flavor, but they will have softened enough to proceed in about 10 minutes or so. It is a nice touch if the raisins are hot when you plate this dish, so reheat them in the microwave for a few seconds just before serving.

Combine the almonds and olive oil in a small pan over medium heat. Cook slowly, stirring constantly, until the almonds just start to turn brown. They will continue to cook in the hot oil, so pull them off the heat before you think they are ready. And do not take your eyes off the pan while you are doing this; it only takes 2 minutes or so. If you try to do something else, they will burn, and you'll have to toss them out. Allow the almonds to cool to room temperature.

Chill the plates you intend to serve the mackerel on for a few minutes (but only a few minutes—if they get too cold, condensation will form on them when they're taken out of the refrigerator, and that water will dilute the food).

To cut the mackerel, use a very sharp, thin-bladed knife. Work from the head of the fillet toward the tail. Place the base of the knife blade at a 45-degree angle on the fillet to make a slice that is about 1/4 inch thick. Gently pull the knife blade through the fish in one smooth stroke. When the knife reaches the skin, gently turn the blade to be parallel with the skin and cut to separate the slice from the skin. (See page 248 for illustrated step-by-step directions.)

With the fish still on the knife, transfer it to one of the chilled plates. Take care how you place the fish on the plate as it will be difficult to move once set. Continue this process, placing a slice on each plate. Slice the fillet in this manner until you reach about an inch from the tail. (This meat has too many connective tissues in it to be used in a preparation like this.)

To serve, season the fish with a few grains of kosher salt. Spoon a small amount of the almonds and the oil over the fish and place a few warm raisins on the plate (there should be about 1 raisin per bite of fish). Garnish with a few mint leaves and serve immediately.

Serves 4 as a first course

Cured Sardines with Celery and Walnuts

This recipe takes a few days, but is a magnificent way to take advantage of fresh sardines—the cured fillets are luscious and intensely flavored. The salad provides a tasty backdrop for the meaty sardines as well as a contrast in textures.

1/3 cup coarse sea salt

8 large fresh sardines, heads removed, scaled and gutted

1 tablespoon red wine vinegar

1/4 cup extra-virgin olive oil

1/2 cup walnuts, toasted (page 15)

4 ribs celery, very thinly sliced

Pinch of red chile flakes

Freshly cracked black pepper

Focaccia bread, sliced and toasted

For the sardines, sprinkle a little of the sea salt in a container just large enough to hold the fish in a single layer. Lay the fish down with the spines on the bottom so that the belly cavity is facing up. (You know, pack 'em in like sardines!) Sprinkle the remaining salt over the top, wrap tightly in plastic wrap, and refrigerate for 2 days.

Wash the sardines in cold water to remove the salt. Gently fillet the fish by running a finger down the spine to release the fillets, which should come off with ease. Taste a small portion of a fillet; if it is too salty, soak the fillets in water for a few minutes. Pat the fillets dry and lay on plates. Sprinkle the fillets with the vinegar, then coat with the olive oil.

Mix the walnuts, celery, chile flakes, and a couple twists of pepper in a medium bowl and toss to combine. Spoon the nut mixture over the fillets and serve with toasted bread.

Serves 4 as a first course

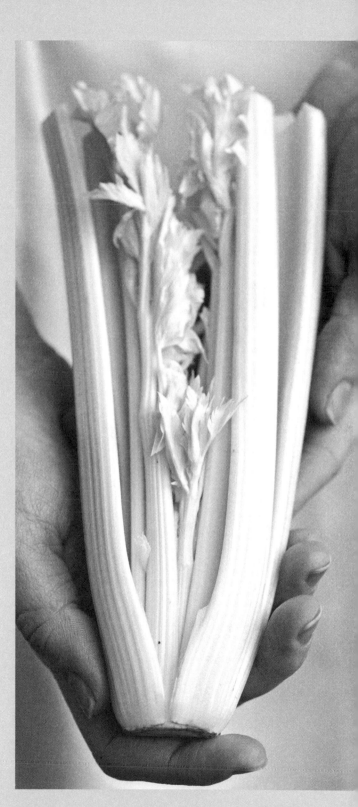

Sardines with Currants and Roasted Pine Nuts

Whole sardines are delicious and easy to cook. They require a little work at the table, but so does lobster, and I don't hear many people complaining about that! This works best as an appetizer but can easily be made into an entrée portion or a light lunch. It's best served with a salad of peppery greens such as young mustard, radish, or turnip greens and arugula.

1 shallot, diced

3 1/2 tablespoons butter

1 cup white wine

1/4 cup currants, or raisins roughly chopped

1/4 cup pine nuts, toasted (page 15)

Leaves from 1 bunch fresh flat-leaf parsley, chopped

Salt

8 sardines, brined (page 249)

1/2 tablespoon canola oil

For the sauce, sauté the shallot in 1/2 tablespoon of the butter over medium heat. When it is translucent, add the wine and currants and simmer until the wine is reduced to about 1 tablespoon. Remove from the heat, cut the remaining butter into small cubes and add them one at a time, swirling each in the pan until it is incorporated. Once they have all been added, you should have a thick, creamy sauce. Stir in the pine nuts and parsley. Season with a little salt.

Preheat the broiler.

For the sardines, gently scale the fish by running your finger from the tail toward the head. Do this under running water so the scales wash away. Using a paring knife, gently cut through the belly cavity and use the back side of the knife to scrape out the innards. Wash the cavity under running water. Pat the fish dry, then brush with the canola oil. Place the fish in a large baking dish in a single layer and season with salt. Broil for about 3 minutes. Flip the fish and broil the other side for 5 minutes.

Turn the fish onto a serving plate. Spoon the sauce over the sardines and serve immediately.

Serves 4 as a first course or light entrée

Pounded Tuna with Spices and Herbs

Tuna is one of the most popular fish in our diets, but there are serious environmental concerns associated with the way it is captured. There are fishermen who do it right, and they deserve to be supported; when buying canned tuna, check the label and look for brands whose tuna is pole- or troll-caught. These can be expensive, but it's the right thing to do. While I don't recommend eating tuna all the time, when you do, treat it as a celebration and get the most out of it. In this recipe, I prepare it as an incredibly tasty and easy party appetizer. You get all the great flavor of the tuna without serving very much of it.

One 6-ounce can albacore tuna, packed in water

1/4 cup extra-virgin olive oil

1 tablespoon whole-grain mustard

Pinch of salt

1 tablespoon chopped fresh tarragon

1 tablespoon chopped fresh flat-leaf parsley

5 slices dark bread, such as rye or pumpernickel

Open and drain the can of tuna. Place the fish in a medium bowl and mash with a whisk until it is a fine paste. Add the olive oil, mustard, and salt. Continue to whisk until all the oil has been incorporated. Add the chopped herbs and mix to combine. Check for seasoning and let sit for at least 20 minutes to allow the flavors to develop. Keep at room temperature if you are serving immediately. If not, then place in the fridge. The mixture keeps, tightly covered, in the refrigerator for up to 3 days.

Preheat the oven to 350 degrees.

Meanwhile, trim the crusts off the bread slices and cut them into quarters. You can do either triangles or squares, depending on your preference. Place the bread pieces on a baking sheet and bake them until they are just crisp, about 4 minutes.

To compose the canapés, take two teaspoons and gather about half a spoonful of the tuna mixture in one of them. Carefully shape the tuna with the other spoon, transferring the mixture between the spoons with a cupping motion until you have an attractive mound. Gently transfer the mound onto a toast and serve immediately.

Makes about 20 canapés

Marinated Clams with Minted Lemon Marinade and Pine Nuts

This is a nice choice for a party because so much of the process can be done in advance. This recipe can be multiplied to make as many pieces as you need. If you can find razor clams, by all means use them. They're available on both coasts and make for an impressive presentation, as their shells (not surprisingly) are shaped like an old straight razor.

12 littleneck or razor clams, rinsed thoroughly (discard any that won't close)

5 fresh mint leaves, thinly sliced

2 sprigs fresh flat-leaf parsley, chopped

Juice of 1/2 lemon

1 tablespoon extra-virgin olive oil

Kosher salt

1 tablespoon pine nuts

1 small serrano chile, thinly sliced

Place the clams in a small pot, cover with cold water, and place over high heat. As soon as they begin to open, remove them from the water one at a time. Discard any clams that have not opened after 5 minutes of boiling. Remove the clam meat from the shells. Scrape the shells clean and set them aside. Place the clams in a small bowl.

For the marinade, mix the mint, parsley, lemon juice, and olive oil. Season with a little salt and stir well. Pour over the clams and mix to coat well. Check for seasoning and add a touch more salt if necessary. The clams can sit at this point in the refrigerator for as long as overnight but are best after an hour or two.

To serve, spoon one marinated clam back into each shell and place on a bed of salt to keep stable. Once all the clams are distributed, discard the unused shells. Pour any remaining marinade into the clams and garnish with roughly chopped pine nuts or grate them on top of each clam using a Microplane. Garnish each shell with one slice of the chile. Serve immediately.

Makes 1 dozen canapés

Steamed Clams and Basil Pesto

Steamed shellfish work with so many different flavors. Here I top clams with a bright basil pesto. It is a super-easy preparation and makes an elegant and easy weeknight meal.

3 dozen littleneck clams, rinsed thoroughly (discard any that won't close)

1 cup white wine

1/2 cup Basil Pesto (page 266)

2 tablespoons butter

1 crusty baguette, sliced and toasted

Place the clams and wine in a covered pot over high heat. As the broth begins to boil, gently stir the clams to ensure that they cook evenly.

Once all the shells are open (discard any that haven't opened after 5 minutes), remove the clams from the pot and place them in serving bowls, leaving as much of the broth in the pot as possible. Carefully pour the broth into a bowl, leaving any sand that has collected in the bottom of the pot. Add the pesto and butter to the clam broth and stir to combine. Pour over the clams and serve with toasted bread.

Serves 4 as an appetizer or light entrée

Clams and Mussels en Escabeche

Both clams and mussels can handle some pretty big flavors. This dish uses a highly spiced marinade with lots of vegetables to enliven the cooked shellfish. The vegetables not only add a layer of complexity but also some heft and texture to the dish.

24 littleneck clams, rinsed thoroughly (discard any that won't close)

1 cup white wine

1 pound mussels, scrubbed and debearded (discard any that won't close)

1 cup extra-virgin olive oil

1 carrot, peeled and sliced into thin rounds

1 bunch scallions, chopped (white and green parts kept separated)

3 cloves garlic, peeled and thinly sliced

2 teaspoons sweet smoked paprika

1 teaspoon coriander seeds

Zest of 1 lemon, removed in strips with a peeler

1 tablespoon sherry vinegar

3 tablespoons chopped fresh flat-leaf parsley

1 loaf crusty bread such as baguette, sliced and gently toasted

To open the clams, place them in a small pot with the wine and bring to a boil. Cover and steam until all the shells have opened, about 5 minutes. Discard any clams that haven't opened. Remove the clams from the pot, leaving the cooking liquid, and extract the meat from the shells. Reserve half the shells.

Add the mussels to the pot and repeat the process, again reserving half the shells.

Strain the broth by allowing it to sit undisturbed for a few minutes so any grit falls to the bottom. Gently pour off the clear liquid from the top and save 1 cup of the broth for the marinade.

For the marinade, put the olive oil in a small pot with the carrot, scallion whites, and garlic. Simmer over medium heat until the carrot slices begin to soften, about 3 minutes. Add the paprika and coriander and cook for another minute. Add the lemon zest and simmer for another 3 minutes. Add the reserved cooking broth and vinegar and bring to a boil. Reduce by about half, then add the parsley and clam and mussel meat. Stir to mix well. Let cool to lukewarm, then refrigerate covered for at least 1 hour and up to overnight (they taste much better if you let them marinate overnight). Stir the mixture as it cools so that everything marinates evenly.

Serve the clams and mussels by placing a spoonful of the mixture in each shell, then set the clams in a serving dish and pour any remaining marinade over them. Let the mixture come to room temperature before serving to get the most flavor from the dish. Serve with toasted bread.

Serves 4 as an appetizer

Chilled Mussels with Toasted Fennel and Sour Cream

In this elegant appetizer I pair the bright, clean flavor of fennel (amplified by the Pernod) with the cool richness of sour cream to balance the brininess of the mussels. When it comes time to serve the mussels, use a layer of Kosher salt on the platter to ensure that the shells stay upright.

2 pounds mussels (25 to 35), scrubbed and debearded (discard any that won't close)

1 cup water

2 tablespoons Pernod or other anise-flavored liqueur

1 bay leaf

3 tablespoons extra-virgin olive oil

1 tablespoon fennel seeds, toasted and ground (page 9)

1 cup sour cream

Place the mussels, water, Pernod, and bay leaf in a pot and bring to a boil, then cook for 5 minutes. Cover and steam until all the shells have opened. Discard any mussels that have not opened after 5 minutes of cooking. Remove the meat from the shells and discard the top shells.

Place the mussels in a small bowl and toss with the olive oil and fennel until evenly coated, then chill in the refrigerator for at least an hour but no longer than one day.

A few minutes before serving, fill each reserved mussel shell with a small dollop of the sour cream and top with one mussel per shell. Divide any remaining marinade among the shells and serve.

Serves 4 as an appetizer

Broiled Oysters with Peach and Paprika

I love me some broiled oysters! Such a broad range of flavors can be paired with their salty brine that you can let your imagination run free. Here, the combination of the sweet jelly with the slight bite of the smoked pepper is one of my favorites. I serve this as a light meal, but the quantities can be reduced to make it an appetizer. These are also great served straight from the oven as a cocktail canapé.

24 oysters, washed thoroughly

2 tablespoons butter

2 tablespoons peach jelly

1/2 tablespoon sweet smoked paprika

1 cup fine dried bread crumbs

Preheat the broiler.

Shuck the oysters (page 33) and discard the top shells. Arrange them on a baking sheet so that they hold their juices; you may need to pour a layer of salt under them to stabilize them.

Melt the butter with the jelly and the smoked paprika in a small saucepan over low heat. Place a small spoonful of the mixture on top of each oyster. Top each with a sprinkling of bread crumbs.

Broil until the edges of the oysters begin to curl and the bread crumbs are crisp and golden brown, about 5 minutes. Serve immediately.

Makes 24 oysters (appetizer for 6)

Mixed Seafood Salad

This chilled marinated salad, inspired by the Italian dish *frutti di mare*, is equally at home at a fancy dinner party or a casual lunch. Use whatever seafood looks best at market, adding Maine shrimp, clams, poached fish, smoked oysters, or anything else that catches your eye.

2 pounds mussels, scrubbed and debearded (discard any that won't close)

1 cup water

Juice of 1 lemon

1/2 pound cleaned squid

Kosher salt

Freshly ground black pepper

2 tablespoons extra-virgin olive oil

1 head frisée lettuce, separated into leaves and heavy stems removed

Leaves from 1/2 bunch fresh cilantro (about 2 cups, loosely packed)

2 ribs celery, sliced as thinly as possible

1/2 small red onion, very thinly sliced

Red chile flakes

Place the mussels in a covered pot with the water and half the lemon juice. Cook over high heat until the shells begin to open. Remove the mussels to a bowl as they open, leaving behind as much of the broth as possible. Discard any mussels that haven't opened after 5 minutes. Remove the mussels from their shells, saving only the meat.

Prepare the squid by slicing the tubes across into the thinnest possible rings. Leave the tentacles intact. Place the squid in the pot with the mussel broth and place over medium heat. Cook until the squid begins to stiffen. Stir constantly so it cooks evenly and does not glom together. After about 5 minutes, the squid will be cooked. Remove it from the broth and add it to the mussels.

To make the dressing, mix 1 tablespoon of the cooking broth with the remaining lemon juice. Season with a little salt and a few cracks of black pepper. Add the olive oil and whisk to combine. Pour over the mussels and squid and mix. Marinate the seafood for at least 1 hour but no longer than overnight.

To serve, mix the frisée with the cilantro, celery, and onion and add the marinated seafood. Check for seasoning and add more salt if necessary. Toss to combine and serve immediately. Offer a pinch of red chile flakes at the table.

Serves 4 as a first course

Txalaparta Bread Dip

I had this dish in a truly fantastic restaurant called Txalaparta in Barcelona when I was traveling with my wife. It's similar to the Italian dip *bagna cauda* but is meant to be served with bread instead of vegetables. Serve it with lots of super-chilled white wine.

1 cup extra-virgin olive oil

3 salt-packed anchovies (page 24–25) or 6 oil-packed anchovy fillets

2 cloves garlic, grated on a Microplane or very finely minced

2 tablespoons chopped fresh flat-leaf parsley

Pinch of red chile flakes

1 loaf crusty baguette, sliced

In a small saucepan, heat the olive oil over medium heat until warm. Add the anchovies and garlic and cook for about a minute, just until the garlic begins to brown. Remove from the heat and add the parsley and chile flakes. The oil will pretty much dissolve the anchovy fillets, giving you an incredibly flavored oil to dip your bread into. Best if served hot.

Serves 4 as an appetizer

Avocado-Dill Soup with Smoked Trout

My great friend and mentor, David Scribner, taught me how to make this soup. He was messing around with new dishes once, trying to impress a girl, and came across the combination of dill and avocado. I have made this soup ever since and love the versatility of the garnish, which can range from sliced crisp vegetables to seafood. With its beautiful green hue, this cold soup is equally well suited to serve at a formal dinner or a picnic.

3 very ripe avocados, each cut in half and pitted

1 bunch fresh dill

3 cups half-and-half, plus more if needed

Juice of 2 limes

Salt

6 ounces smoked trout fillet, skin discarded, shredded

2 tablespoons extra-virgin olive oil

Freshly ground black pepper

Scrape the avocado flesh from the skins into a blender. Reserve a few sprigs of the dill for garnish and add the rest, along with the half-and-half and lime juice, to the blender. Season generously with salt and blend on high speed until you have a very fine purée. If the soup is too thick, add a few extra tablespoons of half-and-half or water. Transfer to a bowl and cover with plastic wrap, pressing the wrap against the surface of the soup to keep the soup from discoloring. Chill in the refrigerator for at least 1 hour (you can refrigerate it up to a day, but there will be some discoloration).

To serve, divide the shredded trout among 4 bowls. Sprinkle with the olive oil and add the remaining sprigs of dill. Season with a few cracks of pepper. Ladle the chilled soup into the bowls.

Serves 4

Barramundi with Toasted Almond Butter and Basmati Pilaf

Barramundi is a great substitute for the not-always-available and usually-not-sustainable snapper. It has the same thin skin, which crisps nicely in the pan, and a similar meaty, firm texture and mild sweetness. Here, I pair it with a simple rice pilaf enlivened with scallions. The almond butter pairs nicely with all kinds of fish—I particularly like it over grilled seafood. Make a double batch to have around, and it will be a great easy addition to any meal. You can even try melting it over roasted vegetables.

2 tablespoons extra-virgin olive oil, plus more for brushing fillets

1 1/2 cups basmati rice

3 cups water

Salt

3 tablespoons slivered almonds

3 tablespoons butter, softened

1 teaspoon prepared horseradish

1 clove garlic, finely grated on a Microplane or very finely minced

1/2 tablespoon chopped fresh flat-leaf parsley

Four 5-ounce portions skin-on barramundi fillet, brined (page 249)

1 bunch scallions, chopped

For the pilaf, heat the olive oil in a medium saucepan over high heat. Add the rice and cook, stirring constantly, until the rice is golden brown and has a rich, nutty aroma. Add the water and bring to a simmer. Season with salt to taste and reduce the heat to low. Cover and let cook until all of the water is absorbed, about 15 minutes.

Preheat the broiler.

For the flavored butter, toast the almonds in a small, dry sauté pan over medium heat. This should take 3 to 4 minutes—watch closely! Continuously shake the pan so the nuts brown evenly all over. When they are golden brown (a little uneven color is okay here), place them in a small bowl and add the butter, horseradish, garlic, parsley, and a pinch of salt. Mix to incorporate and set aside.

For the barramundi, place each of the fillets in an ovenproof pan with the skin side up. Brush the skin of each fillet with a little bit of oil and broil for about 7 minutes. The skin should begin to blister and crisp as the flesh cooks evenly. Pull it from the oven just before the fillets are cooked through, as the pan will hold enough heat to finish the cooking.

To serve, mix the rice with a fork to fluff it, then add the scallions, reserving a little for garnish. Divide the rice between plates and place a fillet on top. Top each fillet with a spoonful of the almond butter and sprinkle with the remaining scallions.

Serves 4

Cobia with Walnut Purée and Asparagus

Cobia is a very meaty fish that can stand up to grilling. It must be cooked slowly, though; it is so dense that the outside will dry out long before the inside cooks if it is subjected to high heat for too long. This recipe also works with the oven and broiler: cook the fish at 250 degrees for 20 minutes, then transfer the fish to the bottom rack while you broil the asparagus until crispy. The asparagus should be browned and the fish will be done by that point.

2 bunches asparagus (about 2 pounds), heavy bottoms trimmed

1 small onion, peeled

3 cloves garlic, peeled

1/2 cup extra-virgin olive oil

1/2 cup walnuts

Juice of 1 lemon

3/4 cup cold water

Salt

Four 5-ounce portions cobia fillet

Blanch the asparagus in boiling water for 2 minutes (if the spears are particularly thin, shock them in ice water and drain). Set aside.

For the walnut purée, place the onion and garlic with the olive oil in a small pot. Simmer over medium heat until the onion begins to soften, about 5 minutes. Add the walnuts and continue to cook for another 4 minutes. Remove the pan from the heat and stir in the lemon juice. Carefully transfer the contents of the pot to a blender. Starting on very low speed, pulse the mixture a few times to get the purée going and begin to gradually increase the speed. Add the water and continue to blend until it is a smooth purée. Season to taste with salt. The sauce will keep, refrigerated, up to 5 days.

For the cobia, prepare a grill according to the instructions on page 250. Place the cobia on the hottest part of the grill and cook for 4 minutes. Rotate the grate so the fish is over the coolest part of the grill and cover the grill. Cook for another 12 minutes. When the fish is almost cooked through, place the asparagus over the hottest part of the grill and cook until charred.

To serve, brush the plates with a generous spoonful of the walnut purée and place the asparagus on it. Place the fish on top of the asparagus and serve.

Serves 4

Halibut with Ginger-Raisin Crust

I love raisins with fish—they have the perfect balance of sweet and acid, which really accentuates the flavors of not-so-strong-flavored fish, a.k.a. slightly bland-tasting halibut. I like to use larger pieces of halibut here as they are easier to deal with than smaller fillets. These larger pieces can be divided at the table.

2 1/2 tablespoons butter

1/4 cup raisins, chopped into a paste

3 tablespoons panko (Japanese-style bread crumbs)

1 tablespoon peeled and grated fresh ginger

2 teaspoons ground mace

Grated zest of 1 orange

Two 10-ounce portions halibut fillet

Preheat the oven to 300 degrees.

For the coating, melt 2 tablespoons of the butter and combine it with the raisin paste in a small bowl. Add the panko, ginger, mace, and orange zest and mix well. You should have a thick, slightly sticky paste.

Pat the halibut as dry as possible, then press the breading paste into the top of the fish and gently massage it so that it sticks.

Heat a large, ovenproof sauté pan over medium-high heat. Melt the remaining 1/2 tablespoon butter in the pan, then place the halibut, breading side down, in the butter. Cook, without moving the fish, until the coating begins to brown around the edges, about 4 minutes. Transfer the whole pan into the oven and cook for 20 minutes for a piece of halibut that is 1 1/2 inches thick. This will ensure that the breading continues to cook evenly and becomes very crispy while protecting the fish and keeping it moist.

Once the halibut is done, it will begin to flake apart if slight pressure is applied to the side. Using a spatula, gently turn the fish out of the pan and onto the serving plates with the breaded side facing up.

Serves 4

Mahimahi with Cilantro-Almond Pesto and Sweet Potatoes

I really like mahi on the grill, as its sweet and meaty flavor is nicely complemented by the smokiness of the fire. In this recipe, I also grill sweet potatoes, making this an easy all-in-one dish. The cilantro pesto is tough to make in small quantities (enough for only one meal), but it freezes well, so go ahead and make a big batch. Split it into a few smaller packs and freeze until needed (it'll keep up to nine months).

2 pounds sweet potatoes, left unpeeled and cut into 1-inch-thick wedges

Tabasco sauce

Salt

1 clove garlic, peeled

1/2 cup slivered almonds

1/2 cup canola oil, plus more for brushing fish and potatoes

1 bunch cilantro

Four 5-ounce portions mahimahi fillet

1 lime, cut into wedges

Place the sweet potatoes in a large saucepan, sprinkle them with a few drops Tabasco, and cover with water. Season generously with salt and bring to a simmer over medium heat. Cook until the potatoes are just tender when pierced with a knife, about 4 minutes. Drain and let cool. The potatoes can be cooked up to a day in advance and refrigerated.

For the pesto, place the garlic, almonds, and oil in a blender and pulse to combine. With the blender on medium speed, begin to add the cilantro a handful at a time. Continue until it has all been added, the leaves are all puréed, and you have a thick paste. Season to taste with salt. (It will keep, tightly covered, up to a week in the refrigerator.)

For the mahimahi, prepare a grill according to the instructions on page 250. Brush the fillets and sweet potatoes with canola oil and season with salt. Place the fish on the hottest part of the grill and sear for 4 minutes. Rotate the grate so the fish is over the coolest part of the grill. Place the sweet potato wedges over the hot part of the fire and cover the grill. Grill until the fish is cooked through and the potatoes are well seared, another 10 minutes or so.

To serve, place a generous spoonful of the pesto onto each plate. Using the back of the spoon, push the sauce toward the edge to create a swoosh. Arrange a mound of the potato wedges in the small of the swoosh and a fillet directly on top of the potatoes. Serve with lime wedges.

Serves 4

Pacific Cod with Ginger-braised Asparagus

Asparagus is so versatile. Here it gets a bit of an Asian treatment with the addition of fresh ginger and garlic. The cod has a nice chewy flake to it and its flavor is a good foil for the ginger.

1 egg white

1 teaspoon whole-grain mustard

Four 5-ounce portions Pacific cod fillet

1/2 cup panko
(Japanese-style bread crumbs)

Grated zest and juice of 1 orange

1 tablespoon butter

2 teaspoons peeled and chopped fresh ginger

1 clove garlic, sliced

2 pounds asparagus, heavy bottoms trimmed

Salt

1/2 cup water

Preheat the broiler.

Whisk together the egg white and mustard well, until the white is no longer stringy. Lightly brush each of the fillets on one side with the egg mixture. Mix the panko and orange zest and sprinkle over the top of each fillet. Gently pat down to ensure that the breading adheres to the fish. Set the fillets on a baking sheet and broil until golden brown. Turn off the broiler and move the cod to the lowest rack in the oven to continue to cook slowly.

For the asparagus, heat the butter, ginger, and garlic over medium heat in a large sauté pan. When the butter begins to froth and the garlic begins to soften, add the asparagus so that all the spears point the same direction. Season with salt and pour in the orange juice and water. Bring to a boil and cook until the liquid has reduced to a glaze.

Serve the cod fillets with the asparagus and spoon any remaining glaze on top.

Serves 4

Sablefish in Aromatic Broth with Pistachio, Celery, Shallots, and Orange

I like the ease of poaching, and I really like this recipe because not only do you end up with a moist, flavorful piece of fish, but the poaching liquid becomes the basis of a rich, easy-to-make sauce. When served over slices of toasted bread, the contrast of the crunchy, slightly charred bread and the delicate sauce makes for inspired eating.

1 orange, cut into segments (page 7), peel reserved

Four 5-ounce portions sablefish (black cod) fillet

1/2 cup unsalted shelled pistachios, toasted (page 15)

2 ribs celery, thinly sliced

1/4 cup extra-virgin olive oil

1 shallot, peeled and thinly sliced

3/4 cup white wine

1/2 cup water

Salt

1 1/2 teaspoons cornstarch

4 thick slices country-style sourdough bread

Preheat the oven to 200 degrees.

Cut a piece of the orange peel into a roughly 1-inch square and slice it into thin strips. In a high-sided skillet just big enough to hold the fish in a single layer, add the orange peel strips, pistachios, celery, olive oil, shallots, wine, and water. Season the broth with salt, bring it to a simmer over medium heat, and let cook for 10 minutes.

Add the sablefish to the pan in a single layer and heat the liquid to 170 degrees, checking the temperature with an instant-read meat thermometer. When it reaches this temperature, remove the pan from the heat and allow it to sit for 9 minutes, covered.

Transfer the fillets to a plate and place in the oven to keep warm. Place the skillet back on the stove and bring to a boil. Mix the cornstarch with enough cold water to form a paste and add it to the boiling liquid, stirring constantly for 30 seconds. The sauce will thicken as it boils. Remove the sauce from the heat.

Toast the bread slices until dark brown and set one in each serving bowl. Remove the fish from the oven and place each piece on top of the toasted bread. Spoon the sauce over the fish and garnish with the orange segments.

Serves 4

Chilled Poached Salmon with Shaved Cabbage and Cilantro Slaw

I love the bold flavors of this dish. Most people don't think of eating fish cold, but with salmon it works very well. This is the perfect choice for entertaining because everything is done ahead.

Four 5-ounce portions wild salmon fillet, preferably Alaskan keta or coho

1 sprig fresh thyme

Juice of 1/2 lemon

Salt

1/2 head green cabbage, cored

2 carrots, shredded

2 tablespoons raisins

2 tablespoons slivered almonds, toasted (page 15)

1 tablespoon whole-grain mustard

Juice of 1 orange

2 tablespoons extra-virgin olive oil

Leaves from 1 bunch cilantro (about 2 cups loosely packed)

For the salmon, place the fillets in a medium skillet and barely cover them with cold water. Add the thyme and a few drops of lemon juice and season generously with salt. Place over medium heat and poach the fish very slowly. Check the temperature with an instant-read meat thermometer. When the water registers about 170 degrees, remove the pan from the heat. The water will continue to cook the fish as it cools. When it is near room temperature, place the whole skillet in the refrigerator to cool completely.

For the slaw, shred the cabbage as thinly as you can and mix it well with 1 1/2 teaspoons salt. Let sit at room temperature for 1 hour to draw out a lot of the moisture in the cabbage. Strain the cabbage and mix with the carrots, raisins, almonds and the remaining lemon juice.

For the sauce, add the mustard and orange juice to a blender and season with a little bit of salt. On low speed, begin to blend and slowly add in the olive oil in a steady stream through the top. It will begin to emulsify and turn into a thin sauce. Continue until all the oil has been added.

To serve, mix the slaw with the cilantro leaves and toss to combine. Divide among the plates. Remove the salmon from the poaching liquid, pat dry, and set on top of the slaw. Drizzle a spoonful of the orange sauce over the plate and serve.

Serves 4

Pink Salmon and Basil Salad

This one of my wife's favorite dishes. The aroma of the basil is a perfect foil for the crisp coolness of the fennel and the bright, meaty-tasting pink salmon. The recipe only takes about a minute to put together, and it can easily be doubled to serve more people.

One 7-ounce can pink salmon

1/2 bulb fennel, very thinly sliced across the grain

Leaves from 2 sprigs fresh basil

Salt

Juice of 1/2 lemon

1 tablespoon extra-virgin olive oil

Gently flake the salmon into a bowl in bite-sized pieces. Add the sliced fennel. Tear the basil leaves into small pieces and add them to the salmon as well. Season with salt, then sprinkle the lemon juice and olive oil over all. Toss to combine and serve immediately.

Serves 2

Striped Bass with Grilled Broccoli Rabe and Sweet Garlic Aioli

Sweet, nutty, garlicky aioli and the crispy crunch of broiled broccoli rabe are balanced with the bite of chile flakes. What a great match for the strong, meaty flavor of striped bass!

1 cup garlic cloves, plus 2 additional cloves

Juice of 1/2 lemon

1 egg yolk

1 tablespoon plus 1 cup water

Salt

1 cup plus 1 tablespoon canola oil

Four 5-ounce portions striped bass fillet

2 tablespoons butter

4 sprigs fresh thyme

2 tablespoons extra-virgin olive oil

2 bunches broccoli rabe, stems peeled

Pinch of red chile flakes

Freshly grated nutmeg

Blanch 1 cup of the garlic cloves according to the directions on page 244. Slice the remaining 2 cloves and set them aside.

For the aioli, place the blanched garlic cloves, lemon juice, egg yolk, and 1 tablespoon of the water in a blender. Season to taste with salt and purée until it is a smooth paste. With the machine running, add 1 cup of the canola oil drop by drop until all of it has been incorporated. The result should be a thick mayonnaise. Check the seasoning and refrigerate, tightly covered, until ready to serve or up to a few days.

In a large nonstick sauté pan over medium heat, heat the remaining 1 tablespoon canola oil. Add the fillets and sear until they begin to crisp and have cooked about halfway through, about 6 minutes. Flip the fillets over and add the butter. Turn the heat up to high and allow the butter to foam and begin to brown. Once this stage is reached, lay the thyme sprigs on top of the fillets, turn the heat back to medium, and, using a deep spoon, baste the fillets with the butter. Continue to do this for a few minutes, until the butter has become clarified (the milk solids have separated from the clear fat) and the fish is cooked through, about 4 minutes. (See page 244 for butter basting instructions.)

Preheat the broiler.

For the broccoli rabe, heat the olive oil in a large ovenproof sauté pan. Add the reserved sliced garlic and cook over medium heat until golden brown. Add the broccoli rabe and arrange so it is in a single layer. Season generously with salt and toss to get the garlic mixed into the leaves. Cook for a minute, then add the remaining 1 cup water. Cover the pan as best you can and allow to steam for a few minutes. Remove the cover and place the pan under the broiler. Broil until the water is mostly evaporated and the broccoli is charred on top. Remove from the oven and sprinkle the chile flakes on top.

To serve, divide the broccoli rabe between 4 serving plates and set a fillet on top. Spoon a large dollop of the aioli on each fillet, then grate a few strokes of nutmeg over the plate.

Serves 4

Wild Striped Bass with Cilantro-Onion Salad and Yogurt-Avocado Purée

Wild striped bass has a clean and assertive taste that is great with the strong flavors of Southwestern cooking. In this dish I like the combination of the rich avocado purée with the fresh, bright tasting cilantro and onion. You have the option of purchasing farmed or wild-caught striped bass. While I prefer the flavor of the wild fish, the farmed fish is fine and is widely available.

1 ripe avocado

Juice of 1 lime

3 tablespoons plain yogurt

Salt

2 tablespoons olive oil, plus more for drizzling

Four 5-ounce portions skin-on striped bass fillet

Leaves from 1 bunch fresh cilantro about 3 cups loosely packed

1 small onion, very thinly sliced

Chipotle Tabasco sauce, optional

Preheat the oven to 300 degrees.

For the avocado purée, cut the avocado in half and discard the seed. Use a spoon to scoop the flesh (make sure to scrape the inside to get all the dark green stuff right next to the skin) into a small bowl; add half of the lime juice and the yogurt. Season to taste with salt and mash together to create a thick sauce. It should be about the consistency of tomato sauce.

For the fish, heat a large ovenproof sauté pan over high heat for 2 minutes. Add 1 tablespoon of the olive oil and place the fish, skin side down, in the pan. Cook over high heat until you see the sides of the skin begin to brown, then, without turning the fish, transfer the pan to the oven and cook 12 minutes per inch of thickness.

Meanwhile, for the salad, mix the cilantro and onion in a medium bowl and dress with the remaining lime juice and 1 tablespoon olive oil. Season to taste with salt.

To serve, spoon a dollop of the avocado purée onto each plate and, using the back of the spoon, push it across the plate to create an attractive swoosh. Place a fish fillet on the sauce with the skin side up and garnish with the cilantro salad. If you like heat, I suggest a few drops of chipotle Tabasco sauce as an addition to the plate. Drizzle with a little more olive oil and serve.

Serves 4

Tilapia with Lemon Brown Butter

This is a take on *beurre meunière,* brown butter and lemon sauce, a classic preparation for fish. I like to add onions to give the dish a little bulk and a balancing sweetness. The tilapia stands up well to the nuttiness of the browned butter.

1 1/4 pounds tilapia fillets

2 tablespoons flour

3 tablespoons butter

1 small onion, very thinly sliced

1/2 cup water

Juice of 1 lemon

2 tablespoons chopped fresh flat-leaf parsley

Salt

Preheat the oven to 250 degrees.

Cut the tilapia crosswise into 1-inch-wide strips. Dredge the strips in the flour until evenly coated. Heat 1 tablespoon of the butter in a large sauté pan over medium heat. When the butter is beginning to brown, turn the heat to high and add the tilapia in a single layer. Sear until the fish begins to brown slightly. Turn each fish strip over and continue to cook for another 3 minutes. Transfer the fish from the pan to a serving platter and place in the oven to keep warm.

To the same pan, add the onion slices and another tablespoon of butter. Sauté until the onion begins to soften. Add the water and lemon juice and bring to a boil. The flour still in the pan will cause the sauce to thicken slightly. Remove from the heat and stir in the parsley and the remaining 1 tablespoon butter. Season generously with salt and stir to combine.

Remove the fish from the oven and spoon the sauce over the top. Serve immediately.

Serves 4

Roasted Trout with Lime-Dill Butter and Roasted Potatoes

Trout is a truly fun fish to serve to friends because it looks so impressive when presented whole. In this recipe, I stuff the fish with fresh dill and sliced lime. Don't eat the lime slices, though; they impart a wonderful perfume to the trout, but they don't taste good.

Two 12-ounce boned rainbow trout, head and tail intact

1 lime, very thinly sliced

1 bunch fresh dill

Salt and freshly ground black pepper

1 pound small red potatoes

4 tablespoons butter, cut into small cubes

4 cloves garlic, sliced

Juice of 1 lime

1 tablespoon water

For the fish, line the belly cavity of each trout with lime slices and a few sprigs of dill; set the remaining dill aside. Arrange the lime and dill so they will not fall out of the cavities. Season the outside of the fish with salt and pepper and reserve.

If the potatoes are larger than a golf ball, cut them into wedges. Place them in a medium pot with enough cold water to barely cover the potatoes. Add 1 tablespoon salt and bring to a boil. Immediately drain and allow the potatoes to air dry for a few minutes.

Preheat the oven to 500 degrees.

Melt 2 tablespoons of the butter with the garlic in a large ovenproof sauté pan over high heat. As the garlic begins to brown, add the potatoes and toss to coat with the butter. Allow the potatoes to sear in the pan until they begin to brown on one side.

Shake the pan so the potatoes are in a single layer—this will be the bed for the trout. Lay the stuffed trout on top of the potatoes and transfer to the oven. Roast until the trout is cooked through, about 12 minutes; check for doneness by gently lifting the belly flap to reveal the meat. If it is an even color all the way through, it is done.

For the lime butter, chop the remaining dill. Combine the lime juice and water in a small saucepan and bring to a boil. Remove from the heat and add the remaining 2 tablespoons butter, swirling the pan until it is all melted into the sauce. Season with salt and add the dill.

I like to serve this family style, so I arrange the trout on plates, placing the potatoes around it. Spoon the dill sauce over top and serve.

Serves 4

Maine Shrimp on Grits with Crispy Prosciutto

Grits are good. Grits are great. I don't often think to make them, but when I do, I remember what I've been missing. The process for making grits is not all that different from mill to mill, but there are a number of great artisanal producers of grits worth seeking out. The difference is that the small guys tend to treat grits as a seasonal crop. The mass-produced grits we are used to always taste old. I learned this in Italy, where polenta is ground only when the corn kernels have dried just long enough on the cobs. In Italy, you eat polenta in the winter and spring, and fresh corn in the summer and fall. Small producers of grits, such as Anson Mills, treat their product in the same way. Look for them locally or online. Here I've paired grits with Maine shrimp, whose season runs from winter to mid spring.

2 cups milk

2 cups water

Salt

1 cup coarse-ground grits

4 slices prosciutto, sliced into very thin strips

2 tablespoons butter

1 small onion, thinly sliced

2 cloves garlic, sliced

1 pound Maine shrimp, picked over for pieces of shell

In a medium saucepan, bring the milk and water to a simmer. Season with salt and slowly whisk in the grits. Stir constantly for about 6 minutes over medium heat. Reduce the heat to the lowest setting possible and cover the pot. Allow to cook for about 20 minutes, then let rest off the heat.

Sauté the prosciutto strips in the butter over medium heat until crispy, then transfer them to a plate. Add the onion and garlic to the butter in the pan. Cook for a few minutes, until the onion is translucent. Add the shrimp and sauté for about 3 minutes, until just cooked through. Remove the pan from the heat. Season to taste with salt.

Divide the grits among 4 serving bowls. Spoon the shrimp and onion mixture over the top, garnish with the crispy prosciutto, and serve.

Serves 4

Linguine with Squid and Poblano Pepper Butter

This dish uses the classic flavors found in the Mediterranean dish, black rice. Known by various names, it combines bell pepper, celery, and onion with squid and its ink. Squid ink is a little adventurous for most cooks, and it's hard to find. But if you want to try it out, just add 1/2 tablespoon of ink to the pan once the vegetables are cooked, then proceed as directed.

Salt

1 pound linguine

6 tablespoons butter

1 medium onion, finely diced

4 ribs celery, finely diced

1 poblano pepper, seeded and finely diced

1 pound cleaned squid, tubes and tentacles, tubes sliced very thinly into rings

Bring a large pot of water to a boil and season generously with salt. Add the linguine and cook until al dente, following the package directions. Drain, reserving 1 cup of the cooking water.

Meanwhile, in a large sauté pan, melt the butter over medium heat. Add the diced vegetables and cook, without stirring, until the celery is soft and the onion translucent, about 5 minutes. Add the squid and toss to combine. Add the pasta and reserved cooking water. Bring to a boil, then reduce the heat and simmer until the pasta has absorbed the broth and is lightly coated in sauce, about 3 minutes. Serve immediately.

Serves 4

Sautéed Greens with Orange, Anchovy, and Red Onion

Greens are among my favorite flavors, and in this preparation, they are elevated beyond the expected. The anchovies melt into the oil, and the sweetness of the orange balances any bitterness. The more bitter greens, like dandelion or puntarella, are ideal here. This dish is a perfect match for Barramundi with Toasted Almond Butter and Basmati Pilaf (page 65) and Dijon- and Peach-crusted Tilapia (page 233).

2 tablespoons extra-virgin olive oil

2 salt-packed anchovies (page 24)
or 4 oil-packed anchovy fillets

1 small red onion, thinly sliced

1 1/2 pounds spinach, dandelion,
or kale, trimmed of any heavy stems
and washed thoroughly

Salt

1 orange, peeled and
cut into segments (page 7)

In a large sauté pan, heat the olive oil over low heat and add the anchovies. After a few minutes, gently mash the fillets with a spoon; they will form a paste with the oil. Add the onion and raise the heat to medium. After a few minutes, the onion will begin to wilt. Add the greens and season with a little bit of salt. Stir to coat all the leaves with the oil and continue to cook until they begin to wilt. Add the orange segments and toss to combine. Serve immediately.

Serves 4 as a side dish

Raw Kale Salad

There is nothing like the chewy bite of raw kale, but you'll want the bright green younger leaves for salad—try a local farmers' market for just-picked spring leaves. Mature kale is fibrous and difficult to eat raw. This exceptionally nutritious salad can be turned into supper with the addition of a few canned sardine fillets and a cup of cooked quinoa. The vinaigrette will keep for a few days, so you might want to make a double batch.

1 bunch kale

2 carrots

1 cup seedless grapes, sliced in half

1/2 cup slivered almonds, toasted (page 15)

Salt

1/2 cup garlic cloves, blanched (page 244)

1 tablespoon sherry vinegar

1/4 cup extra-virgin olive oil

1 tablespoon mayonnaise

Wash the kale thoroughly; it's a magnet for sand and grit. Remove the tough stalk from each leaf, then pile several leaves on top of one another. Slice as thinly as you can across the pile, yielding fine strips of kale. Repeat with all the leaves.

Peel the carrots, discarding the outer skin. Continue to peel the carrot into thin shards, collecting the pieces in a bowl as they fall. This is a nice way to get all the flavor of the carrot while removing the (in this case) distracting crunchy texture. Add in the grapes, almonds, and kale. Season to taste with salt.

For the vinaigrette, purée the garlic with the vinegar and olive oil in a blender and season with salt. Put the mayonnaise in a small bowl and add the purée slowly to it, whisking to combine.

Toss the salad with as much vinaigrette as you like and allow it to sit for at least 10 minutes before serving, to soften the leaves a little and combine the flavors.

Serves 4 as a side dish

Orange and Fennel Salad with Anchovy Vinaigrette

This is a great mid-meal course for a festive dinner. It is refreshing and sets the stage for a more complicated dish to follow; plus, all the prep can be done well ahead of time, and the ingredients tossed together at the last minute.

4 salt-packed anchovies (page 24) or 8 oil-packed anchovy fillets

1 small shallot, peeled

1 teaspoon cider vinegar

Juice of 1 lemon

6 cloves garlic, blanched (page 244)

1/2 cup extra-virgin olive oil

2 fennel bulbs, stalks trimmed and discarded, very thinly sliced

3 oranges, peeled and cut into segments (page 7)

1 small red bell pepper, seeded and cut into the thinnest possible strips

Salt

Freshly grated nutmeg

For the vinaigrette, combine the anchovies, shallot, vinegar, lemon juice, and garlic in a blender. Pulse to begin the purée, then, with the machine running, add the olive oil in a slow, steady stream. Process until it is reduced to a fine purée with no chunks remaining.

Combine the fennel, orange segments, and pepper strips in a medium salad bowl and toss with the vinaigrette until thoroughly incorporated. Season with salt and garnish with a few gratings of nutmeg.

Serves 4

Carrie Anne's Beet Salad

This salad couldn't be easier. I like to make it for my wife, Carrie Anne, at lunch, because I know it will keep her going until dinner. If you can find them, try yellow beets; they have a milder flavor that works better with other ingredients. They also don't stain your cutting board and clothes the way red beets do. Serve this as a light lunch or as a substantial side for a whole grilled fish.

2 pounds beets, stems and greens removed

Salt

Leaves from 1 bunch fresh flat-leaf parsley (about 3 cups loosely packed)

1 Granny Smith apple, quartered, cored, and very thinly sliced

2 bunches scallions, thinly sliced

2 tablespoons Chile Oil or Citrus Oil (page 262)

Juice of 1 lemon

6 ounces goat cheese

Simmer the beets, fully submerged in heavily salted water, until a knife pierces the flesh easily, about 35 minutes for a tennis ball-sized beet. Drain and, using a few paper towels, gently scrape off the skin. You can wait a few minutes so they're not blazing hot, but don't let them cool or else the skin will be tough to get off.

Slice the beets into 1/2-inch-thick rounds and arrange on a large platter. Scatter the parsley leaves, apple slices, and the scallions on top. Drizzle with the oil and season with salt. Just before serving, drizzle with the lemon juice and crumble the cheese over all.

Serves 4

Pan-fried Potatoes with Orange-Sherry Aioli

This preparation is based in part on the Spanish potato dish *patatas bravas*, in which potatoes are topped with a spicy tomato sauce and garlicky aioli. In this version, I spice up the potatoes by sautéing them with slices of garlic in lots of olive oil. The aioli is a great pairing here and also works well as a sauce for grilled vegetables and nearly any protein. It is hard to make small quantities of the aioli, so plan on using the rest over the next week or so. (Be sure to keep it refrigerated in an airtight container.) This dish makes a great snack to put out before dinner; serve with toothpicks.

1 large egg yolk

1 teaspoon sherry vinegar

1 clove garlic, grated on a Microplane, plus 4 cloves, thinly sliced

1 tablespoon sweet smoked paprika

Juice of 1/2 orange

Salt

1 cup canola oil

1 pound russet or Yukon gold potatoes, left unpeeled and cut into 1/2-inch cubes

1/2 cup extra-virgin olive oil

For the aioli, whisk together the egg yolk, vinegar, grated garlic, paprika, orange juice, and 1 teaspoon salt in a medium bowl until well combined. Add the oil in a slow, steady stream so that it is incorporated as you whisk (if you add the oil too quickly, the sauce will break and you'll have to start again). As you whisk and slowly incorporate the oil, the sauce will begin to thicken into a mayonnaise-like consistency. Once all the oil has been added, cover tightly and refrigerate until ready to use.

Place the potatoes in a small saucepan with just enough water to cover them. Season generously with salt and bring to a simmer. You are only cooking the potatoes until they are about three-quarters done, so keep an eye on them and stay close. It should take 4 to 5 minutes. Drain off the water and cool the potatoes in the refrigerator on a plate or small baking sheet.

When the potatoes have cooled, heat a large heavy-bottomed sauté pan over high heat until it begins to smoke. Add the olive oil and sliced garlic and slightly brown the garlic (this will only take a few seconds). As soon as they begin to color, add the potatoes and toss to coat with the oil. Make sure the potatoes are in one single layer and are frying in the oil. There should be enough oil so that the potatoes are about half submerged. When the potatoes are brown on one side, toss to continue cooking the other sides. When the potatoes are crispy, remove the potatoes and garlic slices from the oil using a slotted spoon, then carefully discard the oil.

Check the aioli for seasoning. Place a giant dollop of it on the side of the crisped potatoes and serve immediately.

Serves 4 as a side dish

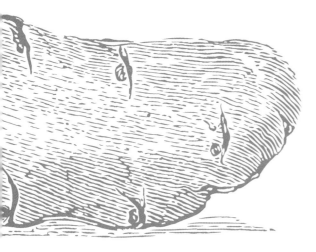

Mushroom Persillade

Oyster mushrooms are among my favorite 'shrooms to cook. Although they cannot compare to the incredible flavors of wild varieties like the chanterelle, they certainly hold their own. The best part about them is their texture—slightly toothsome, a little rubbery, even (in a good way). I like to cook mushrooms so that they sear hard, then braise them in white wine and lots of herbs and finish off with tons of butter. The key to this is lots of herbs, so don't stint on the quantities called for.

1 pound oyster mushrooms, cut in half

1 pound button mushrooms, cut in half or quarters depending on their size

1/4 cup canola oil

Salt

1 medium onion, finely diced

4 tablespoons butter

3 cloves garlic, minced

3 sprigs fresh thyme

2 cups white wine

3 tablespoons chopped fresh chives

3 tablespoons chopped fresh mint

3 tablespoons chopped fresh flat-leaf parsley

In a large dry sauté pan, sear the mushrooms in small batches in the canola oil. When the mushrooms are well colored, season with salt and remove to a bowl.

Sauté the onion in 2 tablespoons of the butter over medium heat, until translucent. Add the garlic and cook, stirring, for another 4 minutes. Add the seared mushrooms and thyme. Toss to combine.

Add the wine, bring to a simmer, and cook over medium heat until the wine has reduced to just a few tablespoons of liquid.

Remove the thyme sprigs, then add the remaining 2 tablespoons butter and the herbs. Remove the pan from the heat and toss to combine as the butter melts. Serve immediately.

Serves 4 as a side dish

Garlic-Yogurt Mashed Potatoes

This is a version of a recipe that I did for Oprah's magazine. I like to use yogurt instead of butter because its acidity heightens the other flavors. My preference is for full-fat Greek-style yogurt, but any unsweetened plain yogurt will do. If you can find *labne*, a Middle Eastern-style yogurt, that's another great choice.

1 1/2 pounds russet potatoes, each peeled and cut into 8 pieces

6 cloves garlic, each cut in half

Salt

1 cup plain Greek-style yogurt

Put the potatoes and garlic in a pan that is big enough to hold them, but not overly large (see photo below). Add enough water to barely cover and season generously with salt. (Potatoes absorb water as they cook, so if the water is seasoned, the potatoes will taste great throughout. If you try to season them at the end, it often doesn't produce the same results. Also, the potatoes' flavor is water-soluble, so the more water you use to cook them, the weaker the taste will be. Try tasting the cooking water when you strain it off. Tastes like potatoes, right? You are pouring flavor down the drain.)

Bring the water to a boil, then reduce the heat to a simmer and cook until the potatoes are soft and just beginning to fall apart. Drain, reserving some of the cooking water. Add the yogurt to the potatoes and mash together. If they are a little too thick, add the reserved cooking water a few tablespoons at a time until it reaches your desired consistency.

Serves 4 as a side dish

Summer brings sexy back. Corn and zucchini, tomatoes and peaches—this is when cooking gets really fun. The coastal waters teem with seafood of all sorts. Little and big are doing their dance, returning to the shallow waters. The weather is steady enough that fishermen can reliably get offshore and out to where they ply their trade. Lobsters bring throngs of vacationing East Coasters northward out of the cities, and little fishing villages come alive with the other trade, tourism. The butter is melted, the bibs are on. In Maryland, the crab feasts become the social activity, and shredded fingertips remind us throughout the week of the slow shelling process for the Sunday meal.

Recreational fishing kicks up, and the diversity of offerings at the store is at its peak. Traditionalists are shunning oysters, but a die-hard group still carries on squeezing lemons and slurping from shells. Salmon runs are in full swing, and once-forlorn coasts bustle with activity again.

The food is simple. The sauces are light or maybe not even necessary. And summer heralds the full return of my favorite thing, the grill. Meals seem more communal, ingredients are more vibrant, and the mood is more relaxed.

> The food is simple. The sauces are light or maybe not even necessary. And summer heralds the full return of my favorite thing, the grill.

Grilled Okra with Charred Onion Dip

This is a great way to prepare okra. Chef John Murphy was trying to replace our best-selling appetizer because the farmers had no more broccoli. It was late summer, and he came up with the idea of grilling okra. I had him test it, and now I'm reluctant to eat okra any other way. You'll need six 6-inch bamboo skewers for this dish; soak them for an hour in water to prevent scorching.

1 tablespoon butter

1 medium onion, diced

1 cup sour cream

1 tablespoon sweet smoked paprika

1 bunch fresh chives, thinly sliced

Salt

24 large okra pods

Canola oil for brushing

For the dip, heat the butter in a heavy skillet over high heat. When the butter is brown, add the onion and let sit without stirring for a few minutes. The point is to char it in order to develop a deep, bittersweet flavor. After a few minutes, toss the onion and add a few tablespoons of water to deglaze the pan. This will release the charred bits and allow the sugars in the onion to stew as the water reduces, thus caramelizing and creating the flavor profile we want. After the water is evaporated, let the onion char again in the dry pan, then add a few more tablespoons of water. Cook until dry, then remove the pan from the heat. The onion should be dark brown but still have a little bit of texture. Allow it to cool, then mix in the sour cream, paprika, and chives, and season with salt. Mix well to combine and let sit for 20 minutes so the flavors meld. The dip will keep, tightly covered, in the refrigerator for up to 1 week.

Thread 4 okra onto each bamboo skewer, leaving a little space between them. Brush the okra with oil and season generously with salt.

Prepare the grill according to the instructions on page 250.

Cook the okra on the hottest part of the grill until the skin begins to char and slightly blister. Rotate the grill grate until the skewers are over the cool part of the grill; cover the grill and cook until tender throughout, about 4 minutes.

Remove the okra from the skewers and serve on a platter with the dip on the side.

Serves 4 as an appetizer

Anchovies and Peppers

This is a great light dish to serve as a casual lunch or to present on a platter for parties. If you offer it as a canapé, serve it with toast points on the side. The key to this dish is good-quality anchovies and olive oil.

3 bell peppers, either red or yellow

1 teaspoon canola oil

6 salt-packed anchovies (page 24) or 12 oil-packed anchovy fillets

3 tablespoons best-quality extra-virgin olive oil

Leaves from 2 sprigs fresh mint

1 lemon, cut into wedges

Preheat the broiler or prepare a grill according to the instructions on page 250. Lightly oil the peppers with the canola oil. If broiling, place the whole peppers on a baking sheet and broil as close to the heat as possible until their skins are blackened and the peppers are tender, turning them every few minutes to cook evenly. If grilling, place the peppers over the hottest part of the fire and blacken in the same way.

Place the blackened peppers in a brown paper bag and fold the top closed. This will trap the heat and steam the peppers, making it easier to remove their skins. Set aside until the peppers are cool enough to handle, then gently flake off the burned skin. It should slip right off, but if necessary you can use a knife to gently scrape the pepper clean. Do not wash it! A little burned skin is better than washing away all the flavor. Remove the stem end and discard all the seeds from each pepper. Tear the peppers into 1-inch strips and place them on a serving plate.

To serve, arrange the anchovy fillets on top of the pepper strips. Drizzle with the olive oil and scatter the mint leaves over the plate. Serve with lemon wedges on the side.

Serves 4 as a light lunch or appetizer

Salmon Carpaccio with Grilled Lemon and Herbs

Carpaccio is a nice way to start a meal and an economical use of great fish. When serving raw fish, buy the very best quality that you can (see Consuming Raw Seafood, page 43). For this recipe I would suggest using only wild Alaskan king salmon, as it has a great richness and a full flavor that you can appreciate when raw. Broiling or grilling the lemon wedges lightly caramelizes the flavor of the juice. Lemon juice will "cook" salmon in the way that a ceviche does. This will change the texture and the color of the salmon, so have your guests squeeze it on at the last minute.

One 10-ounce skin-on wild Alaskan king salmon fillet

Leaves from 4 fronds fresh dill

Leaves from 6 sprigs fresh flat-leaf parsley

1 head frisée lettuce, separated into leaves and heavy stems trimmed

Salt

1/4 cup best-quality extra-virgin olive oil

1 lemon, cut into wedges and grilled or broiled a few minutes

To slice the salmon, use a super-sharp, thin slicing knife. Starting at the base of the knife, draw it through the salmon on a slight bias, creating a 1/4-inch-thick sheet. You should be able to slice all the way down to the skin with one stroke of the knife. If you saw the knife back and forth, you risk ripping the fragile sheets of salmon. Once the knife gets close to the skin, slightly rotate the angle to cut the slice cleanly off and leave most of the dark connective tissue on the skin side. (See page 248 for illustrated step-by-step directions.) Place the thin slices on 4 plates, considering the arrangement before laying them down, as you will not be able to shift them without ripping the fish. Wrap each plate in plastic and chill for no more than a few hours.

To serve, mix the herbs and frisée and place a small tuft on each plate. Season with salt and drizzle with the olive oil. Garnish each plate with a wedge of lemon.

Serves 4 as a first course

Wahoo Crudo with Three Different Flavors

Crudo, an artful preparation of raw fish, has become the darling of the young chef crowd. I was introduced to the idea at Esca restaurant in New York City. While it is always hard to assign credit for the inception of a dish, chef David Pasternack has certainly brought the idea to the forefront of American restaurant cooking. It is a reasonable evolution from sushi, which most Americans are comfortable with. The key to this dish is to use the freshest seafood possible. See Consuming Raw Seafood (page 43).

3/4 pound wahoo loin

1 tablespoon capers

10 celery leaves, picked from the very center of the heart

2 tablespoons maple syrup

1 jalapeño chile, finely sliced

4 tablespoons extra-virgin olive oil

1 orange

2 tablespoons plain Greek-style or regular full-fat yogurt

10 fresh cilantro leaves

Salt

To slice the wahoo, use a knife with a long, thin, sharp blade. Start at the base of the knife and, making 1/8-inch-thick slices, draw it through the loin in one motion. (See page 248 for illustrated step-by-step directions.) Layer the slices attractively on large serving plates in three groups. Position the slices carefully, as moving them is difficult to do without tearing them. If necessary, cover the plates and chill them until you need them.

Just before serving, for each group of slices, arrange the garnishes in these combinations: Place a few capers with the celery leaves and drizzle with the maple syrup. On another group, arrange a few slices of the jalapeño, drizzle with 2 tablespoons of the olive oil, then grate orange zest over the top. On the third grouping, serve a dollop of the yogurt and the cilantro leaves, and drizzle with the remaining 2 tablespoons olive oil. Season each grouping with salt, except the one with the capers.

Try to get this dish to the table as cold as possible.

Serves 4 as a first course

Grilled Clams with Lemon-Chive Butter

I love cooking clams on the grill as an appetizer or canapé while people wait for dinner. After the charcoal has been lit, you have about twenty minutes until it burns down to embers, so why not cook some clams? The shells protect the meat from the intense heat, and it is easy to melt the butter on the side of the grill in a small pan. When the clams pop open, just drizzle a little butter on and serve.

24 littleneck clams, washed thoroughly (discard any that won't close)

3 tablespoons butter

2 tablespoons chopped fresh chives

Juice of 1 lemon

Tabasco sauce

Freshly ground black pepper

Prepare a grill according to the instructions on page 250. Set the clams on the hottest part of the grill and cook until the shells begin to pop open.

For the lemon butter, combine the butter, chives, and lemon juice in a small saucepan. Season to taste with Tabasco and a little black pepper. Set the pan on a low-heat area of the grill to warm it, whisking constantly so that the butter remains creamy.

As the clams open, remove them from the grill and drizzle a little of the melted butter into each shell. Discard any clams that haven't opened after 7 minutes. Serve immediately.

Makes 24 pieces as an appetizer or canapé

Crab and Corn Toast

Corn starts showing up around Washington, D.C., at midsummer, and, for me, it is one of the best times of the year. Driving around on the outskirts of town, one can find little roadside stands piled high with corn and melons, and the dewy scent of the husks fills your car as you drive away. This recipe is a tribute to mid-Atlantic cooking, where corn and crabs are just about the best things going. It is a take on the ever-popular crab dip, which I usually find to be too rich. Here the cream serves just to bind the dish and make it a little saucy.

1/2 onion, finely diced

1/2 bulb fennel, stalks trimmed and discarded, finely diced

2 tablespoons butter

2 ears corn, husked, kernels cut off, and cobs scraped

1/2 cup heavy cream

Pinch of Old Bay Seasoning

Salt

1 pound crab claw meat, picked through for cartilage

Soft baguette, sliced 1 inch thick

In a medium saucepan, sauté the onion and fennel in the butter over medium heat until soft, about 10 minutes.

Add the corn and cook 2 minutes. Add the cream and Old Bay and season with salt. Bring to a boil and add the crabmeat. Cook until the cream is reduced to a thick coating, about 4 minutes.

Toast the bread until golden brown. Serve the crab and corn mixture as a dip with the bread alongside.

Serves 4 as an appetizer

Poached Squid and Green Bean Salad

The combo of crunchy green beans and gently poached squid is a nice balance of textures. All rounded out by the creamy almond dressing, this salad is an easy make-ahead first course or buffet offering.

Salt

1 pound green beans, trimmed and snapped into roughly 1-inch pieces

1 pound cleaned squid, both tubes and tentacles

1/4 cup Chunky Almond Oil (page 262)

2 tablespoons sour cream or buttermilk

Juice of 1 lemon

Tabasco sauce

For the green beans, bring a large pot of water to boil and season heavily with salt. Drop the green beans into the water for 30 seconds, then drain, reserving about 2 cups of the cooking water. Do not shock the beans in ice water but rather allow them to cool on a baking sheet at room temperature.

For the squid, slice the tubes as thinly as you can to make tiny rings. Cut the tentacles into thin strips. Place in a saucepan and cover with the reserved cooking water from the green beans. Place over low heat and cook until the squid has turned white and stiffened, about 4 minutes. You will need to stir every once in a while to make sure that the squid cooks evenly and does not clump together. Drain and set aside.

For the dressing, combine the almond oil, sour cream, lemon juice, a few dashes of Tabasco, and a pinch of salt in a small bowl. Whisk until combined.

Combine the green beans, squid, and dressing in a serving bowl and toss until the beans and squid are well coated with the dressing. Serve immediately or chill to serve cold. Can be made up to a day ahead of time.

Serves 4 as a first course

Squid with Green Beans, Potatoes, and Basil Pesto

This is one of my all-time favorite dishes. I love the combination of pesto with potatoes and green beans—it is traditionally served with the Italian pasta orecchiette. The squid is crunchy with smoky charred flavor, and the warmed potatoes and beans really enliven the pesto and draw out the aroma of the basil. I have served some variation of this to rave reviews in every restaurant where I have been chef. Ask your fishmonger not to remove the delicate purple skin when cleaning the squid, it makes a difference in texture. However, if you cannot find squid with its skin still attached, the recipe will still be delightful.

2 russet potatoes, peeled and cut into 1/2-inch cubes

Salt

1/2 pound green beans, trimmed and cut into 1-inch lengths

8 medium fresh squid, cleaned, about 1 pound

2 bunches frisée lettuce, separated into leaves and heavy stems trimmed

1 cup Basil Pesto (page 266)

Prepare a grill according to the instructions on page 250.

Place the potatoes in a small saucepan and barely cover with cold water. Season generously with salt and bring to a simmer. After about 3 minutes, check the potatoes for doneness. They should be just cooked but not falling apart, about the same doneness that you would use for a potato salad. Drain and allow potatoes to dry on a plate.

Meanwhile, blanch the green beans in boiling salted water for 2 minutes, then drain and add to the potatoes.

Season the squid with salt. Cook the squid on the hottest part of the grill for about 2 minutes per side. If you're using squid that still has the skin on it, the purplish skin will begin to char and the color will become a deep, vibrant hue. For skin-on squid, make sure that the section under the wing gets cooked evenly, as this area can get folded over and stay underdone. Turn the squid to cook the other side for another 2 minutes. The tentacles should cook about twice as fast as the bodies; when they are done, shift them to a cooler part of the grill to stay warm.

Preheat the broiler.

To serve the salad, transfer the potatoes and beans to a baking sheet and reheat briefly under the broiler, then mix with the frisée and a tablespoon or two of the pesto. Season with salt and mix to combine. Divide the remaining pesto among 4 plates, pushing it across the plate with the back of the spoon to create a swoosh, then place a mound of the salad on top. When removing the squid from the grill, shake out the bodies to release any cooking juices that have accumulated inside the tubes. Place the squid on top of the salad and serve immediately.

Serves 4 as a first course or light lunch

Roast Pepper Gazpacho with Smoked Mussels

I'm a gazpacho fan, but I'm often turned off by the flavor of raw peppers—they can be a little overpowering and bitter. So in this version I use roasted peppers; roasting softens their flavor and brings a great harmony to the dish. (Jarred roasted peppers work fine here.) If you like classic gazpacho, then by all means use raw peppers. I like the addition of the smoked mussels; it's an easy and economical way to turn a simple soup into a light lunch.

1 cucumber, peeled and roughly chopped

1/2 yellow onion, roughly chopped

2 large ripe tomatoes, roughly chopped

One 7-ounce bottle roasted peppers, drained, or 2 red bell peppers, roasted, peeled, and seeded

1 clove garlic, peeled

3/4 cup plus 2 tablespoons water

2 tablespoons kosher salt

1 tablespoon vinegar, preferably red wine

1/4 cup extra-virgin olive oil

One 7-ounce can smoked mussels

Combine all the ingredients, except the olive oil and mussels, in a blender. Pulse to engage the blades, then slowly increase the speed until you have a superfine purée. Remove to a bowl and chill for at least 1 hour and up to a day.

Whisk in the olive oil and adjust the seasoning if necessary.

Divide the mussels among the bowls, then ladle the soup into the bowls and serve.

Serves 4

Arctic Char with Blistered Cherry Tomatoes in Garlic Olive Oil

Farmed Arctic char is widely available and is a great substitute for farmed Atlantic salmon. It has a mild flavor and a great texture. It is not quite as fatty as salmon, which is why Rick Moonen calls it "salmon lite." Wild Arctic char from the northern seas is available only for a few weeks every summer when the ice has melted enough for the local fishermen to reach them. It is a sought-after delicacy, and one that will cost you if you can find it, but it is worth it.

This is super easy to cook—it only requires one pan and one hot broiler. For a terrific variation, at the last minute before serving, toss in very thinly sliced shallot and a few fresh basil leaves.

1/4 cup extra-virgin olive oil

4 cloves garlic, each cut in half

2 pints cherry tomatoes (Sun Golds are best, if you can find them)

Salt

Two 5-ounce portions skin-on Arctic char fillet

Preheat the broiler.

Set a large cast-steel or cast-iron skillet on the stove over high heat until it is smoking hot. Add the olive oil and garlic. Cook the garlic until it is blistered and golden brown. Add the tomatoes, but do this very carefully, otherwise searing hot oil will splash up onto you. Cook until the skins of the tomatoes begin to blister in the hot oil, about 1 minute, then season very generously with salt.

Carefully place the char fillets, skin side up, on top of the tomatoes and transfer the pan under the broiler. Cook for 6 minutes, then check on the fillets. The skin should be blistered and bubbling. Remove the char fillets to serving plates. Spoon the tomatoes onto the char fillets and serve immediately.

Serves 2, but the recipe can easily be doubled by using two pans

Barramundi with Creamed Zucchini and Sorrel-Tarragon-Carrot Salad

Sorrel is an absolute treat with barramundi. It is a broad-leafed herb with a bright, lemony flavor and sometimes a peppery bite like arugula. It is great when its very distinctive flavor is somewhat offset by a fat (try it in a compound butter). In this recipe, sorrel is balanced by the olive oil in the salad, as well as the butter and crème fraîche in the zucchini. If you cannot find sorrel, mint leaves with a few drops of lemon juice added makes a great substitute.

Four 5-ounce portions barramundi fillet

1 tablespoon extra-virgin olive oil, plus more for brushing the fillets

1 tablespoon butter

2 cloves garlic, sliced

3 medium zucchini, cut into 1/4-inch-thick rounds, then into half-moons

Salt

2 tablespoons crème fraîche or sour cream

Leaves from 1 bunch sorrel, stacked, rolled, and sliced crosswise as thinly as possible into ribbons

2 carrots, peeled and shredded on a box grater

1 small red onion, very thinly sliced

Preheat the broiler.

Place the fish fillets on a baking sheet and brush with just enough olive oil to give them a sheen. Broil them for 4 minutes. Shift the baking sheet to the bottom rack of the oven and turn the heat off. There should be enough heat in the oven to continue to cook the fish gently as you prepare the rest of the meal. If the oven does not feel hot (or your broiling unit is not part of your oven), then warm it to 225 degrees.

For the zucchini, in a large pan, melt the butter over high heat, then sauté the garlic until it begins to brown. Add the zucchini and toss to combine. Cook for 1 minute, then season to taste with salt and stir in the crème fraîche. Reduce the heat to medium and allow the zucchini to simmer in the sauce. When the sauce has reduced to a thick glaze, about 5 minutes, remove from the heat.

For the salad, in a medium bowl, mix the sorrel, carrots, and onion. Toss with the remaining 1 tablespoon of olive oil and season to taste with salt.

To serve, divide the zucchini into 4 bowls and place a fillet on top of each. Garnish with the salad and serve immediately.

Serves 4

Bluefish with Charred Green Beans and Almond Aioli

There is no better way to prepare green beans than this. I love the burned, crispy skin they develop when cooked on high heat over the grill. They pair well with nearly any type of seafood and are great on their own as a snack.

2 pounds green beans, trimmed

1 egg yolk

1 tablespoon fresh lemon juice

Salt

1 small clove garlic, grated on a Microplane or very finely minced

Dash of Tabasco sauce

1 cup extra-virgin olive oil

2 tablespoons slivered almonds, toasted (page 15)

Four 5-ounce portions bluefish fillet

Spice mix of your choice (pages 260–261)

Bring a pot of salted water to a boil and blanch the green beans for 1 minute. Drain them, shock them in ice water, and drain them again. Set aside.

For the aioli, mix the egg yolk with the lemon juice, 1 teaspoon salt, the garlic, and Tabasco and whisk to combine. Begin to add the olive oil in a slow, steady stream while whisking to incorporate each drop. As the aioli begins to emulsify (thicken), you can increase the flow slightly until all the oil is incorporated. The result should be a thick mayonnaise with a slight yellow color from the olive oil. Add the toasted almond slivers and stir. (This will keep up to a week in the fridge, tightly covered.)

For the bluefish, prepare a grill according the instructions on page 250. Season the bluefish with the spice mix (try the Smoked Paprika and Cinnamon Spice Mix with bluefish). Set the fillets on the hottest part of the grill for 3 minutes, skin side down. Rotate the grate so the fillets are over the coolest part of the grill; cover the grill. It will take about 10 minutes for the fillets to cook through.

Meanwhile, season the cold green beans with lots of salt and cook over the hottest part of the grill. (Place them perpendicular to the grill grates so that they don't fall through, or use a grill basket.) Turn them after a few minutes, when they begin to char. If you don't have a grill basket, this can be tricky; use a metal spatula and tongs for greater control. The beans should be done in about the time it takes the bluefish to cook through.

To serve, divide the beans among 4 serving plates and place a fillet of bluefish on top. Garnish each fillet with a generous dollop of the aioli. Serve immediately.

Serves 4

Bluefish with Creamed Corn and Herb Croutons

Fresh corn is one of the great treats of the summer. This interpretation of creamed corn has just a touch of sour cream and butter added to it to accentuate the natural sweet creaminess of the corn kernels.

For the croutons, preheat the oven to 350 degrees. Melt 1/2 tablespoon of the butter in a medium ovenproof skillet and add the bread cubes. Toss to combine, then season to taste with salt. Place the skillet in the oven and toast the croutons until lightly brown and crunchy throughout. Remove from the oven and set aside. These can be made up to a few days ahead (store them in an airtight container), but their flavor is best the day they're made.

For the corn, take the ears one at a time and, using a paring knife, cut off all the kernels, letting them drop into a large bowl. Scrape the cob with the knife so that the juice and little bits of corn fall into the bowl too. In a large sauté pan over medium heat, melt the remaining 1 1/2 tablespoons butter and cook the onion and garlic until soft, then add the corn. Sauté for another minute, then add 1/4 cup of the water and season generously with salt. Allow to boil, as this will steam the corn and cook it. After a few minutes, combine the remaining 1/4 cup water with the cornstarch and add to the pan. This will thicken the juices immediately and create a creamy, rich sauce around the kernels. Remove from the heat and stir in the sour cream. Keep warm.

For the bluefish, prepare a grill according to the instructions on page 250. Cook the fillets, skin side down, on the hottest part of the grill for 3 minutes. Rotate the grate so the fillets are over the coolest part of the grill; cover the grill. Cook for approximately 10 minutes, until the fillets are an even color throughout and the flesh is beginning to flake when gentle pressure is applied.

To serve, divide the corn among 4 bowls and top with a bluefish fillet. Scatter the croutons and parsley over the top and serve immediately. Serve with Tabasco sauce, if desired.

Serves 4

2 tablespoons butter

4 slices brioche bread or potato rolls, cut into 1/2-inch cubes

Salt

8 ears corn, shucked

1 small onion, finely diced

2 cloves garlic, thinly sliced

1/2 cup water

2 teaspoons cornstarch

2 tablespoons sour cream

Four 5-ounce portions skin-on bluefish fillet

2 tablespoons chopped fresh flat-leaf parsley

Tabasco sauce, for serving

Catfish and Romesco Stew

Romesco sauce—a mixture of fire-roasted vegetables puréed with almonds and olive oil—is often found in the cuisine of Spain. I fell in love with it while I was traveling there and enjoyed its versatility. It goes incredibly well with just about anything you could imagine, so go ahead and make a double batch of it. This dish is similar to a curry, in that the fish is slowly simmered in a flavorful sauce. The best part is eating the remaining sauce with rice pilaf or boiled potatoes.

2 plum tomatoes, each cut in half lengthwise

1/2 medium onion, cut into 1/2-inch dice

2 cloves garlic, each cut in half

1/2 green bell pepper (use a poblano pepper if you like a little heat), seeded and cut into 1/2-inch pieces

6 tablespoons extra-virgin olive oil

1/4 cup sliced or slivered almonds

Salt

1 pound catfish fillets, cut crosswise into 1-inch strips

For the romesco, combine the tomatoes, onion, garlic, bell pepper, olive oil, and almonds in an ovenproof sauté pan. Season to taste with salt and toss to combine. Place under the broiler and cook until the vegetables are charred and the tomatoes have released their juices, about 10 minutes. Transfer to a blender and purée on high speed until smooth (use caution when blending hot ingredients).

Place the catfish strips in a large saucepan and cover with the sauce. Set over low heat and cook until the catfish begins to flake apart, about 10 minutes. Do not stir or the fish will break into small pieces. Check for seasoning and serve immediately.

Serves 4

Slow-grilled Catfish with Roasted Pepper and Cream Cheese Butter

Cream cheese has a nice acidic tang that accentuates great fish. I like it here softened with the taste of butter and smoky sweet peppers. The butter is an excellent topping for nearly anything, but I particularly like it with catfish, inspired as it is by the Southern specialty, pimiento cheese spread. This can easily be made in an oven if a grill isn't available. Serve it with Pecan Quinoa Pilaf (page 243) or a regular rice pilaf.

Four 5-ounce catfish fillets

1 tablespoon canola oil

2 teaspoons Seafood Spice #2 (page 260)

1 roasted red bell pepper, jarred or homemade

1 tablespoon butter, softened

1 tablespoon cream cheese, softened

Salt

For the catfish prepare a grill according to the instructions on page 250. Brush the fillets with the canola oil, season with the Seafood Spice, and place them on the grate as far away from the flame as possible. Cover and grill until the fillets are cooked through, about 15 minutes.

For the butter mince the roasted pepper until it is nearly a purée. Transfer to a bowl and combine with the butter and cream cheese. Season to taste with salt and whisk vigorously until smooth.

When the catfish come off the grill, smear each fillet with a good portion of the butter and serve immediately.

Serves 4

Poached Mackerel Roll with Spiced Mayonnaise

The classic sandwich rolls of New England tradition are among the best ways to enjoy shore-fresh seafood. Nothing tops sitting in the sun holding a lobster roll and a cold beer. Lobster can be expensive, though, so try this version with mackerel. Poached Maine shrimp also work well. Serve the sandwiches with a fresh green or Sweet Potato Salad (page 141).

1 pound skinned Spanish or Boston (not king) mackerel fillets

Juice of 1/2 lemon

2 sprigs fresh thyme

Salt

1/4 cup mayonnaise

1 teaspoon ground mace

1 rib celery, finely diced

1 shallot, finely diced

4 potato rolls

2 tablespoons canola oil or melted butter

Place the fillets in a skillet just large enough to fit them in a single layer. Add the lemon juice and thyme and season to taste with salt. Barely cover the fillets with cold water and place over medium heat. Cook 8 minutes and remove from the heat. Check the doneness of the fillets. If they are still not quite cooked through, let them hang out in the water for another few minutes; the residual heat will continue to cook them. Then strain the water and chill the fillets until cold. They will keep for up to a day before they begin to lose flavor.

Preheat the broiler.

In a medium bowl, combine the mayonnaise, mace, celery, shallot, and a little salt. Mix to combine, then flake in the chilled mackerel. Gently mix by hand to coat it with the mayonnaise.

Brush the potato rolls with the canola oil and place under the broiler. Remove when golden brown and fill each with a generous heap of the mackerel mixture.

Serves 4

Mackerel with Almond-Ginger-Mustard Butter

A whole grilled mackerel is something to behold. It is a beautiful fish to begin with, and the sexy char of grill marks only enhances its good looks. It is easy to prepare a whole fish; just put it on the grill and wait until it tastes good. The butter was inspired by the cooking of a good friend from India. She loves to share her family's recipes when she comes to visit, and I learn a lot every time I watch her cook. The aromatics are simmered in butter, which mellows their sharpness but also infuses the butter with deep, rich flavor. I added the almonds for crunch and substance.

1 Spanish or Boston (not king) mackerel, dressed (about 2 pounds)

2 lemons, 1 sliced and 1 cut into wedges

4 sprigs fresh thyme

3 tablespoons butter

3 cloves garlic, sliced

1 tablespoon peeled fresh ginger grated on a Microplane or very finely minced

2 teaspoons mustard seeds, soaked in hot water for 2 hours and drained

3 tablespoons slivered or sliced almonds

1 tablespoon water

Prepare a grill according to the instructions on page 250. Line the belly cavity of the mackerel with the lemon slices and thyme sprigs and place the fish on the hottest part of the grill for about 5 minutes. Rotate the grate so the fish is over the coolest part of the grill; cover. Grill until the fish is cooked all the way through, about 25 minutes. The best way to check is to make an incision along the backbone and check the color of the flesh at the spine; it should be opaque white. Or you can insert a toothpick into the fish, pushing right down to the spine. Hold it there for a few seconds, then put the toothpick to the bottom part of your lower lip. If it feels hot, the fish is cooked.

Meanwhile, combine the butter, garlic, and ginger in a small saucepan over medium heat. Cook for a few minutes, until the garlic is about half cooked but not yet browning. Add the mustard seeds, almonds, and water and cook until the water is evaporated and the almonds are just beginning to brown, about 4 minutes. Remove from the heat and let sit for a few minutes for the flavors to soften.

The easiest way to move a whole fish off the grill is to remove the entire grate from the heat and lay a plate over the fish. Using a towel to hold the grate, quickly flip the grate and the plate at the same time, inverting the fish onto the plate. If you don't feel comfortable doing this, use a couple of metal spatulas to get under as much of the fish as possible and have someone hold the plate near so as you lift the fish up, your helper quickly slides the plate underneath. Breakage often occurs when the fish is moved away from the grill; both of these methods eliminate that problem.

Fillet the fish using a fork and table knife. Divide the fish among 4 plates, then drizzle the warm butter over the top. Serve with the lemon wedges.

Serves 4

Mahimahi with Gingered Zucchini and Smoked Tomato Sauce

I like the way ginger and cinnamon combine in this dish, the cinnamon bringing out the depth of flavor in the tomatoes. This treatment works with almost any fish possessing substantial texture, such as Pacific cod or amberjack.

3 tablespoons butter

2 teaspoons ground cinnamon

2 teaspoons sweet smoked paprika

4 Roma tomatoes, cut into 1/2-inch dice

Salt

Four 5-ounce portions mahimahi fillet

3 cloves garlic, sliced

1 tablespoon peeled, grated fresh ginger

4 medium zucchini, cut into 1/4-inch-thick rounds, then into half-moons

2 tablespoons water

For the sauce, melt 1 tablespoon of the butter in a small pot over medium heat, then add the spices. Toast them in the butter for 1 minute, then add the tomatoes. Season with salt and bring to a simmer, mashing it all together with a fork. Cook for about 4 minutes until the mixture resembles a chunky salsa. Remove from the heat and set aside.

For the mahimahi, prepare a grill according to the instructions on page 250. Place the fish on the coolest part of the grill and cover. (This dish is best if the fish does not sear at all, absorbing smoke but never caramelizing.) Cook slowly, allowing about 15-20 minutes for a fillet that is 1 1/2 inches thick. The fish should be cooked through but only just beginning to flake when gentle pressure is applied.

Meanwhile, for the zucchini, melt the remaining 2 tablespoons butter in a large sauté pan over high heat. As it begins to foam, add the garlic and ginger. Cook, stirring, until the garlic begins to brown slightly. Add the zucchini and toss to combine. Allow to cook undisturbed for 3 minutes so it begins to develop some color. Season to taste with salt and add the water. Continue to cook until the water evaporates and the zucchini is lightly glazed, about 3 minutes.

To serve, evenly divide the zucchini among 4 plates and set a fillet on top of the zucchini. Spoon a generous portion of the tomato sauce over each and serve immediately.

Serves 4

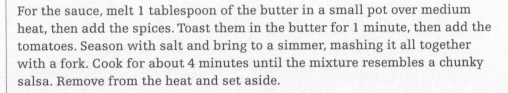

Mahimahi with Grilled Peaches and Buttermilk-Mint Dressing

The flavors in this dish are unexpected and delicious. The charred-sugary-bitter-burned peaches make an excellent foil to the meatiness of the mahi; the creamy mint dressing brings it all together nicely. I love to serve grilled peaches as a dessert with this, too. To do that, set the peach halves on the hot part of the grill and cover it while you enjoy dinner. Clear the table, bring out the vanilla ice cream and aged balsamic vinegar to use as toppings, and your peaches are ready to come off the grill, cooked to smoky, sweet charred perfection.

1 tablespoon extra-virgin olive oil

1 teaspoon Dijon mustard

1 teaspoon sugar

1/2 cup low-fat buttermilk

Juice of 1/2 lemon

Leaves from 8 sprigs fresh mint, chopped

Salt

Four 5-ounce portions mahimahi fillet

4 ripe peaches, cut in half and pitted

1 pound arugula leaves

1 small red onion, very thinly sliced

For the dressing, whisk together the olive oil, mustard, sugar, buttermilk, lemon juice, and mint. Season to taste with salt and allow to sit at room temperature for at least 20 minutes and up to two hours so that the flavors combine.

For the mahimahi, prepare a grill according to the instructions on page 250. Place the fillets on the coolest part of the grill and the peach halves over the hot part of the fire. Cover the grill and cook about 15-20 minutes for fillets 1 1/2 inches thick. The fish should be cooked through but only just beginning to flake when gentle pressure is applied. At that point, the peaches will be slightly charred and beginning to soften.

To serve, mix the arugula and onion, toss with two-thirds of the dressing, and season with salt. Divide the salad among 4 plates. Place 2 grilled peach halves next to the salad. Place a piece of mahimahi on top of the salad and spoon the remaining dressing over it. Serve immediately.

Serves 4

Grilled Sablefish with Shredded Endive and Cherry-Tarragon Salsa

Sablefish can be tough to work with on the grill; it's so flaky that chunks can easily end up in the fire instead of on the plate. The trick is to be very patient. Do not touch or move the fillets on the grill until they are cooked through. The less you touch them, the more dinner you will have to eat. Why take the trouble? Because sablefish infused with grilled smokiness is incredibly good. The cherry salsa adds a sweet-yet-sharp point of contrast as well as striking color. When pitting cherries, wear gloves, as the juice can stain your fingers.

2 tablespoons extra-virgin olive oil

2 shallots, finely diced

2 pints sweet cherries, cut in half and pitted

Salt

1/4 cup white balsamic vinegar or white wine vinegar

Four 5-ounce portions sablefish (black cod) fillet

3 heads Belgian endive, bottoms trimmed and cut crosswise into thin strips

3 tablespoons chopped fresh tarragon

For the salsa, place the olive oil in a sauté pan over high heat. Add the shallots and cook for 1 minute. Before the shallots are fully softened, add the cherries and toss to combine. Cook until the cherries begin to bleed some of their juices, about 2 minutes. Season generously with salt and add the vinegar. Turn the heat down to medium and continue to cook until the liquid in the pan reduces to a slightly thick syrup around the cherries, about 4 minutes. Remove from the heat.

For the fish, prepare a grill according to the instructions on page 250. Place the fillets on the hottest part of the grill and cook for 2 minutes. Rotate the grill grate so that the fish is over the coolest part of the fire; cover. Cook for approximately 10 minutes, or until the fish begins to flake.

To serve, divide the shredded endive among 4 plates. Gently reheat the salsa if necessary and add the tarragon. Toss to combine. Gently set the fish on top of the endive and spoon the salsa over the top. Serve immediately.

Serves 4

Grilled King Salmon with Tarragon Butter

The addition of orange to this dish accentuates the deep, rich flavor of the salmon. Tarragon and all sorts of seafood are a near perfect pairing; try this butter with the fish or shellfish of your choice. If you like, double the butter recipe—any leftovers will keep in the refrigerator for up to a week. You also can wrap up little nuggets of the butter and freeze them; they'll keep for up to a year.

3 tablespoons butter, softened

Grated zest of 1 orange

2 tablespoons chopped fresh tarragon

Salt

Freshly ground black pepper

Four 5-ounce portions king salmon fillet

For the tarragon butter, in a small bowl combine the butter, orange zest, and tarragon. Season to taste with salt and pepper. Using the back of a fork, mash it together until well mixed, and set aside.

For the salmon, prepare a grill according to the instructions on page 250. Grill the salmon skin side down over the hottest part of the fire for 3 minutes to give it nice grill marks. Rotate the fish to the coolest part of the grill and continue to cook for another 12 minutes or so. Salmon is a fish that can be eaten at different temperatures. I prefer it to be cooked through, which is when the flesh is an even color throughout. This can be checked by gently separating the fillet with a knife so the inside is visible.

Gently remove the salmon from the heat and top each fillet with a pat of the tarragon butter. Serve immediately.

Serves 4

Salmon with Minted Cucumbers

I like this dish best with poached salmon, but the minted cucumbers pair well with any grilled fish. Pink salmon is ideal with this preparation as it has the softest flavor of the different types of salmon and contrasts nicely with the crispy texture and bright taste of the cucumbers. The salad gets better the longer it sits—I often have it the next morning for breakfast. Refrigeration muffles the flavor, so be sure to let it come to room temperature before serving it.

Four 5-ounce portions pink salmon fillet

1 cup white wine

1 tablespoon soy sauce

1 teaspoon-sized piece fresh ginger, peeled and thinly sliced

3 cucumbers

2 tablespoons extra-virgin olive oil

1 tablespoon cider vinegar

Salt

Leaves from 10 sprigs fresh mint, stacked, rolled, and cut crosswise into thin ribbons (about 1/4 cup)

1/2 red onion, thinly sliced

Place the salmon, wine, soy sauce, and ginger in a skillet just large enough to hold the salmon pieces in a single layer. Barely cover the fish with cold water. Bring to a simmer and turn the heat off. Make sure the fillets are completely submerged and allow them to sit for approximately 7 minutes. The residual heat of the liquid will be enough to cook the fish through; the flesh should be one even color throughout. Chill the fish in the poaching broth so that it stays moist. This can be done up to a day in advance.

For the cucumbers, peel the cucumbers lengthwise, leaving thin strips of peel in between each stroke for a striped effect. Discard the ends and cut each cucumber in half lengthwise. Cut the halves crosswise into 1/4-inch-thick half-moons and place in a large bowl. Add the olive oil and vinegar and season generously with salt. Toss to combine and allow to sit for a few minutes for the salt to draw out some of the moisture. Add the mint and onion. Toss to combine. You can hold the salad at room temperature for up to 4 hours before it should be chilled.

To serve, divide the salad among 4 plates. Gently remove the salmon fillets from the poaching liquid, pat dry, and place next to the salad on each plate.

Serves 4

Smoked Sardines with Heirloom Tomatoes and Herbs

Couldn't be any simpler than this. In keeping with the ease of a tomato salad, all you have to do here is to open up the can of sardines and chop some herbs. Regular red tomatoes will also work, but heirlooms have interesting and unique flavors and give you the ability to mix and match different personalities on the plate.

2 pounds super-ripe heirloom tomatoes (I prefer a colorful mix of varieties)

Two 6-ounce cans smoked sardine fillets

Salt

1/4 cup chopped fresh soft-leaved herbs such as cilantro, parsley, mint, or chervil

1 bunch scallions, thinly sliced

Slice the tomatoes 1/2 inch thick and distribute them among 4 plates. Flake the sardines over the tomatoes and drizzle the sardine oil over the top. Season to taste with salt and sprinkle the herbs and scallions over all. Serve immediately.

Serves 4

Yogurt-marinated Sturgeon

Sustainably raised farmed sturgeon from the western United States has a meaty texture and a bold flavor that is perfect for the grill, but it can be tough. The great chef José Andrés marinates fibrous fish like shark in vinegar and spices for a couple of days to tenderize it before cooking. Taking my cue from José, in this recipe I let the sturgeon marinate in a mixture of yogurt and vinegar for a day and a half before cooking. Feel free to experiment with spices that you like.

1 cup plain full-fat yogurt, preferably Greek style

2 tablespoons sherry vinegar

4 tablespoons extra-virgin olive oil

1 tablespoon ground coriander

1 tablespoon smoked paprika

1 tablespoon salt

One 1 1/2-pound sturgeon fillet, skinned

In a small bowl, whisk together the yogurt, vinegar, 2 tablespoons of the olive oil, coriander, paprika, and salt until smooth and well combined. Place the sturgeon fillet in a large shallow baking dish. Pour the yogurt mixture over it and turn it several times, until well coated. Cover with plastic wrap and let marinate in the refrigerator 36 hours, turning the fish several times in the marinade.

Prepare a grill according to the instructions on page 250. Set the sturgeon, still coated with the marinade, on the coolest part of the grill. Cover and cook for about 30 minutes. As the fish cooks, you can baste it with the yogurt marinade. Just be aware that the marinade contains raw fish juice, so be sure to cook the fillet for a few minutes after the last basting to ensure that everything is safe.

Check for doneness by applying gentle pressure to the middle of the fillet. It should flake easily. If the fillet is not done, cook for another 5 to 10 minutes with the grill covered.

To serve, drizzle with the remaining 2 tablespoons olive oil.

Serves 4

Tilapia with Minted Nectarine Salad

Nectarines are almost always a letdown to me when I eat them as table fruit. They just never seem to be really ripe. Don't get me wrong—they are fine, but they're not the same as a super-ripe juice-to-the-elbows peach. So here is a way to use the slightly underripe fruit to great effect. Salt and oil help to soften the thin slices, and the mint rounds out the flavors. Pecan Quinoa Pilaf (page 243) is a great side to serve with this dish.

6 nectarines, cut in half and pitted

Leaves from 1 bunch fresh mint

1 red onion, sliced as thinly as possible

Salt

4 tablespoons extra-virgin olive oil

Four 5-ounce tilapia fillets

Preheat the oven to 300 degrees.

For the salad, thinly slice the nectarines and mix with the mint and sliced onion. Season to taste with salt and toss with 3 tablespoons of the olive oil.

For the tilapia, place the fillets on a baking sheet and lightly brush with the remaining 1 tablespoon olive oil. Bake until the fillets easily flake under light pressure, about 8 minutes.

Serve the fillets just out of the oven with a tuft of the salad on the side.

Serves 4

Trout with Warm Cherry Tomato and Dill Salad

Cherry tomatoes are so delicious they really only need salt. Here they are punched up with a little garlic, shallot, and dill, then warmed on top of the trout as it cooks in the oven. It couldn't be easier.

1 pound cherry tomatoes, single variety or mixed, each cut in half

1 shallot, finely diced

Fronds from 1 bunch fresh dill, chopped

1 clove garlic, grated on a Microplane or very finely minced

3 tablespoons extra-virgin olive oil

Salt

Four 5-ounce skin-on trout fillets

Preheat the oven to 300 degrees.

For the salad, mix the tomatoes, shallot, dill, garlic, and 2 tablespoons of the olive oil in a medium bowl. Toss gently to combine. Season to taste with salt and let sit for a few minutes until the tomatoes release their juices and the flavors meld.

Place the trout fillets on a lightly oiled baking sheet, skin side down. Top the fillets with the tomato mixture and place in the oven. Bake for about 10 minutes, checking to see that the fillets cook all the way through. The flesh should be opaque and will easily flake.

Remove from the oven and transfer to plates, taking care to keep the tomatoes on top. Spoon over any remaining juices and serve immediately.

Serves 4

Wahoo with Ratatouille

Wahoo, with its bright, clean taste, is a fantastic fish for the summer, and it cooks just like tuna. In fact, it is a member of the same family and has the same concentric rings in the loins. While it is best to cook it medium rare, much like good-quality tuna, you can cook it to a higher temperature if that is what you prefer, but be aware that it dries out very quickly. The addition of prunes to the ratatouille may be surprising but ties together all the flavors in the stew. If prunes just don't cut it for you, use raisins instead.

3/4 cup extra-virgin olive oil

6 cloves garlic, each cut in half

1 red bell pepper, seeded and cut into 1-inch pieces

1 small onion, cut into medium dice

1 cup slivered almonds

12 prunes, each cut into eighths

2 medium zucchini, cut into 1/2-inch dice

2 medium yellow squash, cut into 1/2-inch dice

Salt

3 ripe beefsteak tomatoes, cut into 1/2-inch dice

1 tablespoon cider vinegar

Four 5-ounce wahoo steaks cut from the loin

For the ratatouille, heat the olive oil in a large saucepan. When the oil is hot, add the garlic, pepper, and onion and cook over high heat until the pepper is blistered and the garlic is browned. Add the almonds and prunes and cook until the almonds begin to brown, about another 5 minutes. Add the zucchini and squash and cook for 4 minutes. Season to taste with salt and reduce the heat to low. Add the tomatoes and vinegar, season again with salt, and cover. Let simmer until the squash is soft and the tomatoes release all their juice, about 15 minutes.

For the wahoo, prepare a grill according to the instructions on page 250. Place the wahoo on the hottest part of the grill and cook for about 1 minute. Turn the fish over and cook for 1 minute more. Rotate the fish to cook the remaining sides for about 30 seconds each and remove from the grill. The fish should be medium rare.

To serve, divide the ratatouille among 4 plates. Thinly slice each portion of wahoo on the bias and arrange portions over the ratatouille.

Serves 4

Soft-shell Crabs with Corn and Black Bean Relish

Soft-shells are among the best things about the approach of summer. Everyone seems to have an opinion on what to use to bread soft-shell crabs before frying them—or whether to bread them at all. I prefer a coating of fine cornmeal, as this helps to mellow their flavor and to add a bit of texture. The key with soft-shells is to cook them over moderate heat so that they get crispy but don't burn. The relish is a nice accompaniment, as the lime zest and butter really make the fresh corn shine.

1 cup fine-ground cornmeal

1 tablespoon Seafood Spice #1 (page 260)

4 large soft-shell blue crabs, gills, face, and tail flap removed

5 tablespoons butter

3 tablespoons canola oil

1 clove garlic, sliced

Grated zest and juice of 1 lime

4 large ears corn, shucked and kernels cut off the cob

Salt

One 16-ounce can black beans, drained and rinsed

Tabasco sauce

For the crabs, combine the cornmeal and spice mix in a shallow bowl. Dredge each crab well in the coating. Heat 2 tablespoons of the butter and 1 tablespoon of the canola oil over medium-high heat in a heavy-bottomed skillet big enough to hold all the crabs in a single layer. When the butter is just melted, add the crabs, shell side down, arranging them so they all fit neatly with the claws in their natural positions. Reduce the heat to medium and cook until the coating is crisp, about 5 minutes. Turn the crabs over with tongs and add the remaining 2 tablespoons canola oil. Cook for another 5 minutes. Remove the crabs from the pan and pat off any excess oil with paper towels.

While the crabs are cooking, make the relish. Heat the remaining 3 tablespoons butter in a large sauté pan. Add the garlic and lime zest and cook for 1 minute. Add the corn kernels, season to taste with salt, and toss to combine. Cook for a couple minutes, until the corn begins to soften. Add the black beans, a few dashes Tabasco, and the lime juice and cook for another 3 minutes to warm the beans through.

Serve the crabs with the corn relish spooned over the top of the shell.

Serves 4

Grilled King Crab Legs

Grilling crab legs is one of the best ways to prepare these treats. You need to thaw them before you put them on the grill, but other than that, there is no prep to this dish. The crab is so flavorful that you do not need an accompanying sauce other than melted butter and a little lemon juice. If you want to offer a dipping sauce, try Orange-Sherry Aioli (page 84) or season the legs with Parsley-Garlic Finishing Mix (page 270) when they come off the grill. The heat of the shells will bloom the aroma of the garlic.

2 pounds Alaskan king crab legs, thawed

Lemon wedges

Prepare a grill according to the instructions on page 250. Place the legs on the hottest part of the grill; cover. Cook for 5 minutes, then turn the legs over with tongs. Cover and cook for another 3 minutes. Shells should be well charred. Remove one leg and check the meat to make sure it is hot all the way through.

Serve immediately with lemon wedges.

Serves 4 as a main course

Grilled Lobster with Spiced Butter

I've always thought that grilling is a most rewarding way to cook and enjoy lobster. Here, the work of cracking open the lobster is done ahead of time, making this a much less messy and labor-intensive way to serve it. However, grilling lobster requires a lot of space and a really hot fire, so don't plan on having everyone eat all at once. To keep everyone happy, though, you can serve each guest a half lobster at a time.

1/4 cup butter, softened

1 teaspoon ground mace

6 drops vanilla extract

Juice of 1 lemon

Four 1 1/4-pound hard-shell lobsters

2 tablespoons canola oil

For the butter, combine the butter, mace, vanilla, and lemon juice in a small bowl. Keep at room temperature.

See page 31 for instructions on how to pre-cook lobsters.

Remove the claws from the water and crack the shells. You can remove the meat entirely from the shell or leave on the claw tips to make it easier to eat.

If using a charcoal grill, prepare a large, hot fire with the coals in the center of the grill. Place the lobster bodies, two halves at a time, directly over the coals, cut side down. Do not move the lobster halves after this if they contain coral, as it is very delicate. The lobsters will cook in about 5 minutes, depending on the heat of your fire.

If using a gas grill, place the lobsters over the hottest flame possible and cook for about three minutes. Reduce the heat to low and turn the lobsters, cut side up, and continue cooking until the tail is cooked through, about another 5 minutes.

Using a large spatula, transfer the lobsters from the grill to a platter. While the body is cooking, the claws can be rewarmed on another part of the grill, as they only need to be heated through.

As soon as the lobster is on the platter, brush with a little of the spiced butter; it will baste the meat and collect in the shell. Serve immediately.

Serves 4

Grilled Greens

Grilled greens are among the simplest yet most guest-praise-worthy, "How did you do that?" dishes that I cook. There is no secret to this. The recipe is basic: add greens to heat, allow to burn, eat. Anyone can handle that. The crunchiness of the leaves and the flaky, fall-apart texture is incredible and, best of all, this dish takes no time to prep, doesn't leave a mess in the kitchen, and is incredibly nutritious. Any type of kale will do, but I prefer the lacinato variety, also known as dinosaur kale.

2 bunches kale

1 tablespoon canola oil

Salt

1/2 cup Chunky Almond Oil (page 262)

Prepare a grill according to the instructions on page 250.

It's easiest to grill the kale with the stems on, but you can remove them by holding the base where the leaf meets the stem between two fingers and pulling down on the leaf to separate. Toss the leaves with the canola oil and salt to taste. Spread the leaves over the hottest part of the grill until they begin to burn and the edges turn black, about 4 minutes. Using tongs, turn the leaves on the grill and cook for another 2 minutes.

Remove the kale to a serving platter and drizzle the almond oil over it. Serve immediately.

Serves 4 as a side dish

Eggplant Stuffed with Smoky Tomato–Anchovy Ratatouille

This is a fun dish to serve to guests in the summer, as you can prepare it ahead and it tastes wonderful at room temperature. The brilliance of the vegetable flavors is really what shines here.

1 cup bread crumbs

2 jumbo eggplants

4 tablespoons extra-virgin olive oil

1 small onion, cut into 1-inch pieces

4 cloves garlic, grated on a Microplane or very finely minced

8 salt-packed anchovies (page 24) or 16 oil-packed anchovy fillets

1 tablespoon sweet smoked paprika

2 medium zucchini, diced into 1/2-inch pieces

4 Roma tomatoes, diced in 1/2-inch pieces

Salt

In a dry pan over medium heat, toast the bread crumbs, stirring constantly, until golden brown. Set aside. Preheat the oven to 400 degrees.

Cut the eggplants in half lengthwise. Heat a heavy sauté pan over high heat, then add 1 tablespoon of the olive oil and sear the cut sides of the eggplant halves until well browned. Transfer them to a baking sheet and place in the oven for 12 minutes. Remove eggplant from oven and let cool, leaving the oven on.

While the eggplant is baking, add the onion, garlic, and 2 tablespoons of the olive oil to the pan and sauté over high heat until the onion begins to soften. Add the anchovies and paprika and cook for 30 seconds to flavor the oil. Add the zucchini and cook for about 4 minutes, without stirring. Add the tomatoes and cook until they break down, about 2 minutes. Remove from the heat and season to taste with salt. Place the tomato mixture in a medium bowl with the bread crumbs.

When the eggplants are cool enough to handle, scoop out the insides, chop them, and add to the bowl. When scraping the eggplant halves, make sure to leave enough flesh on the inside so that the outer skin does not collapse. Season the eggplant hulls with salt. Stir the vegetable mixture well and use it to stuff the eggplants. Return the eggplants to the oven for 10 minutes to warm the stuffing through. Then increase the heat to broil and cook about 4 inches from the heat source until the tops are brown and beginning to char, about 3 minutes.

Drizzle the eggplant halves with the remaining tablespoon olive oil. Serve immediately.

Serves 4 as a main course

Roasted Eggplant Purée

This purée is great as a dip with pita chips or as a sauce served with just about everything. It is best at room temperature, so be sure to take it out of the refrigerator an hour before serving time.

As a wine-pairing note, I have found that eggplant goes particularly well with port.

1 large eggplant, halved lengthwise

Salt

1 cup extra-virgin olive oil

This is really easy. Preheat the oven to the highest temperature possible, short of turning on the broiler. Place the eggplant halves, cut side down, on a baking sheet, and roast for 25 minutes. (Unless your oven is spotlessly clean, don't be surprised if you get some smoke.) After this time, the cut side should be crusted and the whole eggplant should have slightly deflated onto itself. Let cool to room temperature.

Use a spoon to scrape out every last little bit of the eggplant from the skins. A lot of the flavor is close up against the skin. Place the eggplant flesh in a blender or a food processor and start to purée. Season to taste with salt, then, with the machine running, add the oil in a slow, steady drizzle, making sure that it is incorporated. When all the oil has been added, taste for seasoning and adjust, if necessary. Eggplant soaks up salt, so don't be afraid to keep adding a little more and a little more until it has a vibrant flavor. (This will keep, tightly covered, in the refrigerator for up to 3 days.)

Makes about 4 cups

Zucchini Carpaccio

This is a dish that I made for a group of CNN reporters who came to my house to film a segment for Anderson Cooper. I put it together in no time at all, and the results were great. The key is good zucchini, so try a taste before you begin. If the zucchini is sweet and moist with great flavor, then your dish will be a winner. If it is bitter and dry, don't use it here. One more thing: this needs to be prepared just before it is served; otherwise, the zucchini will dry out and become discolored from the oil.

2 large zucchini

One 2-ounce can oil-packed anchovy fillets

3 tablespoons best-quality extra-virgin olive oil

Pinch of red chile flakes

Salt

1 bunch scallions, thinly sliced

Slice the zucchini as thinly as you can into rounds (if you own a mandoline, now would be the time to pull it out) and arrange the slices so they barely overlap on a large platter.

Chop the anchovies, reserving the oil, and scatter them over the zucchini. Drizzle the oil from the anchovies as well as the olive oil over all. Sprinkle on the red chile flakes and season with a touch of salt. Scatter the scallions over the plate and serve immediately.

Serves 4

Watermelon Salad
with Lime and Mint

What could possibly pair better with food hot off the grill than the cool taste of watermelon infused with the bright, friendly flavor of lime and the aromatic pop of fresh mint? I love this salad, and I'm not alone—whenever I serve it, it disappears quickly.

8 cups diced seedless watermelon
(about 1/2 large melon)

1/4 cup Chile Oil (page 262)

Juice of 2 limes

Salt

Leaves from 6 sprigs fresh mint

In a large bowl, combine the watermelon, chile oil, and lime juice. Season to taste with salt. Finely slice the mint leaves and toss to combine with the salad at the last minute before serving. Do not serve this dish too cold, or the flavors will be muted.

Serves 4

Autumn is my favorite time to cook. You've still got good grilling weather, and the fresh produce is peaking, with two seasons of bounty to choose from. Summer fades slowly, leaving in its wake most of the joy that comes with it. Cooking picks up the pace to accommodate the renewed vigor of cooler days. Dishes get a little warmer, a little fuller, and a little more complex. No longer able to bask in the perfection of a simple ripe tomato, we begin to seek partners for flavors on the plate. The remaining tomatoes become sauce, taking on a supporting role rather than being the star.

The cooling waters turn the fish south, as many schools begin their migration to warmer waves. The predators, at the peak of their flavor, are fat from a summer of munching on the little guys. Oysters are crisp again with the turn in the weather, and the salmon runs begin to taper off, the unimaginable multitude of fish swimming upriver now slows to a trickle. Fishing communities put away their neon signs and tourist tchotchkes and focus on getting in one last shot before the weather turns cold.

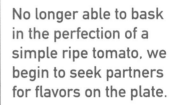

No longer able to bask in the perfection of a simple ripe tomato, we begin to seek partners for flavors on the plate.

Smoked Bluefish Spread with Toasted Bread and Olive Oil

This recipe is a wonderful use of smoked bluefish, which can be strongly flavored. I tend to serve it at parties or enjoy it as an afternoon snack. If you cannot find smoked bluefish, try smoking it yourself, following the directions for hot smoking on page 254. Or you can substitute smoked trout or hot smoked salmon. The taste won't be the same, but it'll still be good.

8 ounces smoked bluefish

3 tablespoons sour cream

Salt

1 loaf crusty baguette, thinly sliced

Extra-virgin olive oil

1 lemon, cut into wedges

Remove any skin from the bluefish and flake the fish into a bowl. Add the sour cream and whip with a whisk until the mixture forms a thick paste and the flakes have all broken down into a purée. Check for seasoning and adjust with a little salt if necessary. (This can be made up to a few days ahead of time; keep refrigerated until ready to serve.)

Brush the bread with olive oil and toast under the broiler (or in a toaster oven) until golden brown.

Serve the spread in a bowl with the toasted bread and lemon wedges surrounding it. Finish the spread with a heavy drizzle of olive oil, then serve.

Serves 4 as an appetizer or snack

Broiled Smelts with Lemon and Oregano

Smelts are easy to prepare. I buy bags of frozen dressed smelts, and because the fish are so small they can be cooked straight from the freezer. Recently they have become widely available frozen with a micro sheet of ice encapsulating them, which protects them from freezer burn. I give them a quick wash to break up the ice layer, then proceed with the dish. Offer a plate of this as finger food at your next party.

1 pound frozen dressed smelts

2 tablespoons flour for dusting

2 tablespoons butter

1 lemon, very thinly sliced

Salt

1 tablespoon dried oregano

Preheat the broiler.

Wash the smelts in a colander for a few seconds under cold running water to rinse off any ice that is on the skin. Pat dry with paper towels, then toss with the flour until they're coated evenly, tapping off any excess.

Melt the butter in a large ovenproof sauté pan over medium heat, then turn the heat up to high. Just as the butter begins to brown, add the lemon slices and cook for 1 minute. Add the floured smelts, making sure they're in a single layer. Season generously with salt and sprinkle with the oregano.

Transfer the pan under the broiler and broil the fish until they become crispy and golden brown, about 5 minutes.

Remove the pan from the broiler and transfer the fish and lemon slices to a large serving dish. Serve immediately.

Serves 4 as an appetizer

Grill-smoked Smelts

This is a hybrid smoking technique that combines the hot-smoke method with grilling to produce food meant to be eaten right after cooking. The smelts cure in a dry rub and are then slowly cooked over a low flame stoked by flavorful wood chips. This is great served with a peppery arugula salad dressed with a fruity dressing such as Blackberry-Shallot Salsa (page 264).

1 pound frozen dressed smelts

2 tablespoons Orange and Rosemary Grill Salt (page 261)

1 cup soaked wood chips (peach is my favorite, but any type of hardwood chips will do)

2 tablespoons extra-virgin olive oil

1 recipe Parsley-Garlic Finishing Mix (optional; page 270)

Gently wash the frozen smelts under cold running water to remove any surface ice. Place the fish in a bowl, toss with the Orange-Rosemary Grill Salt and refrigerate. Let sit for 2 hours, tossing every half hour or so.

Prepare a small charcoal fire according to the instructions on page 250. You won't need more than 6 to 8 briquettes.

When the fire is hot, place the soaked wood chips on the fire and allow to smolder. Pour the fish into a colander to drain off any liquid that has been exuded. Toss the fish with the olive oil in a bowl, then place on the coolest part of the grill. (You can use a grill pan for this to make it easier, or just be careful to lay the fish perpendicular to the grill grates.) Cover the grill to capture the heat and smoke and cook the smelts for about 30 minutes, maintaining the slow heat and smoke of the fire.

Transfer the smelts to a serving platter, sprinkle with the Parsley-Garlic Mix, and serve immediately.

Serves 4 as an appetizer or light lunch

Amberjack on Sweet Potato Salad with Scallions and Honey

Amberjack is a relatively difficult fish to get your hands on. It is not a big commercial catch but is available on both the East and West coasts, where it is caught as a sport fish. It's got a steak-like texture similar to that of swordfish, which makes it an excellent candidate for the grill. If you cannot find amberjack, use U.S. farm-raised cobia or mahimahi.

3 large sweet potatoes, peels left on, cut into 1-inch dice

Salt

1/4 cup mayonnaise

2 tablespoons extra-virgin olive oil

1 tablespoon honey or maple syrup

2 teaspoons ground coriander

2 teaspoons ground mace

2 bunches scallions, thinly sliced

Four 5-ounce portions skinned amberjack fillet

1 tablespoon canola oil

Freshly ground black pepper

Lemon wedges

For the potato salad, bring the sweet potatoes to a boil in cold, salted water to cover and cook until they are just tender, about 2 minutes from the point at which the water begins to boil. Drain and allow to cool to room temperature. Whisk together the mayonnaise, olive oil, honey, coriander, and mace in a medium bowl, then add the cooled sweet potatoes and scallions. Toss to combine. Season to taste with salt. (This can be prepared up to a day in advance and refrigerated. Bring it to room temperature before serving for the best flavor.)

Prepare a grill according to the instructions on page 250. Brush the fillets with the canola oil and season with pepper and salt. Sear over the hottest part of the fire for 1 minute, then rotate the grill grate so the fish is over the coolest part of the grill; cover. Continue to cook until the fish flakes apart easily, about 15 minutes. (If you want to broil the fish, give it a 5-minute sear under the heat, then move it to the center rack of the oven and reset the temperature for 275 degrees. Cook for about 15 minutes.) While the fish is cooking, grill (or broil) the lemon wedges.

Serve with the fish perched on top of the sweet potato salad with the lemon wedges on the side.

Serves 4

Barramundi with Walnut-Cider Dressing and Bacon

Bacon makes nearly everything better. In this salad it is a nice counterpoint to the frisée. Barramundi is a great choice here as it pairs well with the sweetness of the sauce and the smoke of the bacon.

2 cups apple cider

1 tablespoon butter

1/2 cup walnuts, lightly toasted (page 15) and chopped

Four 5-ounce portions skin-on barramundi fillet

1 tablespoon canola oil

4 strips bacon, preferably thick-cut, cut into 1/2-inch pieces

2 heads frisée lettuce, separated into leaves and heavy stems removed

Salt

Freshly ground black pepper

1 lemon, cut into wedges

Preheat the broiler.

For the dressing, reduce the cider by two-thirds in a small saucepan over medium heat, about 20 minutes. Meanwhile, in a small sauté pan over high heat, heat the butter until it is golden brown and has a nutty aroma, add the walnuts and toss to combine. Toast the nuts in the butter for a minute or so, then add the cider reduction. Bring the mixture to a boil and remove from heat.

Brush the fillets with the canola oil and place on a baking sheet, skin side up. Broil for approximately 3 minutes, then turn off the broiler and allow the fillets to cook slowly in the residual heat.

Gently cook the bacon in a small sauté pan over low heat until the pieces are super crispy and most of the fat has been rendered out. Drain off the fat and let the bacon bits cool on a paper towel to absorb any remaining grease.

Toss the bacon bits with the frisée and season to taste with salt and pepper. Arrange on a platter and spoon over the warm dressing. Top with the fish fillets and serve with lemon wedges on the side.

Serves 4

Grilled Bluefish with Bacon-Tomato Butter

Bluefish is a great treat in the fall because its deep, rich flavor pairs well with a lot of the foods we start to crave as the weather turns a little cooler. This dish takes advantage of the last vine-ripened tomatoes before the first frost and the lovely smoky flavor of bacon. If it is too cold to grill, cook the bluefish under the broiler. Either way, serve it with grilled or broiled broccoli. (Try Broccoli with Anchovy Vinaigrette, page 241, and Sweet Potato Mash, page 193.)

The flavored butter can be made in a larger batch and stored in the refrigerator for many weeks (let it soften a bit before using it). Try it on steak or as a garnish for autumn soups made with vegetable purées, such as cream of potato and leek or squash.

3 tablespoons butter

2 strips bacon, chopped

2 Roma tomatoes, diced

Salt

Four 5-ounce portions skin-on bluefish fillet

For the flavored butter, add 1 tablespoon of the butter and the bacon to a small sauté pan. Cook over medium heat until the bacon fat is mostly rendered and the meat is beginning to crisp. Add the tomatoes and cook for a few minutes, until the juices begin to release and the tomatoes break down. Remove the pan from the heat and allow to cool slightly. Add the remaining 2 tablespoons butter and mash together using a fork. This butter shouldn't melt but rather form a paste with the tomatoes. Season lightly with salt.

Prepare a grill according to the instructions on page 250. Put the bluefish on the hottest part of the grill, skin side down, and cook for 2 minutes. Rotate the grate so the fish is over the cool part of the grill and cover the grill. Grill until cooked through, about another 10 minutes.

Set a fillet on each of 4 serving plates and place a dollop of the flavored butter on top.

Serves 4

Catfish with Lemon Butter Okra and Red Pepper Stew

Catfish is one of the most economical and sustainable options at the fish counter. Most catfish farming is done in the South, which is where I got the inspiration for this recipe. I love okra, big time, and here it makes a nice stew with the addition of the red peppers. Try to find smaller okra as they tend to have a more palatable texture.

2 tablespoons butter

1 small onion, diced

1 clove garlic, sliced

2 red bell peppers, seeded and cut into thin strips

1 1/2 pounds okra, bottoms trimmed and pods sliced into 1/2-inch-thick rounds

Salt

Juice of 1 lemon

1 cup water

Four 5-ounce catfish fillets

2 tablespoons Parsley-Garlic Finishing Mix (page 270)

Preheat the oven to 350 degrees.

Melt the butter in a large ovenproof sauté pan over high heat and sauté the onion and garlic. After about 3 minutes, add the bell peppers and cook for another minute. Add the okra and stir to combine. Season to taste with salt and add the lemon juice and water. Bring to a boil, then place the catfish fillets on top of the vegetables. Place the pan in the oven and cook for 12 minutes. Turn the oven off.

Transfer the catfish to a plate and set the plate in the oven to keep warm. Place the pan with the vegetables on the stove and bring to a boil. Let simmer until any remaining liquid is reduced to a thick, syrupy consistency. Check the seasoning.

Divide the stew among 4 serving plates. Place a catfish fillet on top of each and sprinkle with a spoonful of the Parsley-Garlic Finishing Mix.

Serves 4

Smoked Catfish with Fig and Citrus Salsa

Figs are seductive. They have great texture and presence on the plate. Here I mix thin wedges of ripe figs with segments of citrus to create a chunky sauce that marries perfectly with the smoky flavors of the fish. Serve this with a salad of spinach leaves lightly dressed with olive oil and seasoned with salt.

To cold smoke the catfish, follow the instructions on page 258. Use whichever dry rub you prefer to season the fish. For 5-ounce fillets, let them cure no more than an hour.

Four 5-ounce cold-smoked catfish fillets

1 tablespoon canola oil

1 pint fresh figs (about 10)

1 Meyer or regular lemon, peeled and cut into segments (page 7)

1 orange, peeled and cut into segments (page 7)

3 tablespoons extra-virgin olive oil

Freshly ground black pepper

Salt

Preheat the oven to 300 degrees.

Set the smoked catfish fillets on a baking sheet and brush with the canola oil. Bake until they are heated all the way through, about 15 minutes.

For the salsa, stem and slice each fig into about 6 small wedges. Cut each of the lemon and orange segments into 3 pieces. Combine in a medium bowl. Add the olive oil, a few cracks of black pepper, and salt to taste. Mix very gently so as not to crush the figs.

To serve, set a catfish fillet on each of 4 serving plates and top with a spoonful of the vinaigrette.

Serves 4

Halibut and Braised Fennel with Orange and Fennel-Seed Yogurt

Fennel is a classic flavor pairing with seafood, and in this very simple recipe it really shines through. Only a bit of garlic is added to provide a little punch to offset the sweetness of the fennel.

2 tablespoons extra-virgin olive oil

2 cloves garlic, peeled

2 large fennel bulbs, cut into quarters, with stems trimmed but left intact

Salt

1/2 cup water

1 cup white wine

Four 5-ounce portions halibut fillet

2 tablespoons plain Greek-style or regular full-fat yogurt

2 teaspoons fennel seeds, ground (page 9)

1 tablespoon fresh orange juice

Preheat the oven to 400 degrees.

Heat a deep-sided ovenproof saucepan over medium heat, then add 1 tablespoon of the olive oil. Crush the cloves of garlic with the flat side of a knife and add to the oil. Add the fennel bulbs and sear until they begin to lightly brown. Season generously with salt and add the water and wine. Cover the pan, transfer it to the oven, and roast for 35 minutes. Remove the pan, and set aside, still covered. Leave the oven on.

Place the halibut fillets on a baking sheet and season with salt. Transfer the fish to the oven, then turn the oven off. Prop the door open slightly so that the halibut does not cook too quickly. It should take about 15 minutes for a 1-inch-thick fillet to cook.

For the yogurt sauce, combine the yogurt with the remaining tablespoon olive oil, the ground fennel seeds, and orange juice in a small bowl. Season with salt and mix well.

To serve, divide the braised fennel among 4 serving plates, making sure to spoon over any remaining juices from the pan. Place a halibut fillet next to the fennel and top with a large dollop of the yogurt sauce.

Serves 4

Mackerel with Warm Buttered Hummus

I like to prepare this dish with mackerel because its strong flavor stands up to the richness of the chickpea purée, but just about any fish will do. You will, however, want to choose a skin-on fillet, so it can be crisped up.

1 tablespoon canola oil

Four 5-ounce portions skin-on Spanish or Boston (not king) mackerel fillet

Two 16-ounce cans chickpeas, drained

2 cloves garlic, grated on a Microplane or very finely minced

1/4 cup extra-virgin olive oil

2 cups water

Salt

2 tablespoons butter

1 tablespoon chopped fresh flat-leaf parsley

Red chile flakes

Minted Herb Salad (page 270)

Preheat the oven to 300 degrees.

In a large heavy-bottomed ovenproof sauté pan, heat the canola oil over high heat until smoking hot. Place the mackerel fillets, skin side down, in the hot oil. Gently press with a spatula to ensure that the skin is in full contact with the pan. Cook until the edges of the fish begin to brown, about 2 minutes. Transfer the pan to the oven and bake until the fillets are just cooked through, about 7 minutes.

For the hummus, combine the chickpeas, garlic, olive oil, and water in a medium saucepan. Bring to a boil and season to taste with salt. Remove from the heat and transfer to a blender. Purée until you have a smooth consistency. Remove to a large bowl and create a well in the center of the mound. Place the butter in the center and garnish with the parsley and a sprinkling of chile flakes.

Serve the fish fillets with a small tuft of Minted Herb Salad and pass the hummus around the table.

Serves 4

Mackerel Roasted with Grapes and Cauliflower with Brown Butter Mayonnaise

I always hated throwing away the butter solids that were left over from making clarified butter at the restaurant, so I came up with this dish as a way to use them. It became such a popular dish that soon we were making clarified butter just so we would have the solids. Clarifying butter takes some time, but it's easy—just keep an eye on it; the solids can go from golden brown to black in a heartbeat if you get distracted at the wrong time. You'll use some of the clarified butter to cook the cauliflower, grapes, and garlic. (You can use the remainder to cook eggs; it'll keep in the refrigerator, tightly covered, for a couple months.) As for the mayonnaise, it is hard to make in small quantities, so use the remainder in place of regular mayonnaise in a Mackerel Melt (page 225) or on a chicken salad sandwich.

1/4 cup butter

2 large egg yolks

Juice of 1 lemon

Tabasco sauce

Salt

1 1/2 cups canola oil

1 head cauliflower, cut into small florets

1 pound seedless red grapes, separated into clusters

2 cloves garlic, finely chopped

Four 5-ounce portions Spanish or Boston (not king) mackerel fillet

Freshly grated nutmeg

To clarify the butter, put it in a small pan over medium heat. After a few minutes, the fat will float to the top and the solids will collect on the bottom. Cook until the solids have browned and the butter develops a nutty aroma. Separate the clear fat from the solids by spooning it off the top and place both in separate airtight containers. Refrigerate until the solids are chilled.

For the mayonnaise, combine the egg yolks, browned butter solids, lemon juice, and Tabasco and salt to taste in a blender. With the blender running at low speed, add the canola oil in a slow, steady stream until the sauce emulsifies (thickens). The mayonnaise can be made up to a day in advance; keep refrigerated until ready to use.

Preheat the oven to 450 degrees.

In a cast-steel or cast-iron pan, heat 2 tablespoons of the clarified butter over medium heat. Add the cauliflower and cook, without stirring, until lightly golden, about 4 minutes. Add the grape clusters and garlic and toss with the butter. Transfer the pan to the oven and roast until the cauliflower is crisp and the grapes are blistered, about 12 minutes. Season to taste with salt. Remove the pan from the oven and reset the oven to broil.

Place the mackerel fillets on top of the cauliflower and set the pan under the broiler until the fillets are just cooked through, about 7 minutes.

Place a fillet on each of 4 serving plates. Drape the grape clusters over the fish and set the cauliflower alongside. Sprinkle with a few gratings of nutmeg and spoon a dollop of mayonnaise over the top.

Serves 4

Mahimahi on Sautéed Bitter Greens with Spicy Sausage and Dates

Mahi pairs easily with a wide range of flavors, as this single dish demonstrates, by bringing together bitter greens, sweet onions and dates, and spicy sopressata. A pepperoni-like dry sausage, sopressata can be found sliced in deli packages. If you can't find it, use any hard salami or pepperoni. Feel free to experiment with the greens. I like escarole, but kale, chard, chicory, dandelion greens, and spinach are all great alternatives. Or use them in combination.

Four 5-ounce portions skinned mahimahi fillet

1 tablespoon canola oil

1 tablespoon butter

2 ounces sliced sopressata, cut into thin strips

1 small red onion, thinly sliced

10 dried dates, pitted and chopped

Salt

2 heads escarole, chopped into bite-size pieces

Preheat the oven to 300 degrees.

Place the mahimahi in a shallow baking dish and lightly brush with the canola oil. Bake approximately 14 minutes for every inch of thickness. The fillets are cooked when they are an even color throughout and they flake with the application of slight pressure.

For the greens, melt the butter in a large sauté pan over high heat. Add the sopressata and cook, without stirring, until it is slightly crisp and curling at the edges. Add the onion, toss to combine, and cook, without stirring, until it is lightly caramelized, about 4 minutes. Add the dates, toss to combine, and cook for another minute. Season lightly with salt and add the greens. Mix together and cook until the greens are wilted. Check the seasoning and adjust if necessary.

Divide the greens among 4 serving plates, set a fillet on top, and serve immediately.

Serves 4

Mahimahi with Braised Brussels Sprouts and Feta Butter

I often pair the acidic bite of feta cheese with fish. In this recipe the cheese is mellowed out a bit by sweet butter and the meaty taste of the sprouts. This butter would also go great with shrimp and salmon.

6 tablespoons butter

1 small onion, diced

2 cloves garlic, sliced

1 1/2 pounds Brussels sprouts, stems trimmed and each cut in half lengthwise

1 cup water

Salt

Four 5-ounce portions skinned mahimahi fillet

1/4 cup crumbled feta cheese

1 tablespoon chopped fresh flat-leaf parsley

Preheat the oven to 300 degrees.

For the Brussels sprouts, melt 2 tablespoons of the butter over high heat in a large sauté pan. Add the onion and garlic and cook for 1 minute. Add the Brussels sprouts and toss to combine. Continue to cook over high heat until the sprouts begin to brown, about 5 minutes. Add the water and season generously with salt. Cover the pan and reduce the heat to medium.

Gently sear the mahimahi fillets, skin side down, in a small, dry ovenproof sauté pan over medium heat until they just begin to color, about 5 minutes. Transfer the pan to the oven and bake until the fish is an even color throughout, about 8 minutes.

For the flavored butter, mix the feta cheese with the remaining 4 tablespoons butter and the parsley. Mash with a fork to combine, breaking up the feta as much as possible.

When the mahi is done, uncover the sprouts and turn the heat up to high. When the liquid remaining in the pan has reduced enough to just barely coat the sprouts, remove from the heat and toss.

Arrange the fillets and Brussels sprouts on a platter, and put a dollop of the feta butter on each of the mahi fillets. Serve family style.

Serves 4

Warm Poached Salmon in Red Wine Sauce

Cooking salmon in a light red wine brings out the meatiness of the fish. The trick when cooking with wine is to use a wine that you would want to drink. Any flaw in the wine straight from the bottle will only be amplified in the final dish. This recipe calls for about a half bottle, so you can enjoy drinking the rest of it while you are cooking. I like Beaujolais for this as it has a nice upfront fruitiness, plus it's low in alcohol, so you can drink another glass with dinner and not be poached in red wine yourself. Here I call for two 10-ounce fillet portions, rather than four separate pieces, because it is easier to poach larger pieces of fish. The cooking can take place slowly, allowing the fish to absorb as much flavor from the broth as possible.

If you have salmon left over, it is great served cold for another meal. The fish pairs well with the lentils from Sablefish with Lentils and Pomegranate Red Wine Butter (page 185) and with Roasted Sunchokes (page 164).

Two 10-ounce portions salmon fillet, preferably pink salmon

2 cups light red wine, such as Beaujolais or Dolcetto

1 shallot, thinly sliced

2 sprigs fresh thyme

Salt

2 tablespoons butter

Preheat the oven to 200 degrees.

In a sauté pan just large enough to fit the fillets in a single layer, heat the wine with the shallot and thyme over medium heat. Season lightly with salt, keeping in mind that because the wine will be reduced for a sauce later, you shouldn't add too much salt now. When the wine begins to steam, add the salmon fillets and reduce the heat to medium low. You want to keep the temperature of the water at about 170 degrees (use an instant-read thermometer to check this). Poach until the fish is cooked all the way through, about 12 minutes. Check for doneness by gently flaking apart a small section to see if the color is consistent throughout.

Remove the salmon from the wine and transfer to a plate. Keep it warm in the oven. Increase the heat under the wine to medium and reduce until only about 2 tablespoons liquid remain. Remove from heat and discard the thyme. Add the butter and swirl the pan to incorporate it with the wine reduction as it melts. Spoon the sauce over the fillets and serve immediately.

Serves 4

Smoked Sardines with Mixed Greens and Fig-Olive Dressing

This might be the most elegant salad to ever come largely from a can. Sardines are the most economical seafood out there—plus, you get great flavor and versatility. Try to find a greens mix that has a fair bit of arugula in it, as its peppery notes pair perfectly with the other flavors in the salad. The figs create a nice counterpoint to the salty punch of the olives and the smoky rich sardines. If you cannot find fresh figs, dried ones are fine, but be sure to soak them in hot water for a few hours or overnight to soften them up.

6 fresh figs, stemmed and quartered

1/4 cup pitted green olives (my favorite is picholine), chopped

Juice of 1 lemon

2 tablespoons extra-virgin olive oil

Salt

2 roasted red peppers, store-bought or homemade

1/4 pound mixed greens

Two 4-ounce cans smoked skinless sardine fillets

For the dressing, toss together the figs, olives, lemon juice, and olive oil in a small bowl. Season generously with salt and toss to combine.

Cut the peppers into strips and divide between 2 serving plates. Divide the greens between the plates. Drain the sardines and separate the fillets. Place on top of the salad, then spoon over the vinaigrette. Serve immediately.

Serves 2 as a main course

Lobster Linguine with Chive and Tomato

Lobster is one of the great delicacies of the sea and a staple of the New England culinary repertoire. I like to prepare it in ways that take a little of the work out of eating it.

Four 1-pound hard-shell lobsters

6 Roma tomatoes, roughly chopped

4 cloves garlic

1 small yellow onion, finely diced

2 tablespoons extra-virgin olive oil

Salt

1 pound linguine

Chopped fresh chives for garnish

Fill the largest pot you have with at least 1 gallon of water and bring to a boil. Put the lobsters, two at a time, headfirst into the water. (Be sure to do it this way! If you put them in tail first, they will snap it back as they hit the water and could splash boiling water right into your face.) Cook, uncovered, for 2 minutes. This is just enough time to dispatch the lobster and firm up the meat inside the shell. With tongs, transfer the lobsters from the water to a colander to cool. Cook the two remaining lobsters in the same way.

When the lobsters are cooked and have cooled enough to handle comfortably, remove and return the claws to the water to cook for another 5 minutes at a low simmer. (Claws and tails cook at different rates, and it is easier to get the claws out of the shell when fully cooked.) Remove the lobster meat from the tail and cut into 1/2-inch dice. Remove the claws from the water and allow to cool. Do not discard the cooking water. Remove the claw meat from the shell and reserve.

Combine the tomatoes, garlic, onion, olive oil, and 1 cup of the lobster cooking water in a medium saucepan. Season generously with salt and bring to a boil. Reduce the heat to a simmer and cook until the tomatoes begin to break down and the onion softens, about 5 minutes. Remove from the heat.

Add a good amount of salt to the lobster cooking water and cook the linguine, using the timing specified on the package. When the pasta is 1 minute from done, strain off all but 1/2 cup of the cooking water. Add the tomato sauce and continue to cook the pasta for another minute, until it has absorbed most of the liquid. Remove from the heat and toss in the chopped lobster tail meat and the cooked claws. Toss to combine.

Divide the linguine among 4 serving plates. Most of the lobster will fall to the bottom of the pan, making it easy to portion out. (Uneven distribution of the lobster can excite great envy and has the potential to cause fights, so try to get it right.) Place the claws on top of the pasta on each plate and sprinkle with the chives.

Serves 4

Trout and Autumn Squash with Roast Garlic and Pecans

Trout goes nicely with vegetables that have some sweetness to them, like autumn squash. This dish is bound together by the nutty aroma of a whole lot of roasted garlic, along with the slightly smoky flavor of the pecans. If you're not a garlic lover, you can use half the amount called for or omit it altogether.

1 head garlic

1 tablespoon canola oil

1 cup pecans, toasted (page 15)

Grated zest of 1 orange

2 tablespoons
extra-virgin olive oil

Salt

2 tablespoons butter

6 cups diced (1-inch) peeled
autumn squash, preferably
kabocha (about 2 squash)

1/2 cup water

Four 5-ounce trout fillets

Preheat the oven to 350 degrees.

Brush the whole head of garlic with the canola oil and wrap in aluminum foil. Bake until the aroma is sweet and nutty and the cloves are soft, about 45 minutes. Let sit until cool enough to handle. Meanwhile, chop the toasted pecans into rough chunks.

Cut the garlic head in half and squeeze the roasted cloves into a small bowl. Add the orange zest and olive oil and mash with the back of a fork. Season to taste with salt and add the pecans. Mix to incorporate.

Preheat the broiler.

In a large ovenproof sauté pan, melt the butter, then add the squash and shake the pan to arrange it in a single layer. Season generously with salt and place under the broiler. After about 8 minutes, the squash will be soft and beginning to brown. Remove from broiler, pour in the water, and arrange the fillets on top of the squash. Return to the broiler and continue broiling for approximately 6 minutes. The fillets will steam from the bottom and get crisp on the top—they should have a nice brown skin.

Evenly divide the squash among 4 serving plates and top with a trout fillet. Spoon the garlic-pecan mixture over the trout and serve immediately.

Serves 4

Albacore Tuna with Warm Pickled Shiitakes and Chive Risotto

There are only a few recipes in this book for tuna. Although it is one of the most popular species, it is hard to find tuna that has been caught in an environmentally sustainable way. Albacore is particularly good in this dish; its light flavor pairs perfectly with the delicate shiitakes. Because this recipe doesn't call for a lot of tuna (less than a pound), splurge and buy the best-quality pole-caught tuna you can find and really celebrate the flavor. I prefer to use carnaroli rice for risotto, but if you can't find it, arborio is fine.

2 tablespoons extra-virgin olive oil

10 ounces shiitake mushrooms, stemmed and caps sliced

3 tablespoons white wine vinegar

Salt

Two 7-ounce albacore tuna loins

Freshly ground black pepper

1 tablespoon canola oil

1 small onion, finely diced

2 cups carnaroli or arborio rice

2 cups white wine

4 cups water

2 tablespoons sour cream

2 tablespoons finely chopped fresh chives

For the shiitakes, heat 1 tablespoon of the olive oil in a medium sauté pan over high heat, then sear the mushrooms until they begin to color; don't stir them. Add the vinegar and season to taste with salt. Cook, without stirring, until the pan is dry and remove from the heat. Keep warm.

For the tuna, season the loins with salt and pepper. Heat a sauté pan over high heat until smoking hot. Add the canola oil and sear the tuna loins on all sides until they develop a golden crust, but no more than a minute per side. Remove from the pan and set aside.

For the risotto, add the remaining 1 tablespoon olive oil and the onion to a large pot and cook over medium heat, without stirring, for a few minutes, until it is transparent. Add the rice and toss to coat the grains with the oil. Toast the rice for a few minutes, stirring once or twice, until it develops a nutty aroma. Add the wine and season to taste with salt. Cook gently, stirring, until there is no longer any smell of alcohol from the pan and the grains have mostly absorbed the wine. Add 3 cups of the water and stir to combine. Continue to cook over medium heat, stirring every other minute, until the rice has absorbed most of the liquid, about 8 minutes. Add the remaining 1 cup water and the sour cream. Reduce the heat to low and stir constantly until the rice is creamy and thick, about 5 minutes. Stir in the chives and taste for seasoning.

To serve, slice the tuna thinly on a bias. Divide the risotto among 4 serving plates and arrange the tuna slices on top. Spoon the warm shiitakes over the tuna.

Serves 4

Linguine with White Clam Sauce and Coriander

I love the classic combination of clams and pasta. I also love coriander, which provides a freshness not often associated with this dish.

1 gallon water

1 bay leaf

32 littleneck clams, washed thoroughly (discard any that won't close)

Salt

1 pound linguine

2 strips bacon, minced

1 medium onion, diced

1 teaspoon ground coriander

1 cup sour cream

2 tablespoons chopped fresh flat-leaf parsley

Put the water, bay leaf, and clams in a large pot and bring to a boil. Remove the clams with tongs or a small strainer as they begin to open, 5 to 7 minutes, and set them aside in a bowl. Discard any clams that haven't opened. Strain the water into another pot, removing any sand that has accumulated in the bottom.

Set aside 1 cup of the cooking water, season the remainder lightly with salt and return to a boil in the pot. Add the linguine and cook until al dente, following the package directions.

While waiting for the pasta water to boil, start the sauce. Combine the bacon, onion, coriander, and reserved cup of cooking water in a large saucepan. Bring to a boil and continue to cook until reduced by half, about 4 minutes. Remove from heat and whisk in the sour cream. Return the pan to low heat and warm through but don't boil. Season to taste with salt and stir in the parsley.

Drain the pasta and add to the pan with the sauce, along with the clams in their shells. Toss to combine and cook over medium heat until the pasta has absorbed some of the sauce, about 2 minutes.

Serves 4

Mussels in Red Wine with Herbs and Roasted Shallots

Of all the folks I have worked for, Chef Carole Greenwood taught me the most in the shortest amount of time. She was the person who introduced me to cooking over a wood fire, and her incredibly well-developed recipes were often startlingly simple. This is my take on one of the recipes she shared with me at her restaurant in D.C. The rosemary brings this dish together, but it's deliciously surprising how well the smoky flavor of the shallots pairs with the mussels' briny sweetness.

10 shallots, peeled and left whole

1 tablespoon canola oil

4 pounds mussels, scrubbed, debearded, and patted dry (discard any that won't close)

1 cup red wine

Salt

1/4 cup butter

2 sprigs fresh rosemary

3 tablespoons chopped fresh flat-leaf parsley

1 baguette, cut into thick slices and toasted

Preheat the oven to 350 degrees. Toss the shallots with the oil, then wrap them in a double layer of aluminum foil. Bake until they are soft and golden brown, about 1 hour. Remove from the oven and unwrap.

Heat a large heavy-bottomed pot over high heat. Add the mussels to the dry pan and allow to cook until they just begin to open, about 2 minutes. Add the wine and shallots and season the liquid to taste with salt. (Don't season the shells, as that will skew your ability to taste how much salt is in the broth.) Cover the pot and cook until all of the shells have opened, about 4 minutes. (Discard any mussels that haven't opened by this time.)

Add the butter and rosemary and continue to boil until the butter is fully incorporated. Add the parsley and toss to evenly distribute.

Divide the mussels and steaming liquid among 4 serving bowls and serve with the toasted bread.

Serves 4 as a main course

Bacon-wrapped Halibut
with Horseradish Cream and Glazed Beets

I have to admit that halibut's mild flavor doesn't fully grab my attention. But I love halibut when paired with bacon. The flaky lean fish in tandem with the chewy fatty pork makes a really nice combination. Beets also marry well with the smokiness of bacon. The colors are beautiful, too—the caramelized brown bacon and the jewel-colored beets (whether you use golden or red) offer contrast to the snowy white halibut fillet.

1 1/2 pounds beets, golden
or red, trimmed

1 orange, zest finely shredded
and orange sliced into rounds

Salt

Four 5-ounce portions
halibut fillet

8 strips bacon

1 small onion, diced

1 cup water

1 tablespoon butter

1/2 cup sour cream

2 tablespoons prepared horseradish

Place the beets and orange slices in a medium saucepan, cover with water, and add a generous amount of salt. Bring to a boil, then reduce the heat to a simmer and cook until the beets are tender enough to yield when pierced with a knife. Drain and let cool just long enough so that you can handle them. Using your fingers, peel away the skins, then cut the beets into roughly 1-inch pieces.

Preheat the oven to 275 degrees.

Season the halibut fillets with salt, then wrap each one in two strips of bacon. If it helps to keep the bacon on the fillet, use a toothpick or two to secure them. Put the bacon-wrapped fillets in a single layer in a cold, dry sauté pan and set the pan over medium heat. Cook until the bacon is crisp on one side. Leaving the fat in the pan, transfer the fillets to an ovenproof dish. Bake for approximately 10 minutes.

While the halibut is in the oven, add the onion to the bacon fat in the pan. Cook over medium heat for a few minutes, until soft. Add the beets and water. Bring to a boil and cook until the water is almost evaporated. Add the butter and toss with the beets to combine. The beets should be glazed with a sauce just thick enough to coat them but not thin enough to run on the plate.

For the horseradish cream, mix the sour cream, horseradish, orange zest, and salt to taste in a small bowl and whisk to combine.

To serve, spoon a dollop of the sauce onto each of 4 serving plates and use the back side of the spoon to spread it into a swoosh. Evenly divide the beets among the plates and place the halibut fillets on top of the beets. Serve immediately.

Serves 4

Smoked Oyster Stuffing

Thanksgiving is a time of year when seafood slips from our minds. I love to include it on our holiday table, though, and the classic Southern dish of oyster stuffing is a perfect way to do it. Of course you can stuff your turkey with it, but it also works well as a stuffing for whole roasted fish.

One 1-pound loaf brioche bread, cut into 1-inch cubes

4 ribs celery, thinly sliced

1 medium onion, finely diced

1 clove garlic, thinly sliced

3 tablespoons butter

4 fresh sage leaves, chopped

One 4-ounce can smoked oysters, drained, liquor reserved in a measuring cup

Chicken broth or water as needed

Salt

Preheat the oven to 325 degrees.

Place the brioche cubes on a baking sheet and toast in the oven until they are dried out and crunchy, about 20 minutes. Increase the oven temperature to 400 degrees if baking the stuffing separate from the bird.

Meanwhile, in a large sauté pan over medium heat, sauté the celery, onion, and garlic with the butter until the onion is translucent. Add the sage, then the toasted bread cubes and stir to coat the cubes with the butter.

Add enough broth to the measuring cup holding the oyster liquid to equal 1 cup. Add this liquid and the oysters to the pan, stir to combine, and season to taste with salt. Transfer to a baking dish, and bake until hot all the way through, about 30 minutes. If using to stuff a bird, pack it gently into the bird and bake as instructed in your turkey recipe.

Makes about 6 cups

Roasted Endive

A lot of Americans still aren't familiar with endive. It has a distinct watery bitterness that does not do too well as a "mixed green," but it makes a great salad on its own. In this recipe, I sear heads of endive that I've cut in half to slightly caramelize them before putting them in a hot oven to roast. Given this treatment, all they need are a few gratings of nutmeg before serving.

4 heads endive, either red or white

1 tablespoon extra-virgin olive oil, plus more for drizzling

Salt

Freshly grated nutmeg

Preheat the oven to 400 degrees.

Slice the endive heads in half from top to bottom, leaving the stem ends intact. Heat the olive oil in a large ovenproof sauté pan over high heat and, when it just begins to smoke, add the endive, cut side down. Season to taste with salt and transfer the pan to the oven. After 8 minutes or so, check the endive. They should be soft but still retain their contour and a little texture. Remove from the oven and let them sit for a few minutes, to allow the residual steam to cook them through.

Transfer the endive to a serving plate and grate nutmeg over the top. Finish with a drizzle of good-quality olive oil.

Serves 4 as a side dish

Steamed Bok Choy with Turnips and Carrots

Bok choy offers tremendous versatility in a single leaf—the stalk has a wonderful, crisp texture and white color, while the leaves are soft and tender. Bok choy and turnips are a surprisingly great combination as the sweetness of the turnip complements the subtle flavor of the greens. Carrots add color, and the garlic melts into the sauce.

2 tablespoons extra-virgin olive oil

2 cloves garlic, thinly sliced

2 medium carrots, sliced into 1/4-inch-thick half-moons

2 medium turnips, cut into 1/2-inch dice

2 medium heads bok choy, each split in half lengthwise

Salt

1/2 cup water

Heat the olive oil in a large, deep sauté pan over medium heat. Add the garlic and cook for 1 minute. Add the carrots and turnips and let cook without stirring for a few minutes so they begin to brown.

Place the bok choy cut side down on top of the vegetables. Season with salt and add the water. Increase the heat to high, cover the pan, and steam the bok choy for 3 minutes.

Remove the lid and cook over medium heat until the water is reduced to a thick glaze on the vegetables. The oil will emulsify with the water, but if you cook it too long, all the water will evaporate and only oil will remain. If this happens, add 1 tablespoon cold water and swirl the pan to combine again. Toss to mix the caramelized vegetables into the bok choy and serve immediately.

Serves 4 as a side dish

Roasted Brussels Sprouts and Red Onions

Brussels sprouts are one of the most rewarding vegetables to cook; they are so easy to prepare and so delicious. In this recipe, I pair them with onions—their sweetness offsets the slight bitterness of the sprouts. I like to add water to the pan when roasting vegetables because it helps them to cook through without overcaramelizing. This technique also has the benefit of lightly saucing the vegetables and melding the flavors.

2 tablespoons butter

2 red onions, cut into wedges

1 1/2 pounds Brussels sprouts

Salt

1 cup water

Preheat the oven to 450 degrees.

In a heavy ovenproof sauté pan, melt the butter over high heat. Add the onion wedges and cook, without stirring, until they begin to caramelize. Add the Brussels sprouts and toss to combine. Season to taste with salt and continue to cook over high heat until the sprouts begin to take on a bit of color.

Add the water and transfer the pan to the oven. Cook until the water is nearly evaporated, about 15 minutes. Toss the vegetables to glaze with the remaining liquid and serve immediately.

Serves 4 as a side dish

Roasted Sunchokes

Sunchokes have recently begun to show up at grocery stores all over. They're wonderfully easy to prepare—but not much to look at. A grayish, knobby root vegetable, the sunchoke looks like fresh ginger's homely cousin and can vary greatly in size. Look for the ones with relatively thin skin, which you can eat. Before cooking them, give sunchokes a good scrub to make sure no dirt is hiding away in the little crevices. If you can't dislodge all the dirt, just cut out the offending area, as a mouthful of grit can ruin an entire meal.

I roast sunchokes with a little water in the pan so that they can cook through without burning. What's left of the liquid in the pan becomes the flavorful foundation of the sauce. Try this method with carrots, turnips, beets, and nearly any nonstarchy root vegetable. Each will have a different cooking time though, so be sure to check them after a few minutes.

2 tablespoons butter

1 pound sunchokes

5 sprigs fresh thyme

Salt

1 cup water

Preheat the oven to 350 degrees.

Melt the butter in an ovenproof pan large enough to accommodate all of the sunchokes in a single layer. Add the sunchokes and thyme and toss to coat with the butter. Season to taste with salt and add the water. Transfer the pan to the oven and roast sunchokes for 20 minutes. Check for doneness by piercing one with a knife. If it is soft and the water is reduced to a glaze, they are done. If not, cook for another 5 minutes or so. Toss the sunchokes gently to coat them with the glaze. Serve immediately.

Serves 4

Butternut Squash with Dates, Red Onion, and Chives

Butternut squash is often served as a soup, but I enjoy mixing things up a bit. Here I pair it with the sweet bite of red onion and the meatiness of dates, one of my favorite go-to ingredients. This goes particularly well with the meaty flavor of striped bass, cobia, or mahimahi.

2 tablespoons butter

1 medium butternut squash, peeled and cut into 1/2-inch dice

1 small red onion, thinly sliced

2 cloves garlic, sliced

10 dates, each pitted and cut into 8 pieces

1/2 cup water

1/4 cup white wine vinegar

Salt

2 tablespoons chopped fresh chives or flat-leaf parsley

Melt the butter in a large sauté pan over high heat. Add the squash and cook, without stirring, until it begins to brown, about 5 minutes. Toss, then add the onion and garlic. Stir to incorporate and cook, again without stirring, until the onion is soft, about 4 minutes. Add the dates, water, and vinegar. Season to taste with salt and reduce the heat to medium. Cook, without stirring, until the water has evaporated. Add the chives and toss to combine. Serve immediately.

Serves 4 as a side dish

WINTER

Winter is an exciting time to be cooking. While the world slows down for the cold months, a few new products begin to show up in the market as others disappear. Dungeness crab, bay scallops, and Meyer lemons all herald the arrival of the new season. Meals are more a cause for celebration as friends and family gather together. Dishes are a little more intricate as we turn to rich stews and slow simmered flavors in the kitchen. Spices are used to elevate the subtler character of the ingredients we have available, as pantry items like polenta and rice come out of hibernation to supply a bit of inspiration and substance.

Fishermen brave the frigid air and even colder water to ensure that we have delicious fish to eat. Some of the more migratory species have made for warmer climes, and so boat captains will change gear and begin to target different species. Most of our favorites can still be found though, having just arrived from points south where winter's chill is not so fierce.

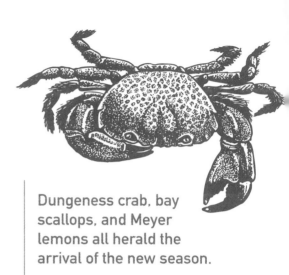

Dungeness crab, bay scallops, and Meyer lemons all herald the arrival of the new season.

Potato Pancakes Topped with Smoked Mackerel and Sour Cream

Every time I eat a potato pancake, I swear that I will never eat potatoes any other way, but they are a challenge to make. Water and starch content can literally vary from potato to potato within one bin, as well as across varieties. The key is to extract as much water as possible from the shredded potatoes. It takes some work, but the result is worth it. The batter should hold together and be a little tacky to the touch. If you need to add more flour, then do so just a little at a time; you can always add more.

1 1/2 pounds russet potatoes, peeled

Salt

2 large eggs

3 tablespoons all-purpose flour

1 teaspoon baking soda

1/2 cup shredded onion

One 7-ounce can smoked mackerel

1/2 cup sour cream

3 tablespoons chopped fresh chives

1 cup canola oil

Shred the potatoes on a box grater. Put the shredded potatoes in a colander and, taking a little bit at a time, squeeze as much water as you can from them. Place the squeezed potatoes on a double thickness of paper towels. When you've squeezed out all the potatoes in the colander, take another double thickness of paper towels and pat the potatoes dry as best you can. Season the potatoes generously with salt and let sit for a few minutes. Change the paper towels and pat dry again.

In a large bowl, mix the eggs, flour, and baking soda, whisking until there are no lumps. Add the onion and potatoes and season again with salt. With a wooden spoon, mix vigorously to incorporate, then let sit for a few minutes to allow the flour to absorb any remaining water.

Preheat the oven to 300 degrees.

Drain the mackerel, put it in a medium bowl, and flake it. Add the sour cream and chives and mix well. Set aside in the refrigerator, covered, until ready to serve.

In a large skillet, heat the oil over medium-high heat. Using an ice-cream scoop, take 1/4-cup portions of the potato mixture and carefully place them in the oil, gently pressing with a spatula to form the cakes. Cook until they are golden brown, then carefully flip them over, trying to minimize oil spatter. When the pancakes are browned on both sides, transfer them to paper towels. Pat them dry and transfer to a baking sheet.

Bake pancakes until cooked through, about 10 minutes; pull one apart to check that the potato is no longer raw in the center.

Top each pancake with a dollop of the mackerel mixture.

Serves 4 as an appetizer

Scallops with Chile-marinated Orange

This is a take on ceviche, with the acid in the orange juice gently "cooking" the scallops. The key to the dish is to dice the jalapeño as finely as possible. If your knife skills aren't the best, consider grating it on a Microplane—but if you do, take care not to let jalapeño juice squirt in your eyes during the process.

1/4 pound bay scallops

1 orange, peeled and cut into segments (page 7)

1 small jalapeño chile, seeded and cut into tiny dice

1 tablespoon extra-virgin olive oil

Salt

20 Belgian endive leaves (optional)

1/4 cup loosely packed fresh cilantro leaves

In a medium bowl, combine the scallops, orange segments and any juice, jalapeño, and olive oil and season to taste with salt. Toss to combine well. Let sit for about 10 minutes to allow the flavors to meld and the acid of the orange juice to gently stiffen the scallops.

Serve a couple of scallops with each orange segment in a cocktail spoon or on a Belgian endive leaf and garnish each with a cilantro leaf.

Makes about 20 canapés or serves 2 as an appetizer

Beet Soup
with Smoked Trout

This soup is a wonderful showcase for the deep, rich flavor of beets. Beets hold a lot of air when they are puréed; as a result, this soup has great body and a silken texture with no fat added. It is also great served chilled, and leftovers make a nice quick lunch. It keeps in the refrigerator for a couple of days, so go ahead and double the batch if you like.

1 pound beets

4 medium carrots

1 small onion

1 clove garlic, peeled

4 cups water

Salt

6 ounces smoked trout

2 tablespoons sour cream

2 tablespoons chopped fresh dill

Peel and roughly chop the beets, carrots, and onion. Place them in a large soup pot. Add the garlic clove to the pot along with the water. Season generously with salt and bring to a boil. Reduce the heat to a simmer and cook until the beets are very soft, about 25 minutes.

Carefully transfer the hot soup to a blender (you may need to do this in batches) and pulse on low speed to release the pressure (use caution when blending hot liquids). As the soup begins to break down, increase the speed until you have a very smooth purée. Check the seasoning and adjust with more salt if necessary.

For the garnish, in a small bowl, shred the smoked trout with a fork and add the sour cream and dill. Mix well and place a dollop in each serving bowl. Reheat the soup briefly and ladle it into the bowls at the table.

Serves 4 as a first-course soup

Butternut Soup with Dungeness Crab

Butternut squash lends itself well to soup, and it seems that every cook has his or her own version, each with some special twist that makes it better than all the others. For my part, I like my butternut squash soup to taste like butternut squash, without a lot of added cream and butter. The crab makes a nice garnish for the silky soup, which has the crisp, pungent bite of shallot and the coolness of olive oil.

To extract the greatest flavor from the squash, it's important to cook it in as little water possible. As is true with root vegetables, most of the flavor in butternut squash is water soluble, so the more water you drain away after cooking, the more flavor you lose. The rule of thumb is to use a pot just big enough to fit all the squash and then to add only enough water to barely cover it.

1 small onion, diced

1/2 cup plus 1 tablespoon extra-virgin olive oil

2 pounds butternut squash, peeled

Salt

1/2 pound Dungeness crabmeat, picked over for shell fragments

1 shallot, finely diced

1 tablespoon chopped fresh herbs of your choice (my favorites are tarragon, chives, and mint)

Grated zest of 1/2 orange

In a soup pot over medium heat, sauté the onion in 1/2 cup of the olive oil until it is soft and beginning to brown, about 5 minutes. Add the squash and just enough water to barely cover it. Season the soup generously with salt, bring to a simmer, and continue to simmer until the squash is soft enough to mash easily with a spoon, about 20 minutes. Drain, then transfer it to a blender (use caution when blending hot liquids) and purée until it is super fine and silky.

For the garnish, mix the crab with the remaining 1 tablespoon olive oil, the shallot, herbs, and orange zest. Toss to combine and season to taste with salt. Divide the garnish among 4 bowls, then ladle in the soup. Serve immediately.

Serves 4 as a first-course soup

Oyster Stew with Sweet Potatoes and Bacon

This is my take on the classic New England dish, in which oysters are very quickly poached in flavored cream. I prefer half-and-half over the usual heavy cream. The sweet potatoes and bacon add complex layers of sweet and smoky flavor.

1 medium sweet potato, peeled and cut into 1/4-inch dice

4 strips bacon, minced

4 cups half-and-half

2 sprigs fresh thyme

24 oysters, shucked (page 33), with liquor and meat reserved

2 tablespoons butter, cut into 4 even pats

1 tablespoon Old Bay Seasoning or Seafood Spice #1 (page 260)

4 slices thick-cut bread, toasted

Blanch the sweet potato pieces in boiling water for a few minutes, until they are soft. Drain and set aside.

Sauté the bacon and sweet potatoes in a large pan over medium heat until the bacon is golden brown and crispy. Pour off the bacon fat, then add the half-and-half, thyme, and oysters with all their juices. Bring to a simmer and cook until the edges of the oysters begin to curl, about 4 minutes.

Remove the pan from the heat and divide the stew among 4 serving bowls. Top each with a pat of the butter and sprinkle with the Old Bay. Serve immediately with a slice of toasted bread.

Serves 4 as a first-course soup

Arctic Char with Ragout of Turnip, Celery, and Chestnuts

Celery and chestnuts are one of the great flavor matchups. I like the way the flavor of the nuts offsets the high-pitch bite of the celery.

6 ribs celery, cut into 1/4-inch-thick slices

3 tablespoons butter

1 pound turnips, peeled and cut into 1-inch pieces

7 ounces jarred shelled chestnuts, cut into 1/4-inch pieces

2 cups water

Salt

1 tablespoon chopped fresh flat-leaf parsley

Four 5-ounce skin-on portions Arctic char fillets

2 teaspoons Smoked Paprika and Cinnamon Spice Mix (page 261)

1 tablespoon canola oil

Sauté the celery in 2 tablespoons of the butter over medium heat. After about 3 minutes, add the turnips and chestnuts. Toss to coat with the butter and continue to cook, without stirring, for another 5 minutes. Add the water, season to taste with salt, and adjust the heat to a simmer. Allow the liquid to reduce to about 2 tablespoons to make a glaze, about 20 minutes.

Add the remaining 1 tablespoon butter and the parsley to the pan and toss to combine. Check for seasoning and make certain that the turnips are cooked through. Keep warm while you cook the fish.

Preheat the broiler.

Set the fillets on a baking sheet, season the flesh side of the fillets with the spice mixture, and let sit for a few minutes to absorb the flavor. Lightly brush the fillets with the canola oil, then place under the broiler for approximately 5 minutes. Turn the oven off and allow the fillets to cook slowly in the residual heat of the oven, about 8 minutes longer.

Divide the ragout among 4 serving plates and top each with a fillet. Serve immediately.

Serves 4

Roasted Whole Arctic Char on Pine Needles with Pine Nut Sauce

This dish is perfect for the holidays—it's a beautiful presentation, and it brings the smell of pine right into the kitchen. The pine needles infuse the fish with a gentle, slightly sweet aroma. (The skin of the char serves to protect the fillets from the pine sap—for that reason, I recommend peeling it off before serving.) Pine needles can be found about anywhere, but I prefer those from a Christmas tree. If you cannot find pine needles, use a mixture of hard-stemmed herbs such as rosemary and thyme. Serve with Roasted Radicchio with Sambuca Dressing (page 198).

1 quart pine needles

1 whole Arctic char, dressed (about 2 pounds)

1 lemon, sliced

3 sprigs fresh thyme

1 cup extra-virgin olive oil

1 small onion, diced

3 garlic cloves, peeled

1/2 cup pine nuts

Juice of 1 lemon

Salt

3/4 cup water

Preheat the oven to 325 degrees.

Make a bed of pine needles, using half the needles, in a large ovenproof pan. Place the char on its side on the needles and layer the lemon slices and thyme sprigs inside the cavity of the fish. Cover with the remaining pine needles. Roast for approximately 40 minutes. The best way to check to see if the fish is done is to gently wiggle a knife into the flesh at the backbone. Lift up to expose the flesh and check that it is an even color throughout. Or another method used in professional kitchens is to stick a toothpick into the flesh, pushing it right down to the spine. Hold it there for a few seconds, then pull it out and immediately place the toothpick under your lower lip. If it feels hot, the fish is done. You can also peek inside by gently lifting the belly flap and poking around, but try not to disturb the needles too much.

While the fish roasts, prepare the sauce. Place the olive oil, onion, and garlic cloves in a small saucepan over medium heat and cook, without stirring, until the onion begins to soften, about 5 minutes. Add the pine nuts and cook for a few minutes to warm them through. Transfer the contents of the pan to a blender, add the lemon juice, and season to taste with salt. Begin to pulse on low speed so that pressure does not build up (use caution when blending hot liquids). As soon as the mixture is turning smoothly, increase the blender speed to high and add the water. Once it reaches a silky smooth consistency, pour the sauce through a fine-mesh sieve to remove any pieces that did not purée. Taste the sauce for seasoning and allow it to reach room temperature before serving.

To serve the char, remove the pine needles from the top and run a knife just under the skin to separate it from the flesh. Fold back the skin and, starting at the tail, push a dinner fork or table knife to the backbone and slide it across the bone to lift off the fillets. Do this in small, manageable pieces so that you don't have a disaster. The meat should separate right at the bones, and you should be able to take the fillets off either side. Divide the fillets among 4 serving plates and garnish with a dollop of the pine nut sauce.

Serves 4

Pan-seared Catfish with Frisée-Apple Salad and Pecan Sauce

Pecans are simply one of the greatest things on this planet. They pair perfectly with just about everything and are as welcome in desserts as they are in savory dishes. I like to use them in puréed sauces after first simmering them in oil with aromatics. Apples are like carrots in that they are great in salads, but often their texture can be a distraction. So here I shave them super thin; you still have a bit of the crispness, but not an overwhelming chunky texture.

1 small onion, diced

3 garlic cloves, peeled

1 cup plus 1 tablespoon extra-virgin olive oil

1/2 cup pecan pieces

Juice of 1 lemon

1/2 cup water

1/4 cup maple syrup

1 large egg, beaten

1 tablespoon milk

1 cup fine dried bread crumbs or panko (Japanese-style bread crumbs)

Four 5-ounce catfish fillets

3 tablespoons canola oil

Leaves from 1/2 bunch fresh mint (about 2 cups loosely packed)

2 heads frisée lettuce, separated into leaves and heavy stems removed

2 Gala or Honeycrisp apples, cut into quarters

Salt

Preheat the oven to 300 degrees.

For the sauce, simmer the onion and garlic cloves in 1 cup of the olive oil until the onion begins to soften, about 5 minutes. Add the pecans and cook for 1 minute. Remove from the heat and stir in the lemon juice. Transfer to a blender and pulse to release the pressure. Gradually increase the speed, add the water and maple syrup, and process until you have a very fine purée. Set aside.

In a large shallow bowl, mix the egg and milk together well with a fork. Pour the bread crumbs onto a large plate. One at a time, dip the fish fillets in the egg mixture, coating them fully, then dredge them in the bread crumbs, patting the crumbs to help them adhere in an even layer. Heat the canola oil in a large ovenproof skillet over medium-high heat. Add the catfish fillets and sear until golden brown, about 3 minutes. Flip the fillets and transfer the pan to the oven. Cook for approximately 5 minutes for fillets less than an inch thick and up to 10 minutes for thicker fillets.

While the fish cooks, mix the mint leaves and frisée in a large bowl, then shave the apple quarters into very thin sheets with a peeler and add to the mix. Dress with the remaining tablespoon olive oil, season to taste with salt, and toss to combine.

Spoon the warm sauce onto 4 serving plates and place a big handful of the salad to the side of the sauce. Top the salad with a catfish fillet.

Serves 4

Stewed Catfish and Black-eyed Peas

Black-eyed peas are the tastiest of all the beans. Their flavor is all their own, and it perfectly suits the taste of catfish. Here I take some of the elements of gumbo and turn them into a hearty wintertime stew.

4 strips bacon, minced

4 ribs celery, diced

1 small onion, finely diced

12 ounces dried black-eyed peas, soaked overnight in a generous amount of water and drained

2 cups chicken broth

3 cups water

1/4 cup cider vinegar

1 bay leaf

12 ounces catfish fillets, cut into 1-inch pieces

One 10-ounce can stewed tomatoes with green chiles

Salt

Good crusty bread, sliced and toasted

Anchovy Butter for Seafood (page 263)

In a large soup pot, sauté the bacon over medium heat until crispy. Add the celery and onion and cook, without stirring, until the onion is soft, about 5 minutes. Add the drained black-eyed peas, broth, water, vinegar, and bay leaf. Bring to a simmer and cook covered, until the beans are soft, about 1 hour.

Add the catfish pieces and tomatoes and cook for another 20 minutes. Season to taste with salt and remove from the heat. Allow to sit for 10 minutes for the salt to be absorbed and then taste and season again if necessary.

Serve with toasted bread brushed with the Anchovy Butter.

Serves 4

Oyster Risotto with Butternut Squash, Crème Fraîche, and Fresh Herbs

Oysters are a great addition to risotto, as the heat of the rice itself gently cooks the mollusks and the liquor from the oysters infuses the whole dish with sweet, briny, delicate flavor.

1 small onion, diced

2 tablespoons butter

2 cups carnaroli or arborio rice

2 cups white wine

Juice and grated zest of 1 orange

2 cups peeled, diced (1/2-inch) butternut squash

4 cups water

Salt

1 cup crème fraîche or sour cream

3 tablespoons chopped fresh flat-leaf parsley

1 tablespoon chopped fresh tarragon

24 large oysters, shucked (page 33), with liquid and meat reserved

Sauté the onion in the butter in a large, heavy-bottomed pot over medium heat until translucent. Add the rice and toss to coat with the butter. Cook until the rice begins to toast and has a nutty aroma, 3 to 4 minutes. Add the wine and orange juice and zest and cook until there is no longer an aroma of alcohol and the rice has absorbed most of the liquid. Add the squash and water. Season to taste with salt and stir as you continue to cook over medium heat. When the rice has absorbed most of the water, about 12 minutes, add the crème fraîche and herbs. Bring to a boil, then turn off the heat and allow the rice to absorb the remaining liquid, about 5 minutes.

Add the oysters and their liquor and stir to combine. The residual heat of the rice will cook the oysters; the dish is ready to serve when the edges of the oysters begin to curl, about 3 minutes. Serve immediately in shallow bowls, doing your best to distribute the oysters evenly.

Serves 4

Sablefish with Crisped Polenta and Scallion Salsa

Sablefish is the most beguiling food that I have ever put in my mouth. Problem is, it is almost too smooth. So here I pair it with a crisp salsa of crunchy almonds and fresh vegetables. I give specific instructions for cooking the polenta, but each brand has slightly different cooking times. Refer to the recipe on your package to help gauge this.

4 cups water

2 cups milk

Salt

2 cups coarse-ground cornmeal

1 tablespoon extra-virgin olive oil

Four 5-ounce portions skin-on sablefish (black cod) fillet

1 bunch scallions, very thinly sliced

2 red bell peppers, seeded and cut into very thin strips

1/2 cup raisins

1/2 cup Chunky Almond Oil (page 262)

For the polenta, bring the water and milk to a boil in large saucepan and season generously with salt. Add the cornmeal in a slow, steady stream while whisking to incorporate. (This is the step that ensures a smooth, lump-free polenta, so don't hesitate to use elbow grease.) Once all the cornmeal has been added, simmer for approximately 25 minutes over very low heat. Taste the polenta, and if there is any remaining grittiness to the cornmeal, continue to cook for another few minutes until it is soft.

Pour the polenta into a 9-inch square baking dish and even it out with a spatula. Cover and refrigerate until the polenta is set, at least 2 hours and up to overnight.

Preheat the oven to 350 degrees.

Cut the polenta into small triangles or whatever shape you like. In a large cast-iron pan over medium-high heat, heat the olive oil, then sear the polenta triangles in batches until browned on one side. Transfer the browned triangles to a baking sheet and heat through in the oven, about 20 minutes.

Place the sablefish on another baking sheet and put it in the oven for the last 7 minutes of the polenta cooking time.

For the salsa, combine the scallions, peppers, raisins, and Chunky Almond Oil in a small bowl. Season to taste with salt.

To serve, divide the polenta and sablefish among 4 plates. Garnish with the salsa and serve immediately.

Serves 4

Sablefish with Lentils and Pomegranate–Red Wine Butter

This is a take on a dish created by my good friend David Scribner. He was the chef at my first restaurant job and this was the best-selling item on the menu. He ended up resenting this dish because, as sometimes happens, a signature dish becomes so popular that it simply cannot be taken off the menu. So there we were in the middle of the nasty August heat in D.C., cooking hearty lentils and red wine reductions, because customers were coming in and demanding it.

It is, however, a wonderful winter dish, elegant yet very easy to prepare. The lentils can be made ahead of time and rewarmed, and the fish cooks so slowly that it is very easy to enjoy the company of your dinner guests while you cook. One note though: the lentils will not cook thoroughly if you add salt at the beginning of the process. Wait until they are fully cooked.

1 small onion, diced

1 clove garlic, grated on a Microplane or very finely minced

2 tablespoons extra-virgin olive oil

2 cups green lentils (French du Puy lentils are the best)

1 tablespoon sweet smoked paprika

4 cups water

Salt

Four 5-ounce portions skinned sablefish (black cod) fillet

1 tablespoon canola oil

2 cups pomegranate juice

2 cups red wine

1/4 cup butter, cut into small pieces

1 tablespoon chopped fresh flat-leaf parsley

In a large pot over medium heat, sauté the onion and garlic in the olive oil. When soft, add the lentils and toss to coat with oil. Cook for 3 minutes to toast the lentils, then add the paprika. Stir the paprika into the lentils and add the water. Bring to a simmer, reduce the heat to low, and simmer until the lentils are soft, about 25 minutes. Season to taste with salt and set aside off the heat.

Place the fillets on a baking sheet and lightly brush with the canola oil. For a 1-inch-thick fillet, bake for 35 minutes. For every additional 1/4 inch of thickness, add about 5 minutes to the cooking time.

While the fish cooks, prepare the sauce. In a medium saucepan, reduce the pomegranate juice and wine over medium heat until there is just about 1/2 cup left. Remove the pan from the heat and swirl in the pieces of butter one at a time, allowing the slowly melting butter to emulsify into the sauce. When it has all been incorporated, you should have a thick, rich sauce with no visible fatty sheen to it.

To serve, bring the lentils to a boil, taste, and season with more salt if necessary. Stir in the parsley and divide among 4 serving plates. Place a piece of sablefish on top of the lentils and drizzle the sauce around the plate.

Serves 4

Tilapia with Cauliflower Purée and Maple-Cranberry Sauce

I love the bold, romantic flavors of winter cooking. In this combination, tangy cranberries are matched with the bite of shallots and the sweetness of maple syrup. Cauliflower has the property of holding air when it is puréed, enabling you to make a purée that has the texture of soft butter without using a bit of fat. Just make sure to cook the cauliflower until it is soft and falling apart. The tilapia fillets are baked in a very low oven to preserve their moistness and flavor.

1 head cauliflower (about 1 pound)

Salt

1 tablespoon butter (optional)

Four 5-ounce tilapia fillets

2 tablespoons extra-virgin olive oil

1/2 cup unsweetened dried cranberries (if using sweetened, omit the maple syrup)

1 tablespoon maple syrup

1 small shallot, finely diced

3 cracks freshly ground black pepper

Cut the cauliflower into similar size pieces. It will usually break off at the stem, then all you have to do is to chop the core. Place the cauliflower in a saucepan just large enough to hold it all and cover with cold water. Season generously with salt and bring to a boil. Reduce the heat and cook at a simmer until the cauliflower is soft and just beginning to fall apart, about 10 minutes. Drain, reserving about 1 cup of the cooking water. Transfer the cauliflower to a blender or food processor. Purée, adding 1 tablespoon of the cooking water at a time to facilitate the process. The purée should be perfectly smooth and silky. If you like, you can add the butter for richness. This can be made ahead and gently rewarmed in a microwave or on the stovetop over low heat for serving.

Preheat the oven to 250 degrees.

Place the tilapia fillets on a baking sheet and brush with 1 tablespoon of the olive oil. Bake just until cooked through, 20 to 25 minutes for a 1-inch-thick fillet. During the last few minutes of cooking, set the serving plates in the oven to warm. This method of cooking fish, while it guarantees moistness, doesn't ever get the fish really hot, so warming the plates is key to keeping the fillets from cooling too quickly.

While the fish is cooking, make the sauce. Put the cranberries in a pan and cover with water. Bring to a boil, then reduce the heat and simmer for about 5 minutes to plump them. Drain, then combine the cranberries with the maple syrup, the remaining 1 tablespoon olive oil, the shallot, and pepper in a medium bowl. Season with a pinch of salt.

To serve, divide the cauliflower purée among the 4 warm serving plates, spreading it over the surface. Set a tilapia fillet on top, spoon the salsa onto it, and serve immediately.

Serves 4

Tilapia with Roasted Spaghetti Squash, Caper Yogurt, and Smoky Balsamic Reduction

This recipe contains several components that work together beautifully, and you'll want to use them separately in other dishes. For example, when you make the balsamic reduction go ahead and double the recipe—use it to drizzle over fresh fruit or on broiled vegetables. The sauce gets a hint of wood-fire flavor from the addition of smoked paprika—although the paprika's flavor is fat soluble, the vinegar will gain just enough smokiness to make it appealing. The reduction will keep for weeks, tightly covered, at room temperature. The caper yogurt, an invention by my friend Josh, is a delightful accompaniment to just about anything, especially grilled chicken, and is great as a substitute for mayonnaise in pink salmon salad sandwiches.

Spaghetti squash is a remarkable vegetable. When raw, it is a dense, hollow gourd with pale yellow skin. When cooked, its flesh turns stringy like spaghetti and has a wonderful nutty taste. It can be served in the skin or shredded out with a fork and then sautéed in butter with herbs.

1 large spaghetti squash	Preheat the oven to 350 degrees.
1/4 cup water	
1 cup balsamic vinegar	For the spaghetti squash, cut the squash in half lengthwise and place cut side down on a rimmed baking sheet. Pour in the water. Bake until the flesh is soft and easily shredded with a fork, about 30 minutes. Leave the oven on.
1 tablespoon sweet smoked paprika	
1 shallot, thinly sliced	For the balsamic reduction, mix the vinegar, paprika, and shallot in a small pot and simmer over medium-low heat until it is reduced by about two-thirds and is a thick syrup, about 20 minutes.
1/4 cup capers, drained and rinsed	
1/2 cup plain Greek-style yogurt	For the yogurt sauce, chop the capers as fine as you can, until they make a paste. Mix the capers, yogurt, and 2 tablespoons of olive oil in a small bowl and whisk to combine. Refrigerate until ready to use. (This will keep up to a week, tightly covered, in the fridge.)
2 tablespoons extra-virgin olive oil, plus more for brushing fillets	
Four 5-ounce tilapia fillets	Brush the fish with a little olive oil, season with salt, and place on a baking sheet. Bake until the fillets are cooked through, about 10 minutes.
Salt	

To serve, shred the squash, leaving it in its skin, and set the halves on a platter. Drizzle with the warm basalmic reduction, set the fillets on the platter, and serve family style, with the yogurt sauce on the side.

Serves 4

Classic New England Clam Chowder

There are as many recipes for clam chowder as there are cooks who love clams. I prefer a very milky style as opposed to the rich, creamy, flour-bound style that is prevalent in some areas of New England. Serve this with lots of oyster crackers or toasted bread. They will help to thicken the soup and provide some heft to the meal.

12 chowder clams (the very large quahogs) or 24 smaller clams, such as littlenecks, washed thoroughly (discard any that won't close)

1 cup water

3 strips bacon, minced

1 medium onion, finely diced

1 teaspoon ground mace

2 russet potatoes, peels left on, cut into 1/2-inch dice

3 cups half-and-half

Oyster crackers or toasted bread, for serving

Place the clams and water in a large soup pot and cover. Cook over high heat until the clams open, about 8 minutes. (Discard any clams that haven't opened by the end of the cooking time.) Remove the opened clams from the water and strain the liquid into a bowl to remove any sand that has collected in the bottom. You need about 3 cups of broth, so if you have less, make up the difference with water. Reserve this cooking broth. Remove the clams from their shells and chop the meat. Rinse out and dry the pot.

Sauté the bacon in the pot over medium heat until crisp, then add the onion. Cook, without stirring, until the onion is soft, then add the mace, potatoes, clam meat, and reserved broth. Simmer until the potatoes are soft, about 10 minutes, then add the half-and-half. Bring to a simmer, but do not boil.

Remove the chowder from the heat and let sit for a few minutes for the flavors to develop. Serve with crackers or toasted bread.

Serves 4

Dungeness Crab Fettuccine

Chefs argue about which is better, the blue crab of the East Coast or the Dungeness of the West. I like them both—for the Dungeness, what stands out for me is its delicious sweetness, which this recipe amplifies.

Salt

1 pound fettuccine

3 strips bacon, minced

1 small onion, diced

1 red bell pepper, seeded and finely diced

1 teaspoon ground coriander

2 cups heavy cream

1 pound Dungeness crabmeat, picked through for shell fragments

3 tablespoons chopped fresh flat-leaf parsley

Bring a large pot of salted water to a boil and cook the pasta until it is al dente, following the package instructions. (Note: when draining the pasta, reserve a few tablespoons of the cooking water.)

While the pasta water comes to a boil, sauté the bacon in a large skillet over medium heat until all the fat has been rendered and the meat is beginning to crisp. Add the onion and bell pepper and cook until soft, stirring occasionally so the onion does not brown. Stir in the coriander and cook for another minute.

Add the cream to the skillet and reduce the heat to a simmer. Reduce the cream by half, then add the crab meat. Add the drained pasta as well as a few tablespoons of the pasta cooking water and bring to a boil. This final cooking will heat the crab through and allow the pasta to absorb the flavors of the sauce.

Pile the pasta onto the plates, garnish with parsley, and serve immediately.

Serves 4

Smoked Mussel Chowder with Fennel and Potato

I had the best chowder of my life while traveling up the Atlantic coast of Nova Scotia. We stopped in every town, and almost every restaurant offered chowder in some form or another. So we made a contest out of it—who had the best chowder? The winner was a little café in Lunenburg. They served a smoked mussel chowder that to this day remains a topic of conversation in our family. So here is my cool-weather interpretation of what we ate on that perfect blue-sky afternoon.

2 strips bacon, minced

1 tablespoon butter

1 medium onion, finely diced

4 ribs celery, very thinly sliced

1 large fennel bulb, stalks discarded and bulb finely diced

2 sprigs fresh thyme

1 teaspoon fennel seeds, ground (page 9)

4 large russet potatoes, peels left on, cut into 1-inch pieces

Two 4-ounce cans smoked mussels (about 40 mussels)

4 cups water

2 cups half-and-half

Freshly grated nutmeg

Heat the bacon and butter together over medium heat in a large saucepan. When most of the bacon has been rendered and the meat begins to turn dark brown, add the onion, celery, fennel bulb, and thyme. Cook until the vegetables are translucent, stirring occasionally, about 5 minutes. Add the ground fennel seeds and cook for another minute. Add the potatoes, mussels, and water. Bring to a simmer and cook until the potatoes begin to fall apart, about 20 minutes.

Add the half-and-half and turn the heat off. Stir to combine and let sit for 20 minutes so all the flavors can meld. Remove the thyme sprigs.

Divide the chowder among 4 soup bowls and garnish with a few gratings of nutmeg.

Serves 4

Mussels with IPA and Roasted Garlic

I cooked a dish similar to this in a restaurant when I was first starting out. The dish was great, but the chef had to take it off the menu because the line cooks kept drinking the beer. Kind of silly—but an eye-opening introduction to some of the realities of restaurant work. In this version, I use whole cloves of roasted garlic and a strong-flavored beer to create a very robust dish.

2 heads garlic

1 tablespoon canola oil

2 shallots, thinly sliced

4 tablespoons butter

4 pounds mussels,
scrubbed and debearded
(discard any that won't close)

Salt

One 12-ounce bottle IPA
beer, at room temperature

Good crusty bread,
sliced and toasted

Preheat the oven to 350 degrees.

Brush the heads of garlic with the canola oil and wrap in aluminum foil. Roast until the cloves are soft and the aroma is nutty, about 45 minutes. Remove the garlic heads from the oven and slice in half around the equator. Squeeze out the roasted cloves and set aside.

In a large soup pot, sauté the shallots with 1 tablespoon of the butter for 2 minutes over high heat. Add the mussels and let sit for a few minutes until you begin to see shells opening a little bit. Season to taste with salt, pour in the beer, and add the garlic cloves. Cover the pot and let the mussels steam open, about 6 minutes. Add in the remaining 3 tablespoons butter and toss to combine with the mussels as it melts. (Discard any mussels that haven't opened.)

Divide the mussels among 4 serving bowls, spooning any remaining cooking broth over them, and serve with toasted bread.

Serves 4 as a main course or a hearty appetizer

Almond Milk–Poached Scallops with Sweet Potato Mash

This is an unusual take on a poaching broth, but the almond milk provides great flavor that matches well with the sweet potatoes.

1 1/2 pounds sweet potatoes, peeled and cut into large chunks

Salt

Juice of 1 orange

1/2 cup plain yogurt

1 tablespoon butter

1 teaspoon ground coriander

2 cups almond milk

2 sprigs fresh thyme

1 shallot, thinly sliced

1 teaspoon fennel seeds

1 1/4 pounds bay scallops

For the potato mash, place the sweet potatoes in a small pan and barely cover with water. Season generously with salt and bring to a simmer. Continue to simmer until the potatoes are soft, about 8 minutes, then drain, combine the potatoes with the orange juice, yogurt, butter, and coriander and mash well to incorporate. Set aside.

Combine the almond milk, thyme, shallot, and fennel seeds in a large saucepan and bring to a simmer. Allow to cool to 170 degrees (use an instant-read meat thermometer to confirm the temperature), then add the scallops. Maintain the heat so the scallops cook slowly, keeping the liquid at 170 degrees. This will take just 3 or 4 minutes, so watch the scallops carefully. When the scallops are done, they will be just firm and opaque all the way through. Remove them from the liquid with a slotted spoon.

To serve, place a mound of sweet potato mash on each of 4 serving plates, then ladle the scallops over the sweet potatoes.

Serves 4

Linguine with Bay Scallops and Sage Butter

Bay scallops are super easy because you can add them to nearly any preparation. Here I gently flavor butter with the highly potent herb, sage, then use the pasta cooking liquid to create a rich coating sauce. I like to finish with parsley because sage can taste a little musty all on its own—the parsley provides a fresh, bright note that really perks up the dish.

1 pound linguine

Salt

1/4 cup butter

1 clove garlic, thinly sliced

Leaves from 2 sprigs fresh sage, thinly sliced across

Juice of 1/2 lemon

1 pound bay scallops

3 tablespoons chopped fresh flat-leaf parsley

Cook the linguine in boiling salted water, according to the timing listed on the package, until about 1 minute from al dente. Drain, reserving 1 cup of the cooking water.

While the pasta cooks, gently warm the butter with the garlic and sage in a large deep-sided pan. It should be just hot enough to soften the garlic but the butter should not brown. Add the lemon juice and scallops. Cook for 1 minute, then add the drained pasta along with the reserved pasta cooking water. Bring the sauce to a boil and cook for a minute to reduce the liquid to a thin sauce. The pasta will absorb most of the water as it cooks fully. Season to taste with salt, sprinkle with the parsley, and toss to combine.

Serves 4

Sautéed Bay Scallops and Chorizo over Roasted Acorn Squash

Chorizo and squash are a fun combination. I first started playing around with these flavors using chorizo as a garnish for squash soups. In this dish, I add fresh scallops and just a hint of wine to make an elegant main course or a filling appetizer.

2 acorn squash, each cut into quarters and seeded

6 tablespoons butter

Salt

1 shallot, diced

2 ounces dried Spanish chorizo, finely diced, or 6 ounces fresh chorizo, casing removed

1 pound bay scallops

1/2 cup white wine

1 tablespoon chopped fresh chives

Preheat the oven to 350 degrees.

Put the quartered squash pieces on a large baking sheet. Place 1/2 tablespoon of the butter in the hollow of each quarter, season with salt, and spear the flesh multiple times with the tines of a fork; this allows the heat and butter to penetrate the flesh of the squash. Bake until the pieces are soft and the skin is beginning to blister, about 30 minutes, or perhaps longer, depending on the squash.

Melt the remaining 2 tablespoons butter in a sauté pan. Add the shallot and chorizo and cook slowly over medium-low heat to render out the fat evenly. If using fresh sausage, use a spatula to break it up into small pieces. Once the chorizo begins to crisp, turn the heat to high and add the scallops. Season with salt and sauté for 1 minute. Add the wine and turn off the heat. The wine will all but evaporate and leave just a thick glaze on the scallops.

Remove the squash from the oven, spoon the scallop mixture over the top, and garnish with the chives.

Serves 4 as a main course

Maine Shrimp with Radicchio and Orange-Cashew Dressing

Maine shrimp are difficult to serve as an entrée course because they are so small. But here they provide great flavor and a bit of bulk to a nice mix of colorful bitter greens.

2 heads radicchio

Leaves from 1 bunch fresh flat-leaf parsley

1 head frisée lettuce, heavy stems trimmed and leaves cut in half

2 tablespoons extra-virgin olive oil

Salt

2 tablespoons butter

1 pound Maine pink shrimp, shelled and deveined

1/2 cup cashew nuts, toasted (page 15) and crushed

Pinch of red chile flakes

Juice of 1 orange

Freshly grated nutmeg

Shred the radicchio as thinly as you can. Add to a medium salad bowl with the parsley leaves and frisée and toss to combine. Pour the olive oil over the greens, season to taste with salt, and toss again.

Heat 1 tablespoon of the butter in a heavy-bottomed 12-inch sauté pan over medium heat until it is foamy and golden brown. Add the shrimp in a single layer to the browning butter and let sit for 1 minute without stirring. Add the crushed cashews and chile flakes and let toast for about 20 seconds without stirring. Add the orange juice and toss. Add the remaining 1 tablespoon butter and mix well to incorporate. Season to taste with salt.

Divide the salad among 4 serving plates and spoon the warm shrimp over the top. Garnish each with a sprinkling of freshly grated nutmeg.

Serves 4

Pumpkin and Pear Panzanella with Pumpkin-Seed Vinaigrette

Try serving this dish with a strongly flavored fish like striped bass—its touch of sweetness provides a welcome counterpoint. It's also delicious topped with crumbled fresh goat cheese.

3 cups cubed (1-inch) peeled pumpkin, such as Sugar Pie, or autumn squash, such as Hubbard

5 tablespoons extra-virgin olive oil

Salt

2 cups cubed (1-inch) bread, preferably brioche or soft baguette

Juice of 1/2 orange

1 tablespoon sherry vinegar

2 teaspoons whole-grain mustard

1 head frisée lettuce, separated into leaves and heavy stems removed

Leaves from 6 sprigs fresh mint

1/2 cup toasted pumpkin seeds

1 pear, quartered lengthwise, cored, and very thinly sliced

Freshly grated nutmeg

Preheat the oven to 400 degrees.

Toss the pumpkin cubes with 2 tablespoons of the olive oil and salt to taste on a baking sheet. Bake until the cubes are soft and begin to brown, about 20 minutes. Remove from the oven and let cool to room temperature. Reduce the oven temperature to 350 degrees.

On another baking sheet, toss the bread cubes with 1 tablespoon of the olive oil and salt to taste. Bake until crunchy and golden brown, about 8 minutes.

For the vinaigrette, combine the orange juice, vinegar, mustard, and remaining 2 tablespoons olive oil in a small bowl. Whisk to combine.

In a large serving bowl, toss the pumpkin with the croutons, frisée, mint leaves, pumpkin seeds, and pear slices. Season with salt and add the vinaigrette. Grate a little fresh nutmeg over the top, toss to combine, and serve immediately.

Serves 4 as an appetizer or side dish

Roasted Radicchio with Sambuca Dressing

Bitter radicchio is most often found in bagged mesclun mixes. It has absolutely no place there. Why would anyone want a tough, fibrous, dried-out, often-too-big-to-fit-in-your-mouth piece of lettuce? I don't get it. But I do love radicchio. When pan seared and roasted, the bitterness fades into a complex sweetness that is at once smoky and bitter. Here I prepare it as a side, complemented with an anise/licorice dressing. This would be great with a broiled fillet of meaty bluefish or mackerel over the top.

4 tablespoons extra-virgin olive oil

2 large heads radicchio, cut in half through the stem

Salt

1 tablespoon sambuca or other anise-flavored liqueur (either the clear or the dark works well)

Juice of 1 orange

1 teaspoon ground oregano

Pinch onion powder

Preheat the oven to 400 degrees.

Heat a large ovenproof skillet with 1 tablespoon of the olive oil over high heat. Place the radicchio, cut side down, in the pan and cook for a few minutes. Transfer the pan to the oven and cook the radicchio until it is wilted, about 12 minutes. Flip the radicchio, season to taste with salt, and set aside.

For the dressing, pour the sambuca into a small bowl. Carefully light a long match and hold it near the liqueur. It will catch on fire; let it burn until most of the alcohol smell is gone. Add the remaining 3 tablespoons olive oil, orange juice, oregano, and onion powder and whisk vigorously. Pour the dressing over the roasted radicchio and serve.

Serves 4

Clove-braised Swiss Chard and Fennel

The flavor of cloves provides a wonderful depth and intrigue to dishes. Be discreet with its use though; it works best as a subtle background flavor, as in this preparation. To avoid serving whole cloves in the dish, I prepare a quick clove-flavored broth that I use to cook the chard and fennel.

6 cloves

1 1/2 cups water

2 tablespoons butter

1 bunch Swiss chard, stems chopped into 1/2-inch pieces and leaves ripped into thirds

1 fennel bulb, stalks trimmed, bulb sliced 1/4 inch thick

Salt

Combine the cloves and water in a small pan and bring to a simmer for 10 minutes, then strain. Set aside.

In a large deep-sided sauté pan, melt the butter over medium heat. Add the chopped chard stems and fennel slices and cook until they begin to soften, about 5 minutes. Add the chard leaves and toss to combine. As soon as the leaves begin to wilt, add the strained clove broth and season to taste with salt. Cover the dish and let cook at a low simmer for 10 minutes. Remove from the heat and check the seasoning. Serve immediately.

Serves 4 as a side dish

Creamed Carrots à la Ris

I had the pleasure of hosting the esteemed Washington, D.C., chef Ris Lacoste in my kitchen one afternoon for a Slow Food fund-raising dinner. I have always admired her cooking and was delighted to have the opportunity to cook alongside her. She prepared an incredible dish of shrimp, but what I really remember are the carrots that she had simmering away for hours. Their sweet aroma, perfumed with the addition of Pernod and cream, filled the kitchen. This is an unfaithful and much quicker interpretation of that dish—I hope she doesn't mind too much!

1 1/2 pounds carrots, cut into
1-inch-thick rounds

3 cups water

1 tablespoon Pernod or other
anise-flavored liqueur

Salt

1 1/2 cups heavy cream

Pinch of saffron threads (about 10)

Grated zest and juice of 1 orange

Place the carrots, water, and Pernod in a small pot, season lightly with salt, and bring to a boil. Cook for about 5 minutes. Drain, reserving 1 cup of the cooking water and setting the vegetables aside. Return the reserved cooking water to the pot, stir in the heavy cream, and cook over low heat until reduced by about half, about 10 minutes. Add the carrots, saffron, and orange zest and juice and stir to combine. Continue to cook over low heat until the carrots are glazed and the sauce is reduced to a thick syrup, about 5 minutes more.

Serves 4 as a side dish

Broccoli Rabe
and Potato Gratin

This is my wife's favorite dish, and we have it with dinner a couple times a week. It has also become a favorite of our friends when they come for a meal. It makes fantastic leftovers too, either chilled or reheated.

5 medium Yukon gold potatoes (about 1 pound total)

3 tablespoons olive oil

3 cloves garlic, sliced

Salt

1 bunch broccoli rabe, stems peeled

1 cup water

1/4 cup slivered almonds

Pinch of red chile flakes

Slice the potatoes in half and then again into 1/4-inch-thick half-moons. Heat a large ovenproof pan with the olive oil and garlic over medium heat. When the garlic begins to brown, add the potatoes and toss to coat with the oil. Cook until the potatoes begin to brown, about 5 minutes, without stirring. Season to taste with salt, then add the broccoli rabe in a single layer over the potatoes. Season the broccoli with salt and add the water. Cover the pan as best you can to trap some of the steam.

After about 2 minutes, remove the cover and place the pan under the broiler. Broil the broccoli until it begins to brown and the leaves char, about 10 minutes. Add the almonds and toss to mix all the vegetables. Place the pan back under the broiler until the almonds are just beginning to burn, about another 5 minutes. (Don't be afraid of a little color on the food here; it's providing flavor. But don't burn them to death either.)

Remove the pan from the oven and sprinkle with the chile flakes.

Serves 4 as a side dish

Cider-glazed Parsnips

I love the meaty texture and sweet flavor of parsnips—the "white carrots" you see in the stores. Although they have a different texture than carrots when raw, they are a fantastic stand-in for their orange counterparts in cooked dishes. Parsnips tend to be sweet, so I pair them with an acid, in this case, cider vinegar. This preparation bathes them in a rich sweet-and-sour sauce that will complement nearly any seafood—I especially like it with rockfish or smoked tilapia or catfish.

2 pounds parsnips, peeled and cut into 1-inch-thick rounds	Cook the parsnips in boiling salted water until soft, about 7 minutes. Drain and let air-dry for a few minutes.
Salt	
4 tablespoons butter	Heat 2 tablespoons of the butter in a large sauté pan over medium heat until it is dark brown and has a nutty aroma. Add the parsnips and shake the pan so they are mostly in a single layer. Let cook for a few minutes without stirring so they can develop some color, then season to taste with salt and add the vinegar. When the vinegar is reduced by two-thirds, about 5 minutes, add the remaining 2 tablespoons butter and the parsley and remove the pan from the heat.
3/4 cup cider vinegar	
2 tablespoons chopped fresh flat-leaf parsley	

Toss the vegetables while the butter melts into the sauce, creating a thick coating. When you serve the parsnips, a puddle of sauce should accumulate underneath them on the plate, but it should not run all over the place. Serve immediately.

Serves 4 as a side dish

Maple-roasted Potatoes

Sometimes I'm in the mood to jazz potatoes up a bit. Here, maple syrup adds unexpected sweetness, while the kick of the Tabasco provides a nice counterpoint to their creaminess. Serve with Roasted Whole Arctic Char on Pine Needles with Pine Nut Sauce (page 178).

1 1/2 pounds baby red potatoes

Salt

2 tablespoons butter

2 cloves garlic, sliced

1 tablespoon water

1/2 cup maple syrup

Tabasco sauce

Place the potatoes in a large ovenproof deep-sided skillet, such as a Le Creuset braiser or sauté pan. Cover with water, season very generously with salt, and bring to a boil. Simmer until the potatoes are just cooked through, about 10 minutes. Drain and allow the potatoes to dry.

Preheat the oven to 400 degrees.

In the same skillet, melt the butter, then add the garlic. Add the potatoes and sear over high heat until the garlic is dark brown but not burned. Add the water and maple syrup and bring to a boil.

Transfer the skillet to the oven and roast the potatoes for 12 minutes. Shake the pan so that the potatoes are covered in the thick glaze. If there seems to be too much sauce, then transfer the pan back to the stovetop and boil until it has a syrupy consistency. Season with a couple dashes of Tabasco.

Serves 4 as a side dish

Broiled Pears with Orange and Honey

This is a particularly nice partner for seafood of all sorts. I like the way the spice of the Tabasco offsets the sweetness of the honey. Serve this at your next dinner party—it's easy to put together and will make for an unexpected and memorable side dish.

4 Bosc pears (not too ripe or they will fall apart)

Juice of 1 orange

2 tablespoons honey

Dash of Tabasco sauce

Freshly ground black pepper

Salt

Preheat the broiler.

Cut the pears into quarters and remove the core from each. Put them on a baking sheet.

Mix the orange juice, honey, Tabasco, a couple of cracks of black pepper, and salt to taste in a small bowl and whisk to combine.

Place the pears under the broiler and broil until they begin to brown, 2 to 3 minutes. Pour the honey mixture over the pears. Put the pears back under the broiler and cook until the liquid has reduced to a thick syrup, about 5 minutes. Remove from the broiler and baste the pears with the reduced syrup.

Serves 4 as a side dish

A SEPARATE SEASON

The easiest way to think of this season is to say "Tuesday night." You are in a rush, the kids are coming late from practice, and you need a recipe you can rely on. Many of the fish and shellfish in this section are farmed, so they have no season and are always at market—you can count on them. The recipes I've included are meant to inspire easy and elegant solutions to your busy life.

Some of these dishes are new, more sustainable takes on classics. Some are meant to broaden your approach to seafood, help you think inside the can! And I've also suggested a number of fun and easy ideas for entertaining that won't break the bank.

Some of these dishes are new, more sustainable takes on classics. Some are meant to broaden your approach to seafood, help you think inside the can!

Roasted Olives

You can find a wonderful array of olives in most every supermarket. I love to eat olives hot as their flavor seems to bloom with the heat, accentuating the differences in each variety.

As I do with fish roe, I rebrine olives when I get them home to take away some of the salt and to allow their natural fruitiness to shine through.

When buying olives, I look for a mix of green olives. Some of my favorites include arbequina, lucques, manzanilla, and picholine. If you prefer black olives, try kalamata or black cerignola.

2 cups mixed olives

Pinch of salt

3 tablespoons extra-virgin olive oil

Zest of 1 orange, removed in strips with a vegetable peeler

4 sprigs fresh thyme

2 cloves garlic, cut in half

Preheat the oven to 350 degrees.

To rebrine the olives, drain them, then cover with water and add the salt. Allow to sit for a few hours, then drain and pat dry.

In a medium ovenproof skillet, heat the olive oil with the orange zest, thyme, and garlic over medium heat. After 2 minutes, the oil will take on the aromas of these ingredients.

Add the olives, toss to coat with the oil, and transfer the pan to the oven. Roast the olives until they are hot all the way through and just beginning to wrinkle, about 8 minutes. Toss again to coat with the flavored oil. Serve immediately.

Makes 2 cups

Radishes with Anchovy-Herb Butter

The French snack of radishes with fresh butter and salt is a classic. It's easy to prepare and a nice change from the typical vegetable platter served with ranch or blue cheese dressing. Here I add a little twist, serving the radishes with an anchovy-herb butter.

1 salt-packed anchovy (page 24) or 2 oil-packed anchovy fillets, minced

2 tablespoons butter, softened

1 tablespoon chopped fresh flat-leaf parsley

1 teaspoon chopped fresh dill

Salt

1 pound radishes, trimmed, the large ones cut in half

For the flavored butter, combine the anchovies, butter, and herbs in a small bowl and mix well, mashing to incorporate. Season with a little salt. Store at room temperature if using the same day; otherwise, refrigerate. (This will keep for several weeks, tightly covered.)

To serve, put the butter in a small crock and set on a plate with the radishes. It's best to put a small smear of the butter on a couple of the radishes so that people get the idea. After that, let them dip the radishes in it, just like a vegetable tray.

Serves many

Bread with Anchovy and Butter

One of my favorite restaurants in D.C. serves this classic Italian preparation. My wife and I order it all the time, along with a couple of espresso shots. The flavor is amazing, but the preparation is incredibly simple. I like to use the salt-cured anchovies for this as they have a more developed flavor and provide a nice counterpoint to the rich butter. If you use oil-packed instead, serve it with red chile flakes, not the Chile Oil.

6 tablespoons unsalted butter, at room temperature

6 slices sourdough bread, each cut in half

12 salt-packed anchovies (page 24) or 24 oil-packed anchovy fillets

Chile Oil (page 262) or red chile flakes

This is best presented as a serve-yourself dish. Set the butter, packed into a small crock, on a platter. Place the bread on the platter in a couple of attractive stacks. Arrange the anchovy fillets on the platter. If using the salt-packed variety, drizzle them with Chile Oil; if using oil-packed, sprinkle them with red chile flakes. Set the platter out for guests, providing a butter knife and small fork so they can help themselves.

Serves 4 as an appetizer

Marinated Boquerones

I love these little fishies, whether you call them *alici* (Italy), *boquerones* (Spain), or white anchovies. I worked at a restaurant where these were always on the menu, and the chef liked to have them at room temperature. The door to the service kitchen was in a narrow hallway that backed up to the salad station, and so I had to walk past these little guys every time I went in or out. Let's just say I ate a lot of them. But that is really the way to enjoy them, in abundance. You can often find these small fillets in the prepared seafood section of your grocery store. They are not raw, and they are not canned, so sometimes you have to look around for them a little bit.

1/2 pound vinegar-cured white anchovies

1 red onion, sliced paper thin

1 sprig fresh thyme

1 clove garlic, sliced paper thin

1/2 cup extra-virgin olive oil

1 teaspoon red chile flakes

Lemon wedges

Sliced crusty baguette

Arrange the anchovies attractively on a platter. Layer with the sliced onion, thyme, and garlic slices and pour the olive oil over all. Sprinkle with chile flakes and place the lemon wedges on the side. This preparation is best if you allow the anchovies to sit in the marinade for an hour or so at room temperature. Serve with sliced bread and lots of crisp white wine.

Serves 4 as a snack

Gravlax

This classic preparation can be used with any type of fresh salmon, but you'll get the best results with a high-fat salmon like wild king (Chinook) or a farmed salmon from a top-quality source such as Loch Duart in Scotland. The curing process results in a very creamy, rich texture that is great on bagels, toast, crackers—hell, it's even good eaten off a spoon.

1/2 cup kosher salt

1/2 cup firmly packed
dark brown sugar

1 pound skin-on salmon fillet

1 small onion, thinly sliced

4 sprigs fresh dill

1 tablespoon extra-virgin olive oil

In a small bowl, mix the salt and brown sugar together well. Put a large sheet of plastic wrap on a plate and sprinkle a thin layer of the salt mixture on the plastic wrap. Place the salmon on top and layer on the onion slices and dill sprigs. Press the remaining salt mixture evenly over the top of the salmon and wrap the fillet tightly with the plastic. Let sit in the refrigerator for 3 days, flipping the salmon over after 18 hours.

Wash off the cure mix and discard the dill and onion. Pat the fillet dry and brush with the olive oil. I like to let the fillet sit another day in the refrigerator, covered, before I use it; this extra time helps to soften the bite of the salt on the outer part of the flesh.

To serve, use a long, thin-bladed knife to cut thin slices of the fillet on the bias down to the skin but not through it. Place the slices on a plate and garnish with whatever you like, much as you would smoked salmon. (The unsliced fish will keep for about a week, tightly covered, in the fridge.)

Serves 8 as an appetizer

Smoked Salmon Panzanella with Feta, Dill, and Grapes

I like unexpected combinations. It turns out that feta cheese has a bright acidity that pairs very nicely with the smoke of hot-smoked salmon. This is a wonderful presentation for a light lunch or as part of a dinner buffet. Unless you are hot-smoking your own salmon (page 254), there is no prep here beyond opening a few packages and making it look pretty.

Juice of 1 orange

2 tablespoons extra-virgin olive oil

1 tablespoon sour cream

Salt

1 head frisée lettuce, separated into leaves and heavy stems removed

1/2 pound arugula

Leaves picked from thick fronds of 1 bunch dill

1 1/2 cups seedless grapes, cut in half

2 cups croutons, preferably brioche

1/2 pound hot-smoked Pacific salmon, flaked

1/2 cup crumbled feta cheese

In a small bowl, mix the orange juice, olive oil, and sour cream until smooth, then season to taste with salt.

In a large bowl, combine the frisée, arugula, dill, grapes, and croutons. Toss with the dressing until the salad is well coated, then season again with salt.

Arrange the salad on a large platter. Scatter the flaked salmon and crumbled feta over the top.

Serves 4 as an appetizer salad or light lunch

Smoked Sable Brandade

This French dish usually is made with salt cod, but sablefish (also sold as black cod) is a much more environmentally sustainable choice. You often can find smoked sablefish in Jewish delis, and many upscale grocery stores carry it as well. Because the sablefish is smoked and then cooked again, its final texture ends up resembling that of the reconstituted salt cod.

4 ounces smoked sablefish

1/2 pound russet potato, peeled and diced

6 cloves garlic, peeled

3 tablespoons extra-virgin olive oil, plus more for toasting bread and serving

1 crusty baguette, sliced 1 inch thick

1 tablespoon chopped fresh herbs, such as chives and tarragon (optional)

Combine the sablefish, potato, and garlic in a small saucepan and barely cover with water. Bring to a simmer and cook until the potato pieces are soft and beginning to fall apart, about 12 minutes. Drain, reserving about 1/2 cup of the cooking liquid.

Preheat broiler if using to toast the bread.

Transfer the potato, fish, and garlic to a medium bowl and begin to mash with a whisk. Add the olive oil in a slow stream, whisking constantly to incorporate it as you add it, then whisk in about 3 tablespoons of the cooking liquid until the purée has the consistency of peanut butter. (The brandade will keep for several days, tightly covered, in the refrigerator.)

Brush the bread slices with a little oil and toast under the broiler or in a toaster oven until golden brown. Serve the brandade in a bowl, topped with a drizzle of olive oil and a sprinkling of herbs, if desired. Offer the toasted bread alongside.

Serves 4 as a canapé or light appetizer

Trout Roe with Cava and Brioche Toasts

Almost any kind of roe I have ever purchased has been oversalted. For that reason, I rebrine it in a quick bath that extracts a lot of the salt and brings out the sweet, clean flavor. I love serving this with brioche bread, as it has a buttery quality that enhances the sweetness in the roe.

4 ounces trout roe

Pinch of salt

Brioche bread, sliced 1/2 inch thick

2 tablespoons extra-virgin olive oil

2 tablespoons cava or other white sparkling wine

1 red onion, very thinly sliced

2 tablespoons crème fraîche or sour cream

To rebrine the roe, place the eggs in a small bowl, cover with cold water, and add the salt. Mix gently with your finger to dissolve the salt and let sit for about 2 hours, discarding any broken egg cases that may have floated to the top. (It may seem counterintuitive, but salt must always be in equilibrium, so the excess salt in the roe will migrate to the almost unsalted water it is soaking in.)

Preheat broiler if using to toast the bread.

Toward the end of the rebrining time, brush the brioche with 1 tablespoon of the olive oil and toast under the broiler or in a toaster oven.

Drain the roe in a fine sieve, then gently wash the roe in cold water. Transfer the roe to a small serving bowl. Add the remaining tablespoon olive oil, then pour in the cava. Allow to sit for a few minutes, then place on a tray along with the sliced onion and brioche toasts. Provide a small bowl of the crème fraîche for dolloping.

Serves 4 as a snack

Trout roe marinating in cava

Pouring cava over rebrined roe

Smoked Clam and Olive Skewers

This is a fun canapé to serve at parties. Make sure you rinse the olives well to remove a little of their brine, which can otherwise overpower the flavor of the clam.

One 4-ounce can smoked baby clams

About 30 pitted cocktail olives, with or without pimiento, rinsed

Chile Oil (page 262)

Thread a clam onto a toothpick, then add an olive. Continue assembling skewers until all clams and olives are used. Arrange on a plate and drizzle with the Chile Oil. Serve at room temperature.

Makes about 30 pieces

Sweet Wine Mignonette for Oysters or Clams

Americans love salty-sweet foods. Take Cracker Jacks, Chinese food, and Snickers Bars. These are all a balance of salty and sweet, which is what I love about this preparation. Rather than the typical vinegary bite of a traditional oyster topping, I use dessert wine. This works best with briny northern oysters, which have a real zip to them that is better suited to a less piquant sauce. I first read about this idea in Julia Child's *Mastering the Art of French Cooking*, when she mentioned that the French Royal Court preferred to pair their oysters with Sauternes, the famous sweet wine of the Bordeaux region. The wine is sweet due to a naturally occurring fungus (called botrytis) that eat small holes in the grape skins, causing the grapes to shrivel up and concentrate their sugars. Wines made from these grapes are unctuous and incredibly well flavored. Pairing them with oysters struck me as a good idea. Ask your wine merchant for a botrytis wine—and you don't need an expensive bottle for this.

3/4 cup dessert wine

1 small shallot, very finely diced

Juice of 1/2 lemon

Freshly ground black pepper

In a small bowl, mix the wine, shallot, and lemon juice, then give it a few coarse grinds of black pepper. Allow to sit for at least 10 minutes and up to several hours (but no longer) for the flavors to meld. Serve with chilled raw oysters or clams.

Makes 1 cup (enough for about 2 dozen oysters)

Bloody Mary Raw Bar Shots

This is a great way to start a party. The shots are light on the alcohol, so think of them more as a slightly boozy canapé than a cocktail. You can top them off with raw oysters or clams to make them shooters.

1 cup V-8 vegetable juice

1/2 cup bottled clam juice

1 tablespoon prepared horseradish

1 tablespoon Worcestershire sauce

1/4 cup vodka

1 tablespoon fresh lime juice

1 lime wedge

1 tablespoon Old Bay Seasoning or Seafood Spice #1 (page 260)

1 dozen shucked oysters or clams

Combine all the ingredients, except the lime wedge, the Old Bay, and the oysters or clams in a cocktail shaker with a few ice cubes and mix well. Use the lime wedge to moisten part of the rim of the glasses and press the shot glasses into the Old Bay seasoning. Pour the Bloody Mary mix through a strainer into the shot glasses and top each with an oyster or clam.

Makes 12 shots

Oyster Shooters Three Ways

I'll say it—there's nothing more fun than eating oysters. Well, maybe a shot of booze with an oyster in it. Here are three variations on that theme; choose the one that sounds best to you, or try all three at once. Any of the spice mixtures in the back of this book (pages 260–261) would work well as a seasoning for these shots. Let your imagination go. Make sure that you get your oysters clean before serving them—nothing ruins an oyster shot like a mouth full of grit.

For each of the combinations that follow, mix the spices/aromatics, then wet the rim of small glasses (yes, shot glasses are fine). Dip the moistened rim in the mixture, then fill with a sip or two of the designated chilled booze. Top each glass with an oyster.

Sake and Ginger

Sake is available in many styles and flavors that range from soft and creamy to bold and brightly acidic. I urge you to try a few different kinds until you find the one that suits you best.

2 teaspoons peeled and grated fresh ginger

Grated zest of 1 orange

1 teaspoon salt

1 teaspoon sugar

Sake

Guinness and Smoked Salt

Guinness is a classic pairing with oysters, and here I play off its dark, rich flavor by adding a little smoke to the spice blend.

| 1 teaspoon sweet smoked paprika

1 teaspoon kosher salt

1 teaspoon powdered or dried oregano

Pinch of cayenne pepper

Pinch of ground cinnamon

Guinness stout

Mezcal and Lime

The slow, gentle roasting of the agave before it is distilled gives Mezcal a smoky, deep, rich taste. To my mind, it tastes like tequila with bacon in it. Awesome! If you can't find the Mezcal, substitute an aged tequila.

| 1 teaspoon ground or dried oregano

1 teaspoon onion powder

1 teaspoon kosher salt

1 teaspoon sugar

2 limes, cut into wedges to serve as a palate cleanser after the shot, frat-bar style

Mezcal

Ritz Cracker–Coated Catfish with Buttermilk Sauce

While preparing dinner at a friend's house, I realized he didn't have any bread crumbs. Unless I wanted to run to the store, I had to improvise with whatever I could find. Ritz crackers are so good, I thought. How could the dish go wrong? Well, in fact, it went really right, and I was hooked.

1/4 cup sour cream

1 cup buttermilk

1 tablespoon honey

3 dashes Tabasco sauce

1 tablespoon chopped fresh flat-leaf parsley

1 tablespoon chopped fresh mint

Salt

1 tablespoon Dijon mustard

1 pound catfish fillets, cut into finger-size strips

1/4 cup fine-ground cornmeal

1 sleeve Ritz crackers, crumbled into a powder

2 cups canola oil

Preheat oven to 275 degrees.

For the sauce, combine the sour cream, 1/2 cup of the buttermilk, honey, Tabasco, and herbs. Season to taste with salt and whisk to combine.

For the fish, mix the mustard with the remaining 1/2 cup buttermilk in a medium bowl and whisk to combine. Add the fish to the mixture and toss to coat. In a shallow bowl, mix together the cornmeal and cracker crumbs. Dredge the catfish strips in the crumbs, making sure that they are evenly coated.

Heat the canola oil in a large saucepan over medium-high heat. When the oil begins to swirl, drop in one piece of catfish. It should sizzle and be enveloped in bubbles as it fries. If you find that the oil is not hot enough, use that first piece as a tester. When it is cooking at a good rate, gently add a few more pieces. When they are golden brown, use a spatula or slotted spoon to gently transfer them to a baking sheet lined with paper towels and place them in the oven to stay warm. Repeat the process until all the fish pieces have been fried. Serve immediately with the sauce in a bowl on the side.

Serves 4

Mackerel Melt

Mackerel is very similar to tuna in flavor, so I thought to try this substitution one day and loved the results. Serve with a salad for a light lunch or with Pecan Quinoa Pilaf (page 243) and Sautéed Greens with Orange, Anchovy, and Red Onion (page 80) for an easy dinner.

Two 7-ounce cans smoked mackerel

1/4 cup mayonnaise

Pinch of celery salt

4 slices whole-grain bread

4 ounces white Cheddar cheese, thinly sliced

Preheat oven to 400 degrees.

Open the cans, drain the mackerel, and flake it with a fork in a medium bowl. Mix in thc mayonnaise and celery salt. Evenly divide the fish among the slices of bread and cover with the cheese. Place on a baking sheet and bake until the cheese is melted and the mackerel is warmed through, about 8 minutes.

Makes 4 open-faced sandwiches

Spaghetti with Mackerel Sauce

This is a take on the classic Italian dish of *tonnato*—or tuna—sauce, which I first encountered as a topping for a veal cutlet. Here I use canned smoked mackerel and olives to create a bright and substantial sauce for a simple pasta dish. I also like this with canned pink salmon, but I think the mackerel gives the best results. The residual heat of the pasta will gently cook the egg in the sauce and cause it to thicken around the pasta.

1 pound spaghetti

Salt

One 7-ounce can smoked mackerel, drained

1/2 cup pitted green olives, with or without pimientos, rinsed

1 large egg yolk

Juice of 1/2 lemon

1 cup extra-virgin olive oil

2 tablespoons chopped fresh flat-leaf parsley

Cook the pasta in boiling salted water until al dente, following package directions.

While the pasta is cooking, combine the mackerel, olives, egg yolk, and lemon juice in a food processor. When the mixture is reduced to a fine purée, with the machine running, add the olive oil in a slow, steady stream. Season to taste with salt.

Drain the pasta, return it to the pot, add the mackerel sauce, and toss until well coated. Serve immediately, sprinkled with chopped parsley.

Serves 4

Smoked Salmon and Goat Cheese Sandwich

This sandwich was one of the first things I put on the menu when I became a chef. It sold ridiculously well, and it was a challenge to keep up with making the smoked salmon as it took a day for us to thaw the fish, two days to cure and dry it, and yet another day to smoke it. It seemed that we always had salmon everywhere in various stages of preparation. Fortunately, you can buy your salmon already smoked—there are a number of great brands at markets. This sandwich can be made with both hot and cold smoked fish, however I prefer the cold for its luscious texture. I buy smoked Alaskan salmon, specifically, smoked sockeye, when it's available.

Once you've got your fish, this takes as long to make as a ham and cheese sandwich. The combination of goat cheese and salmon is a surprising twist. You can present this as a canapé. Just place a piece of salmon on a toast point and top it with a little bit of the mayonnaise mix.

4 soft sandwich buns

4 ounces fresh goat cheese

3 tablespoons mayonnaise

Handful arugula leaves

8 ounces smoked Alaskan salmon

Sliced ripe tomato or Sun-dried Tomato Pesto (page 267)

Salt

It's best to toast the buns in the oven, warming them all the way through. This creates a good contrast in temperatures and adds another level of interest. Mix the goat cheese with the mayonnaise, whisking to make it smooth. Spread the mixture on the toasted bread and place a few leaves of arugula on next. Layer on a few slices of the smoked salmon, then top with a tomato slice. If you can't find great tomatoes, don't use any (a tasteless tomato will only detract from the sandwich) or spread a little Sun-dried Tomato Pesto over the salmon. Season the tomato with salt to taste, and eat, eat, eat!

Makes 4 sandwiches

Pink Salmon Cakes with Dill and Mustard

This has become a weeknight favorite at our house. The cakes are inexpensive and easy to put together. Add a side dish, and you have dinner for four.

Two 7- to 8-ounce cans pink salmon

Salt

2 tablespoons mayonnaise

2 teaspoons whole-grain mustard

Pinch of ground mace

1/4 cup panko (Japanese-style bread crumbs) or fine dried bread crumbs

1 tablespoon chopped fresh dill

2 tablespoons butter

Lemon wedges

Preheat the oven to 400 degrees.

Drain the salmon. Flake the fish into a bowl, being careful to remove any small bones or skin that may be mixed in. Season with salt and add the mayonnaise, mustard, mace, bread crumbs, and dill. Mix gently with your fingers until it is well combined. Form into four even patties about 1 inch thick and allow to sit for about 5 minutes to allow the bread crumbs to absorb the flavor.

In a large sauté pan over medium-high heat, heat the butter until foaming. Add the salmon cakes and cook until they begin to turn golden on the edges, about 5 minutes. Don't touch them while they're browning. Once the edges have browned, transfer the pan to the oven and bake for 5 minutes to heat through. Flip the cakes onto plates and serve with lemon wedges.

Serves 4

Sardine and Capered Egg Salad Sandwiches

I remember my grandfather eating sardine sandwiches when I was young. They always struck me as a little odd. He would put lettuce, mayonnaise, and a can's worth of sardines between two slices of Wonder Bread; it made him happy as a clam . . . so to speak. Here I have added a few of what my grandfather might have considered "gourmet" touches (caper and egg) to make for some really good eating.

4 large eggs

2 tablespoons capers

2 tablespoons mayonnaise

4 soft sandwich rolls

Two 6-ounce cans sardines (any type—I like smoked boneless-skinless for this), drained

1 bunch scallions, thinly sliced

1 large ripe tomato, thinly sliced

Salt

Preheat the broiler if using to toast the sandwich rolls.

Place the eggs in a small saucepan and cover with cold water. Bring to a boil and cook for 4 minutes; drain. Allow to cool slightly, then peel. Place the eggs in a bowl with the capers and mayonnaise and mash with a fork to make a chunky mixture.

Slice the sandwich rolls in half and toast under the broiler or in a toaster oven till golden brown. Spread the egg mixture on one side of each roll, then evenly divide the sardine fillets among the sandwiches. Sprinkle with the scallions and top with tomato slices. Lightly season the tomatoes with salt.

Makes 4 sandwiches

Tilapia with Ginger Glaze

In cookbooks on New England cookery I often see recipes that call for coating seafood in mayonnaise and then broiling it. That always struck me as old-fashioned, until I tried it—for so little effort, you reap great taste results. Here I combine the mayonnaise with ginger, garlic, and soy for an Asian twist. Try this dish with spinach salad dressed with orange juice and olive oil, or Roasted Brussels Sprouts and Red Onions (page 163).

2 tablespoons mayonnaise

1 tablespoon soy sauce

Juice of 1 lemon

One 1-inch knob fresh ginger, peeled and finely grated

2 cloves garlic, finely grated

1/2 bunch scallions, thinly sliced

Four 5-ounce tilapia fillets

Preheat the broiler.

For the glaze, combine the mayonnaise, soy sauce, lemon juice, ginger, garlic, and scallions in a medium bowl and whisk to combine.

Add the tilapia fillets to the glaze and toss to coat with the mixture. Place the fillets on a baking sheet and spoon any remaining glaze over them. Broil for about 6 minutes. The mayonnaise will brown slightly and form a light crust on the fish. Remove and serve immediately.

Serves 4

Dijon- and Peach-crusted Tilapia

Tilapia is not always the most interesting fish to eat, so it does well paired with big flavors. Here, the spice of the mustard and the sweetness of the peach balance beautifully to accentuate the flaky, meaty texture of the fillet. Topped with breadcrumbs or panko, the combination makes a simple breading that you can try with just about any type of fish. Sablefish and halibut would also be good choices. Serve with Garlic-Yogurt Mashed Potatoes (page 87) or Sautéed Greens with Orange, Anchovy, and Red Onion (page 80).

2 tablespoons Dijon mustard

1 tablespoon peach jelly (not too chunky, or you will end up with uneven breading)

Four 5-ounce tilapia fillets

1 cup fine dried bread crumbs or panko (Japanese-style bread crumbs)

Extra-virgin olive oil

Preheat the broiler.

Combine the mustard and jelly and mix well. Brush the mixture over the fillets, then sprinkle with the bread crumbs, gently pressing them to make sure they adhere.

Place the breaded fillets on a baking sheet and drizzle with a little olive oil. Broil until the breading is crisp and golden brown, about 7 minutes. If the fish is not yet cooked through, turn off the broiler and allow the fish to sit in the oven to continue cooking for a minute or two.

Serves 4

Spinach- and Parmesan-crusted Tilapia

This recipe is a little different, in that the crust is as thick as the fish. It is a tasty way to make vegetables an integral part of the meal. I use frozen spinach here.

1 1/2 cups frozen chopped spinach, thawed and squeezed to extract any excess moisture

1/2 cup fine dried bread crumbs or panko (Japanese-style bread crumbs)

2 tablespoons freshly grated Parmesan cheese

2 tablespoons butter

1/2 tablespoon canola oil

Four 5-ounce tilapia fillets

Preheat the broiler.

Place the spinach, bread crumbs, Parmesan, and butter in a food processor. Pulse until the mixture forms a paste, about 30 seconds. Brush a baking pan with the canola oil and lay the fillets in it in a single layer. Evenly divide the topping among the fillets and pat it down to create an even layer. Broil until the topping looks golden brown and crispy and the fillets are cooked through, about 9 minutes.

Serves 4

Trout with Almond Potatoes and Lemon Salsa

The sharp, almost bracing taste of this lemon salsa makes this dish special. If I am grilling, I'll brown thin slices of lemon over a low flame until they are deeply caramelized and smoky, then chop them finely for the salsa. It's key that the potatoes are well seasoned and highly flavored. Bland potatoes will make the lemon stand out too much, and the dish will be out of balance. I use almond extract in the cooking water for the potatoes. Although this is a bit unusual, you will be surprised by how well it works with their creamy texture.

2 pounds red potatoes, cut into 1/2-inch dice

1 teaspoon almond extract

Salt

1 large lemon

1/4 cup extra-virgin olive oil

2 cloves garlic, finely grated

Leaves from 1/2 bunch fresh flat-leaf parsley (about 2 cups loosely packed) finely chopped

3 tablespoons Chunky Almond Oil (page 262)

Four 5-ounce trout fillets

For the potatoes, place them in a saucepan just large enough to hold them. Barely cover with cold water, add the almond extract, and season generously with salt. Bring to a boil, then reduce the heat to a simmer and cook until the potatoes yield when pierced with a knife, about another minute. Drain.

For the salsa, slice the lemon very thinly, discarding the thick-skinned end pieces. Cut the slices into as fine a dice as you can manage, reserving as much of the juice as you can. (This will be a little messy.) In a small sauté pan, heat the olive oil over high heat. When the oil begins to swirl, add the lemon bits, juice and all. Cook over high heat until the lemon juice evaporates and the bits have begun to soften, about 3 minutes. Add the garlic and toss to combine. Cook for another 30 seconds, then remove from the heat. Add the parsley and toss to combine. Set aside at room temperature; the salsa will keep for up to a few hours.

Preheat the broiler.

Strain the oil from the almond slices. Set the almond pieces aside and put the oil into a large ovenproof heavy-bottomed sauté pan. Heat over high heat, then add the potatoes in a single layer. Cook until they begin to brown, about 3 minutes. Add the almond slices, about 2 tablespoons, and lay the trout fillets over the potatoes, skin side up. Place the pan under the broiler and broil the potatoes until the skin is crisped and the flesh is cooked throughout, about 6 minutes.

Spoon the salsa over the fillets and serve immediately.

Serves 4

Linguine with Mussels, Pine Nuts, and Orange

This dish combines the great flavor of mussels with the ease of pasta. Mussels are inexpensive and provide some of the best eating around. The orange adds an interesting touch. This is definitely a dinner-party-worthy recipe.

3 pounds mussels, scrubbed and debearded (discard any that won't close)

1 cup white wine

1 pound linguine

Salt

1 tablespoon extra-virgin olive oil

2 cloves garlic, sliced

1 cup pine nuts

Juice and grated zest of 1 orange

Leaves from 1/2 bunch fresh flat-leaf parsley (about 2 cups loosely packed)

In a large pot, add the mussels and wine. Cover and bring to a simmer. Once the mussels have opened, about 7 minutes, strain them and reserve the liquid. (Discard any mussels that haven't opened by this time.) Allow the liquid to sit so that any sand falls to the bottom; then pour off the sand-free broth and set aside.

Cook the linguine in boiling salted water as per the instructions on the package.

While the pasta is cooking, heat the olive oil in a large sauté pan over medium heat. Add the garlic and pine nuts and cook, stirring occasionally, until the garlic just begins to brown. Add the orange juice and 2 cups of the mussel cooking broth. Bring to a simmer and season to taste with salt.

When the pasta is cooked about 90 percent of the way through (about 5 minutes less than the time recommended for al dente on the package), drain and add it to the sauté pan. Bring to a simmer and continue to cook for 5 minutes. The sauce should reduce to a consistency that coats the pasta, with a small amount in the bottom of the pan.

Remove from the heat and add the orange zest, the parsley, and the mussels. Season again with salt and toss to combine. Serve immediately.

Serves 4

Mussels Saint-Ex

This was the favorite dish on my first menu as head chef at a restaurant named Café Saint-Ex. It is a highly spiced way to make mussels, and it is a bit of a departure for those who might be used to mussels steamed with white wine and herbs. While it has bold flavor, it's a mellow and balanced combination, well suited to the briny sweetness of the shellfish.

1/2 cup canola oil

1 shallot, peeled

4 cloves garlic, peeled

1 tablespoon sweet smoked paprika

2 teaspoons ground coriander

2 teaspoons ground fennel seeds (page 9)

4 pounds mussels, scrubbed, debearded, and patted dry (discard any that won't close)

3/4 cup white wine

Salt

3 tablespoons butter

4 ounces dried Spanish chorizo, thinly sliced

Toasted bread

In a blender, combine the canola oil, shallot, garlic, and spices. Purée until you have a fine paste with no lumps.

In a large pot, sauté the spice mixture over high heat. When it has changed color and the aroma is no longer strong with the smell of raw shallot, add the mussels and allow to sit without tossing. After a few minutes, the mussels on the bottom will begin to open. As soon as this happens, add the wine and season to taste with salt. Cover the pan and allow the mussels to steam open.

When the mussels have opened, uncover the pot and add the butter and chorizo. Reduce the heat to medium, cook until the butter is incorporated, then toss to coat the mussels in the sauce. Discard any mussels that haven't opened by this point. Divide the mussels among 4 shallow bowls and serve with the toasted bread.

Serves 4 as a main course or a hearty appetizer

Mussels with Mustard and Scallions

This is another dish that I came up with when filming a piece with Anderson Cooper's team in my kitchen. They wanted some action shots, and I just happened to have a couple pounds of mussels in the fridge. It worked perfectly because it really proved that sustainable seafood can make for an easy meal that comes together in five minutes. I also like the way that mussels slow down a meal and encourage your family to spend time together. This is wonderful served with Spinach Salad with Warm Apple and Pistachio Dressing (page 240).

1/4 cup extra-virgin olive oil

3 cloves garlic, crushed with the back of a knife

4 pounds mussels, scrubbed and debearded (discard any that won't close)

1 1/2 cups white wine

1/4 cup whole-grain mustard

Salt

1 bunch scallions, sliced

1 loaf crusty baguette, sliced and toasted

Heat the olive oil in a large pot over high heat. Add the garlic and cook until it begins to brown. Add the mussels and wait a few minutes until you begin to see some of the shells open. Add the wine and mustard and season the liquid with salt. Cover the pot and cook for 4 minutes. Toss once to allow all the shells to open. If any are not open, cover and cook for another few minutes before removing the pan from the heat. Discard any mussels that haven't opened at this point. Add the scallions and toss to combine. Divide the mussels and steaming liquid among 4 shallow bowls and serve with toasted bread.

Serves 4 as a main course

Braised Greens with Anchovy Pestata

I learned this technique from the incredible Lidia Bastianich when I was fortunate enough to cook an inauguration dinner with her in D.C. She made a purée of all the aromatics for a dish, then used that as the flavor foundation. In this way, the texture of the main ingredient, in the case of this recipe, the greens, becomes the focal point. It's a brilliant technique, and I think it works particularly well in long-simmering dishes.

4 oil-packed anchovy fillets

1 small carrot, peeled and roughly chopped

4 cloves garlic, peeled

1/2 small onion, peeled

2 strips bacon, roughly chopped

2 pounds sturdy greens, such as kale or collards, washed thoroughly, heavy stems removed, and cut into 2-inch-wide ribbons

1 cup water

Salt

Put the anchovies, carrot, garlic, onion, and bacon in a food processor and pulse until smooth.

Place the purée in a large pot over low heat. When the fat in the bacon begins to render, increase the heat to medium and cook until the purée starts to brown slightly. Add the greens and toss to combine. Add the water and season lightly with salt. Cover and continue to cook until the greens are fully cooked, about 20 minutes.

Serves 4 as a side dish

Spinach Salad with Warm Apple and Pistachio Dressing

This is a wonderful accompaniment for mussels, poached whole salmon, or a meaty fillet like cobia. It also goes nicely with simply spiced and baked Arctic char fillets.

2 tablespoons butter

2 apples, preferably Gala or Honeycrisp, peeled, cored, and diced

2 cloves garlic, sliced

1 cup shelled unsalted pistachios, toasted (page 15)

Juice of 1 lemon

1 tablespoon water

Salt

1 1/2 pounds spinach leaves, heavy stems removed, washed thoroughly

Freshly ground black pepper

For the dressing, in a large sauté pan over high heat, heat the butter until it foams. Add the apples and garlic and cook without stirring until the apples begin to caramelize, about 4 minutes. Add the pistachios and toss to combine. Add the lemon juice and water and season to taste with salt. Reduce the heat to medium and simmer until the liquid is a thick glaze, about 5 minutes. Taste for seasoning and add more salt if necessary. Remove the pan from the heat.

Add the spinach leaves to the pan and toss with the warm dressing. Divide the salad among 4 plates and garnish with a few cracks of fresh black pepper.

Serves 4 as a side dish

Broccoli with Anchovy Vinaigrette

This just might be my favorite dish ever. Broiled broccoli is so good because it takes on a char and slight crunch that will surprise most people. This vinaigrette usually makes its way into my dinners a couple of times a week. I especially like it with vegetables such as fennel or endive. A batch of it will last up to a week in the fridge, but keep it tightly covered or everything in your fridge will taste like it. If anchovies aren't your thing, or for a change of pace, you can substitute a dollop of Caper Yogurt (page 189) for the vinaigrette.

2 heads broccoli

Salt

1/2 cup extra-virgin olive oil

4 salt-packed anchovies (page 24) or 8 oil-packed anchovy fillets

1 teaspoon cider vinegar

Juice of 1 lemon

1 small shallot, peeled

6 cloves garlic, blanched (page 244)

Preheat the broiler.

Cut the florets from the broccoli stalks, reserving the stems for another use. In a large pot of heavily salted boiling water, blanch the florets until they are soft, about 4 minutes. Drain and arrange in one layer on a baking sheet. Brush with a little of the olive oil and broil until the florets are darkly charred and crunchy, about 10 minutes.

For the vinaigrette, put the anchovies, vinegar, lemon juice, shallot, and garlic in a blender. Pulse to begin to purée, then, with the machine running, add the remaining olive oil in a slow, steady stream. Purée until very smooth.

Transfer the broccoli to a platter or serving bowl and drizzle with the vinaigrette. This dish is great served hot or at room temperature.

Serves 4 as a side dish or appetizer

Split Pea Purée

I like using split peas as a side dish because they're an incredibly cheap and easy way to add nutrition and bulk to a meal. In this preparation, the peas essentially mash themselves as they cook. Any leftovers can be turned into soup by adding a few cups of water to the purée as it reheats. You can also experiment with the flavorings. Try adding fennel seeds and dried lavender buds for a Mediterranean spin, or caraway seeds for a more Eastern European take.

2 cups dried split peas, rinsed and picked over

2 tablespoons butter

1 sprig fresh rosemary

4 cups water

Salt

Combine the peas, butter, rosemary, and water in a small pot. Bring to a simmer, cover, and let cook until the peas are soft, about 20 minutes.

Once they are done, remove the rosemary sprig and use a fork to whisk the mushy peas into a thick purée. Season to taste with salt.

Serves 4 as a side dish

Pecan Quinoa Pilaf

A complete protein (meaning it contains nutritionally significant quantities of the essential amino acids our bodies require), quinoa is a superfood. It is also inexpensive and delicious. I make big batches of this (leaving out the onion) and eat the leftovers for breakfast, with maple syrup and milk added.

2 cups quinoa

1 small onion, finely diced

2 tablespoons butter

1 cup pecan pieces

3 cups cold water

Salt

Rinse the quinoa in a colander for 3 minutes under cold running water and set aside. In a large saucepan over medium heat, sauté the onion in the butter until translucent. Add the quinoa and toast in the butter for a few minutes, until the grains start to change color. Add the pecans and water. Season with salt and bring to a boil. Reduce the heat to a simmer and cook until all of the water has been absorbed, about 20 minutes. The grains should be uncoiled and tender to the bite. Fluff the quinoa with a fork, taste for seasoning, and adjust if necessary.

Serves 4 as a side dish

Techniques

When I cook (and prep), there are several methods that I fall back on time and time again. I also do things a little differently in a number of cases. Here I discuss my favorite methods and how I have tailored them to seafood cookery.

Blanching Garlic Garlic is legendary for its delicious flavor but lingering aftereffects. Blanching it first will give you all the lovely aroma and flavor, minus the bitter indigestibility that can accompany it. After just a few turns in the boiling water, the cloves lose their bite and become soft, sweet, and nutty and develop a flowery aromatic quality. Plus you can avoid the need for breath mints later.

To blanch garlic, start with freshly peeled cloves that are free of spots or bruises. Place them in a pan and cover them with cold water. Bring the water to a boil, cook for about a minute, then strain the garlic. Cover it again with cold water and repeat the process. In all, you will need to do this three times, the third time adding a pinch of salt to the water.

Once the cloves have been blanched, they will keep covered in the fridge for just a couple days, so don't make too much. You can slice and sauté the cloves just as you would normally, but note that they will cook faster. Also, these cloves make a nice addition to salad dressing or to sauces that traditionally include raw garlic, such as pesto or salsa.

Butter Basting I am not a big fan of sautéing fish. I think you are far more apt to ruin a piece of fish if you are trying to brown it. Plus, frankly, I don't much care for the flavor of deeply caramelized fish flesh—or the way this method spews vaporized seafood smell all over your house (probably the number-one complaint I hear about cooking fish at home). I think that broiling and grilling offer more control. However, if you must sauté, I suggest you employ the method described below. The fillet is first slightly crisped on one side, then treated to a constant basting of browned butter solids flavored with thyme. The solids are deposited on the fish skin, and the added fat serves to protect the rest of the fillet and keep it super moist.

1. Sear your fillet, skin side down, over medium heat in a non-stick sauté pan.

2. Once it begins to crisp and the fillet is cooked about halfway through, flip the fillet over and add about 1 tablespoon butter for two fillets.

3. Turn the heat up to high and allow the butter to foam and begin to brown. Once this stage is reached, lay thyme sprigs on top of the fillets, turn the heat back to medium, and, using a deep spoon, baste the fillets with the butter. Continue until the fish is cooked through, about 5 minutes.

A Rant Against Stirring

People do too much stirring. The purpose of cooking is to apply heat to ingredients. If you are busy tossing the pan and stirring the whole time, then the food doesn't come in contact with the heat. If you are cooking at the right temperature, then burning is not going to be an issue, as the cooking will be gentle and moderated. Stirring just complicates the process and detracts from the purpose. So have patience and confidence—turn the heat down and put away the spoon.

Poaching

Poaching is a low-heat technique that I don't frequently employ, but when I do, I always marvel at the results. I am a big fan of cooking slowly, and poaching is a great way to do that. I don't allow the temperature of the poaching liquid to exceed 170 degrees, which helps retain maximum flavor and moisture.

Poaching also adds great flavor because of the cooking liquid. For Sablefish in Aromatic Broth with Pistachio, Celery, Shallots, and Orange (page 70), the broth, which contains pistachios, orange, and other aromatics, eventually becomes part of the final dish. So let your imagination go a little wild. I like to use ingredients that might not otherwise show up in a seafood dish, such as red wine. In poaching you have a chance to add a dash of creative flavor without necessarily complicating a dish.

Broiling

Broiling is a technique I use often. If I can't get outside to grill, then the broiler it is. While it certainly does not impart the flavor of live-fire cooking, it delivers some pretty spectacular results. Often I start a recipe on the stovetop, then throw the whole dish under the broiler to meld the flavors (see Arctic Char with Blistered Cherry Tomatoes in Garlic Olive Oil, page 103). Or sometimes I place the dish under the broiler and then turn off the heat, in effect searing and then slow roasting as the oven temperature gradually falls (see Barramundi with Creamed Zucchini and Sorrel-Tarragon-Carrot Salad, page 104). In general, though, broiling is a very convenient and quick way to cook while maintaining control over the heat.

Low-Heat Versus High-Heat Cooking

One of the things I like to tell my cooks is that the flash and drama you see on food TV does not make good cooking. One of the most impressive images you're likely to see is a chef dipping a sauté pan into the flames of a burner on high heat, the contents of the pan flaring up to eyebrow-singeing effect. While this looks great on camera, it's very likely not going to taste great. The fact is, the two biggest mistakes home cooks make are (1) not using enough salt and (2) using too much heat.

Cooking is, scientifically, the application of heat to a food product. Rarely is it a good idea to apply super-hot heat to food. When searing or broiling, yes, but at all other times, slow, consistent heat produces the best results. The reason has to do with proteins. When protein cells are exposed to heat, they seize up, expelling moisture. The more slowly heat is applied, the more gentle the process is, which results in greater retention of moisture and, consequently, of the food's natural flavor—moisture is a vehicle for flavor. If a fillet of fish is moist and tender, with all its natural flavor, then you need to use less fat to compensate for the moisture lost in the cooking. And you, the cook, get a lot more leeway in terms of cooking time. If you are cooking at 500 degrees, the time between underdone and overdone might be a matter of seconds. At a lower heat, such as 300 degrees, you might have a window of a few minutes or even more before the seafood is overdone (meaning dried out). So going slowly makes things taste better, makes them easier to cook, and can decrease the need for added fat to make up for lost moisture.

With some types of seafood, such as salmon, I like to use very low temperatures. Try brushing a salmon fillet with a little olive oil and cooking it at 225 degrees. It will take about 30 to 40 minutes, but the results are stunning. The flesh does not change color or exude the milky fat that courses through it (it's those protein cells, seizing up at a higher temperature, that squeeze the fat out). The salmon has a meaty, delicate texture rather than the dry, flaky results yielded by high heat. The only downside to cooking like this is that the fish never gets super hot to the tongue, so try to pair it with an accompaniment that will retain some heat on the plate, such as a risotto or mashed potatoes.

Filleting a Fish

Filleting fish is a hard thing to learn how to do. Our modern world does not give us much opportunity to interact with whole fish, as the convenience of fillets cannot be matched. However, when purchasing seafood most of the quality factors that help me make a decision are lost when the fish is presented as fillet. A whole fish cannot deceive a buyer.

Eyes, scales, shimmer, and smell don't lie. So if you can buy whole fish, then you are normally getting better quality–that is if you don't mangle the fish while cutting the fillets. I taught fish butchery for the Culinary Institute as a fellow and, believe me, it is a hard thing to pick up. **But the best advice is this; be brave.** You know what a fish fillet looks like. Visualize the fillet and then use the knife to make it happen.

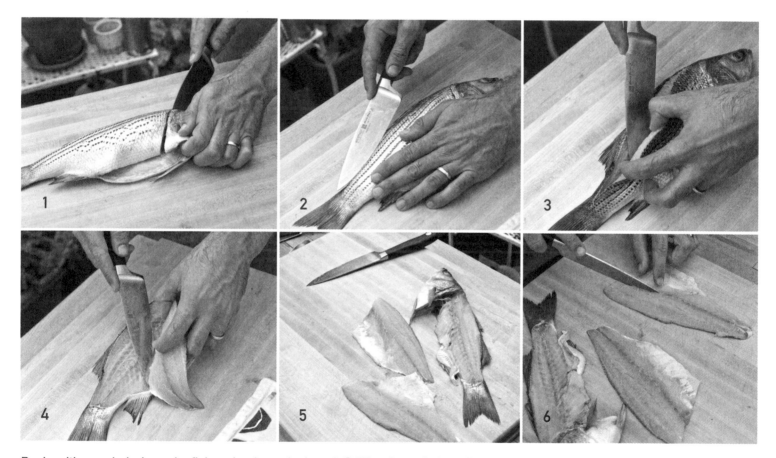

Begin with a scaled, clean, dry fish and a clean, dry board. ❶ Slice through the collar of the fish down to the spine just behind the gill plate. ❷ Beginning at the tail, slice the fillet from the bone by drawing the knife from tail to head along the spine. ❸ When you reach the spine, gently peel back the fillet and continue to follow the contour of the bone. ❹ Cut through the tail section to release the fillet. Follow the contour of the rib cage to separate the belly flap of the fillet from the bone. Do this by angling the knife down so that it glances off the bones. ❺ Repeat the process on the other side of the fish for the second fillet. I find that it is easiest to cut fish while standing at a corner of a table so that you can easily change your angle on the fish just by taking a step to the side. ❻ Remove the tiny pin-bones from each fillet by cutting v-shaped notches in the fillet, each about an inch long. Feel with your fingers to see how far the bones go into the fillet, then cut neatly on either side of them just down to the skin but not through it. Lift out the small pieces of flesh with the bones and discard. Trim off any discolored belly meat and you are ready to cook.

Fish Skin—On or Off?

I know that most restaurants serve seafood with the skin on, but I don't care for its flavor much. It certainly helps to protect the moisture in the fillet and to keep the fillet intact during cooking, just as it protects the fish swimming in the sea. By all means, buy your fillets with the skin on (or leave it on when filleting a fish yourself), but you can simply remove the skin when you are done cooking the fish. In most cases, it takes just a fork and not a lot of effort to peel it off.

Cutting Raw Fish

Slicing fish fillets for raw preparations is an art form in and of itself. Sushi chefs spend years mastering just this one basic skill. So, with no disrespect, here is a 3-step process for cutting raw fish at home. The purpose is to yield thin slices which have some texture but also melt in the mouth with great flavor.

❶ Begin at the head of the fillet cutting toward the tail. Positioning the base of the knife against the flesh at an angle, slowly draw the knife through the flesh, slicing off a thin sheet in one smooth stroke.

❷ When you reach the skin, gently turn the knife towards the tail to separate the thin sheet of flesh from the rest of the fillet.

❸ Continue slicing down the fillet until you no longer can cut usable pieces.

Brining

Brining seafood is commonly only done in the preservation of fillets (think of smoked trout). But it can have the same effect on seafood as on chicken, namely preserving moisture and enhancing flavor. Care must be taken, though, because a piece of fish that has been brined incorrectly is a ruined piece of seafood before it even hits the pan.

During cooking, protein cells contract and lose a significant amount of their natural water. Giving a protein a turn in a brining solution beforehand counteracts this. The cells throughout the meat are able to absorb more water because they have been gently salted by osmosis. The salt attracts more water into the cells, which have broken down slightly during this process. This in turn leads to better moisture retention in the final product. Add too much salt or let the protein sit in the brine for too long, and the flavor becomes affected. This is fine if your goal is to cure the fish (in smoking, for example), but not if your purpose is to preserve moisture. A piece of seafood should remain in the brine for only a few minutes to up to 40 minutes, depending on the density of the seafood.

Try an experiment. The next time you cook seafood in a simple way, such as baking a salmon fillet, brine half of the portions only. Then prepare the meal as you would normally. Taste the difference for yourself.

When I brine, I like to use a mixture of kosher salt, sugar, and water. I think the sugar helps to balance the flavor of the salt and enables you to use less sodium to achieve the same results; like salt, sugar is hygroscopic, meaning it attracts water.

Fish Brine

This recipe is enough to cover four 5-ounce fillets. If you need more (say, for a whole fish), simply double or triple the recipe. Also, I use kosher salt for everything, especially brining, as it gives a consistent measurement of sodium.

2 cups cold water	Mix the ingredients together and stir until dissolved. Pour over seafood to cover completely. Cover with plastic wrap and refrigerate for the amount of time indicated in the chart below.
1 tablespoon kosher salt	
1 tablespoon sugar	After brining, remove the seafood from the brine and pat dry before proceeding with your recipe.

Brining Times for Seafood

Please don't experiment with these brining times. Seafood is far more delicate than a turkey or pork tenderloin, and 10 minutes too long in brine could ruin it. Brining should take place in the refrigerator, and the seafood should always be patted dry afterward. Please note: The one fish I don't brine is tuna, as the process changes its color and texture. Also, brining is only done for fish that will be cooked, not seafood intended to be served raw or cooked rare.

Fish	Brine Time
Trout, shrimp, sardine fillets, and other delicate seafood	15 minutes
Bass, barramundi, sablefish, and other flaky fillets	20 minutes
Halibut, mahimahi, Pacific cod, and other flaky, meaty fillets	30 minutes
Salmon, mackerel, Arctic char, and other meaty, full-flavored fish	35 minutes
Amberjack, cobia, and other dense, steaklike fish	40 minutes

Grilling

Grilling, in my opinion, is the finest way to cook anything. I love it because the cooking method itself becomes an ingredient in the final dish. Smoke is one of the best base flavors to work with: I have largely been able to remove stock and cream from my cooking because I have replaced them with smoke. In every restaurant I have helmed, a wood-fired grill has been the centerpiece of the kitchen.

Smoke, like salt, enhances foods' natural flavors. The key to grilling, and why I love it so much, is that it allows for the gradual and purposeful application of heat. **I always set up my grill so that I have a hot spot—useful for searing and charring—but then I use the grill more as an oven to deliver slow, flavorful heat.** I prefer a live-heat grill, meaning either wood- or charcoal-fired. This is where the flavor comes from. Not to be dismissive, but to me food cooked directly over gas tastes flat, although I acknowledge its convenience.

To prepare a grill, follow these steps.

For a charcoal grill set all the coals in one small area of the grill and light. Burn them down to red embers.

Because seafood is a much more delicate protein than poultry or meat, moving it once it hits the grill can be risky. My answer to this is not to move the seafood, but to move the grate it is cooking on. **Because your fire is located in a confined area, you can control the amount of heat that you apply to foods by changing their placement.** My usual method is to oil the grill grate and lay a fish fillet directly over the hot fire. When the skin begins to char and develop some color, I rotate the entire grill grate, repositioning the seafood (still skin-side down) away from the fire, then put other ingredients over the hot spot. I cover the grill to capture the heat, which creates an ovenlike atmosphere. The seafood slowly roasts in the covered grill with all the flavor of the charcoal but without being subjected to the drying effects of direct heat.

For a gas grill the same effect can be created by having two adjacent zones on the grill. Heat one area to the lowest heat possible, and turn the adjoining one to high. Sear the seafood over the hottest part of the grill. After a few minutes turn those burners off. Use the heat of the ones next to or around the seafood. Cover the grill and allow to roast slowly. This way you don't have to move grates around.

❶ Burn coals down to embers. ❷ Place fish skin side down directly over the fire. ❸ Once the skin begins to color, rotate the grill grate so the fish is away from the fire. ❹ You now have the hot spot to cook other ingredients. ❺ Cover the grill to capture the heat and slowly roast the fillets.

Smoking

I love to smoke fish as much as I love to grill it. It is a great way to extend the use of seafood as you only need small portions because of the highly accentuated flavor. And I think I really love it because it allows me to participate in the process. **All too often seafood cooking is a matter of finding the freshest product, then cooking it simply and quickly.** Most chefs will tell you that their favorite things to cook are the long, slow braises of tough cuts of meat. We love the layering of flavors and the slow development of a dish that is better than the sum of its parts. This is why I like smoking fish. It is the one opportunity we have as cooks to layer and develop flavors with seafood.

There are two ways of smoking, hot smoke and cold smoke. Hot-smoked fish is first brined and then smoked with some heat, cooking the fillets slowly as the wood coals smolder with flavor. This method is common to the Pacific salmon smokehouses, and I consider it to be a West Coast style. Salmon smoked this way will break into flakes. The fish is preserved once smoked and will keep for many months.

Cold smoking is more of a flavoring process. The fillets are usually dry cured with a rub of salt, sugar, and spices. They are then washed and smoked in a controlled environment where the smoke is applied without heat, so the fillets absorb the flavor but do not cook. This is what I consider the East Coast or European style; it's the way lox is prepared. Unlike hot-smoked salmon, lox-style has a silken, buttery texture and is sliced super thin on a bias. Most cold-smoked products are eaten raw, but in some cases the smoking is used as a flavoring for fish that will later be cooked (see Smoked Catfish with Fig and Citrus Salsa, page 147).

Get the Right Kind of Smoke

For smoking at home, all you need is a grill. I have seen people craft smokers from old refrigerators, dryers, and whatever else might be lying around the yard. **But for me, in my urban neighborhood, a Weber grill does just fine.** Preparing the smoke is the hardest part of the process. Smoke can have very different personalities depending on the heat of the fire, the type of wood chips used, and the way in which they're added to the fire. Too much heat, and the smoke is black and acrid—this will be the flavor of the fish as well. Too little heat, and you don't really get any flavor. You might have noticed that when you add wood to a fire, at first there is the super-sweet-smelling gray or white smoke, which billows out in cloudlike plumes. Then it turns to black smoke as the chemical reactions really begin. And then it settles into a fast-rising smoke that accompanies the coals. Think about these different stages. The soft, white, billowy beautiful smoke smells of an aged cabin in the woods, with its rustic aroma of romantic fires and warmth on a chilly autumn night. Got that? Then there is the smell of burning tires. Which do you want on your food?

Think about these different stages. The soft, white, billowy beautiful smoke smells of an aged cabin in the woods, with its rustic aroma of romantic fires and warmth on a chilly autumn night.

Keep the Skin On

When hot or cold smoking, be sure to use skin-on fillets. It helps to keep the flesh intact during the process. Remove it before serving.

Hot Smoking For the piece of fish involved, the hot-smoking process begins with a bath in a brine. The brines used for smoking are a lot stronger, in terms of their salt content, and are used for a different purpose than the brine on page 249. The science works the same, but in this case, the purpose is to heavily salt the fillet so that bacterial growth will be stunted after the smoking is completed. This allows for the much longer shelf life of smoked fish. If you were to cook the fillet using normal cooking methods after a turn in brines this strong, the fish would be dry and salty. But the purpose here is to cook the fish very slowly, adding a lot of additional layers of flavor through the smoke and creating an inherently dry product, which you will use in small quantities.

Hot-smoked King Salmon, ready to serve

Fish Brine 1 for Hot Smoking

This classic brine gives a nice mellow flavor to fish such as trout, char, and salmon. Brush the fillets with Pernod or Sambuca before smoking them.

4 cups water	Bring 1 cup of the water to a boil. Add the salt, sugar, lemon juice, onion powder, and garlic powder and stir to dissolve. Stir in the remaining 3 cups water and chill before use.
1/2 cup salt	
1/4 cup sugar	
1/3 cup fresh lemon juice	Pour the chilled brine over fish fillets to cover them completely. Cover with plastic wrap and refrigerate. (See chart on page 256 for brine times.)
1 tablespoon onion powder	
1 teaspoon garlic powder	After brining, remove the fish from the liquid and pat dry.

Makes enough to cover 2 to 4 pounds of fillets, depending on the container used

Fish Brine 2 for Hot Smoking

This is a woodsier flavor combination and is great for sturgeon, strongly flavored salmon such as sockeye or king, and silken sablefish. Give the fillets a finishing rub of Bourbon before smoking.

4 cups water	Simmer 1 cup of the water with the remaining ingredients for 5 minutes. Stir in the remaining 3 cups water and chill before use.
1/3 cup salt	
1/3 cup firmly packed brown sugar	
1/3 cup orange juice	Pour the chilled brine over the fish fillets to cover them completely. Cover with plastic wrap and refrigerate. (See chart on page 256 for brine times.)
10 juniper berries	
1 teaspoon ground fennel seeds (page 9)	After brining, remove the fish from the liquid and pat dry.
2 tablespoons Pernod or other anise-flavored liqueur	*Makes enough to cover 2 to 4 pounds of fillets, depending on the container used*
1 cinnamon stick	

Fish Brine 3 for Hot Smoking

This is a very well-flavored brine, so use neutral-flavored vodka as the finishing rub before smoking. Use this with salmon if you prefer an intense flavor. It works well with most fish, but be aware that the flavor will overpower a more delicate fillet.

4 cups water	Simmer 1 cup of the water with the remaining ingredients for 5 minutes. Stir in the remaining 3 cups water. Chill before use.
1/3 cup salt	
1/4 cup firmly packed brown sugar	
2 tablespoons brewed coffee	Pour the chilled brine over the fish fillets to cover them completely. Cover with plastic wrap and refrigerate. (See chart on page 256 for brine times.)
1 tablespoon molasses	
6 cloves	After brining, remove the fish from the brine and pat dry.
1 tablespoon Worcestershire sauce	*Makes enough to cover 2 to 4 pounds of fillets, depending on the container used*

Brine Times for Hot Smoking

All brining should take place in the refrigerator. Pat fish dry after brining.

Weight of Seafood to be Smoked	Brining Time
1/2 pound	30 minutes
Up to 1 pound	1 1/2 hours
Up to 2 pounds	3 hours
Up to 3 pounds	4 hours
Up to 4 pounds	6 hours
Up to 5 pounds	8 hours

For hot-smoke preparations, if you are using a charcoal grill, it is best to start a small fire just as you would do for grilling (page 250) and allow it to burn down to embers. Place about 1/2 cup of soaked wood chips on the embers and give them a few minutes to catch fire and then smolder; this is the flavor you want. Place the fillets on the grate as far away from the smoke source as possible and cover the grill. You should be able to create an environment where the temperature is just about 275 degrees. This is, in effect, the same process as grilling, except that you want to prolong the cooking for as long as possible so that you coax the maximum flavor from the fire. For larger fillets or whole fish, you will need to stoke the fire with another application of wood chips and possibly another few pieces of charcoal.

❶ When the fire is burned down to embers add a handful of wood chips and place the fillets on the grill away from the fire. ❷ Cover the grill to capture the smoke and slowly cook the fillets.

If using a gas grill, adjust the burner of one side of the grill to create an ovenlike temperature of 275 degrees inside the closed grill. Place the fish as far away from the heat as possible, laying it on a wire rack or directly on the grates. Place an aluminum foil package filled with soaked wood chips over the burner; allow it to smolder and fill the grill with smoke. Most types of fish need to smoke for about 45 minutes to get the best flavor, so refresh the wood chips if need be.

Make the Smoke Stick!

Salt is hygroscopic, meaning that it draws moisture to it. As the water is drawn out from within the fillets, water-soluble proteins come with it. When you dry the fillets after washing the salt off (for cold smoking or hot smoking), these proteins, now deposited on the surface of the fillet, dry into a sticky film that will trap the flavors of the smoke very effectively. The technical term for this film is a "pellicle." Whether you are hot or cold smoking, you want to encourage the development of the pellicle as much as possible, and one way to do that is to brush the fillets with a little booze. It may sound counterintuitive, but alcohol hastens the evaporation of moisture on the fillets, actually speeding up the process. Plus, it is another opportunity to add great flavor. I like to use Sambuca or Pernod, which impart a licorice-like quality to the fillets. I use Bourbon or Scotch when a stronger flavor is called for.

Cold Smoking Cold smoking is much the same process as hot smoking, but you want to eliminate any heat at all. The pigments in smoke do not activate in a cooler fire, so you will not see as much of the woodsy brown caramel color that is a hallmark of commercial smokers. The key to the texture of the final product is that the fat never renders in the fillet, so all that luxurious moisture and meltingly tender goodness stays locked in the flesh.

Also, instead of brining, the cold smoking process begins with a curing period. Cure mixes, or rubs, draw moisture out of the fillets, leaving you with a silken texture in preparations like this where the fat content remains largely intact. Dry-cure times are different for each type of fish, depending on the texture, but there is a general rule you can apply with good results. For fillets, lightly coat a baking sheet with a thin layer of the rub mix. Place the fillet, skin side down, on the sheet and then lightly pack on the remaining mix. It should be about 1/2 inch thick all over the fillet. If you are using a whole salmon fillet where the belly is thinner, then use less rub on the thin parts and increase the amount over the thickest parts. Cure the fish for 1 hour in the refrigerator for every pound that the fish weighed when whole. So if a salmon weighed 10 pounds when it was caught, you should cure the fillets for 10 hours.

When the allotted cure time is up, gently wash the fish under cold running water, making sure to remove all the salt. Pat it dry, place it on a baking sheet, and brush it with 1 tablespoon of the spirit of your choice. Allow the fillets to air-dry, uncovered, in the fridge for a few hours and as long as overnight. Then follow the instructions on the next page for cold smoking.

If you are buying fillets instead of a whole fish, use this math to estimate the original whole weight:

(Weight of 1 fillet x 2) / 0.7

Seventy percent is an approximate yield of fillet to whole fish, so while it might not always be biologically correct, the formula will give fine results for this purpose.

Dry Rub 1 for Cold Smoking

This simple dry rub accentuates the true flavors of the fish. Great for sablefish and Arctic char.

2 1/2 cups kosher salt	Combine all the ingredients and mix well.
1/2 cup sugar	
1 tablespoon ground mace	*Makes about 3 cups*
1 tablespoon ground coriander	
Pinch cayenne pepper	
1 tablespoon onion powder	

Dry Rub 2 for Cold Smoking

This rub works well for king salmon and other more robustly flavored fish, as the orange zest really adds zip.

2 1/2 cups kosher salt	Combine all the ingredients and mix well.
1/2 cup firmly packed brown sugar	
1 tablespoon ground juniper berries	*Makes about 3 1/4 cups*
1 tablespoon ground fennel seeds	
1 teaspoon garlic powder	
Finely grated zest of 1 orange	

Dry Rub 3 for Cold Smoking

This is a full-flavored dry rub that works equally well for meaty flavored fish like mackerel, and as a seasoning for roasted pork.

2 1/2 cups kosher salt	Combine all the ingredients and mix well.
1/2 cup sugar	
1 tablespoon freshly ground black pepper	*Makes about 3 1/4 cups*
1 tablespoon ground fennel seeds (page 9)	
Pinch of cayenne pepper	
1 tablespoon ground celery seeds	
1 tablespoon ground oregano	
1 tablespoon sweet smoked paprika	

As mentioned, the goal in cold smoking is to smoke the fish without exposing it to heat. The way to do this is to make a bed of ice wrapped in tin foil and lay the fillets on top of it so they have a cool microclimate on their side of the grill. Also, you want to have a less-intense heat source, so a small charcoal fire of only a few briquettes is adequate. You will need to continuously add a few water-soaked wood chips or a handful of moistened sawdust in order to fuel the smoke, which should be a soft, billowy white. The fillets should smoke for as long as you can keep them cold, 45 minutes to 1 hour.

To accomplish this on a gas grill, lay the fish on the ice on one side of the grill. On the opposite side, place a few wood chips in an aluminum foil bowl over the gas and turn the heat on low. After a few minutes, the wood chips will begin to smolder and produce a billowy smoke. Cover the grill to trap the smoke. Make sure the fish stays cool; smoke it for 45 minutes to 1 hour, adding more wood chips if necessary.

Place the fillets in a piece of foil and place over a bed of ice cubes wrapped in foil. This keeps the fish from cooking while it absorbs the smoke flavor.

Pantry Recipes

The following recipes are flavoring staples that I make use of regularly in my cooking. It is wonderfully convenient to have them at the ready when you want a flavor punch.

Seafood Spice Mix 1

This is a great multiuse spice mixture that goes with just about any well-flavored seafood, such as sardines, salmon, or mahimahi. Use it just as you would salt—sprinkle it on the fillets a few minutes before cooking them. Also try it with grilled vegetables or on steaks and chicken. Its flavor profile is a lot like Old Bay Seasoning, which reminds me of my childhood.

2 tablespoons kosher salt

1 teaspoon ground celery seeds

1 teaspoon ground coriander

1 teaspoon ground mace

1 teaspoon sweet smoked paprika

Combine all the ingredients and mix well. Keeps up to 3 months.

Makes about 2 tablespoons

Seafood Spice Mix 2

This spice mix is a nice choice if you'll be serving red wine with dinner. It's best used with well-flavored seafood, such as mackerel, sardines, and salmon. Sprinkle it over the seafood a few minutes before cooking it.

2 tablespoons kosher salt

1 teaspoon ground juniper berries

1 teaspoon ground fennel seeds (page 9)

Pinch of cayenne pepper

1 teaspoon ground thyme

Combine all the ingredients and mix well. Keeps up to 3 months.

Makes 3 tablespoons

Grill Salt

When I season food that is meant for the grill, I use a mixture of salt and sugar. The sugar is not meant to sweeten; rather, as it melts over the heat of the fire it gets sticky and helps the smoke to adhere to the fillet. The sugar also helps to balance the salt and to enhance the natural flavors of the fish.

For salmon and steaklike fish such as amberjack, I use brown sugar as it brings a smoky flavor of its own. For all other types of fish, I use regular granulated sugar.

3/4 cup kosher salt

1/4 cup granulated sugar or brown sugar

Mix together and use as you would normally use plain salt, seasoning just a few minutes before placing on the grill.

Makes 1 cup

Orange and Rosemary Grill Salt

Orange and rosemary are an aromatic match made in heaven. The floral tones of the orange really enliven the woodsy rosemary. Sprinkle this over foods just as you would salt a few minutes before they are to be cooked. I particularly like it with meaty, dense fish such as amberjack or cobia, and it also tastes great with fresh sardines cooked under the broiler.

1 small sprig fresh rosemary

2 tablespoons kosher salt

Grated zest of 1 orange

1 tablespoon sugar

Mix a few of the rosemary leaves with the salt in a microwave-safe container. Microwave for 20 seconds; this will release the flavorful oils in the rosemary. Add the orange zest and sugar. Cover, and shake vigorously for a minute to mix all of the flavors. Remove the rosemary leaves. Use immediately, or cover and refrigerate up to 1 week.

Makes about 3 tablespoons

Smoked Paprika and Cinnamon Spice Mix

The cinnamon adds an unexpected depth of flavor when sprinkled over vegetables before roasting them. I particularly like this with salmon and char, but it works nicely with any well-flavored fish.

1 tablespoon sweet smoked paprika

1 tablespoon kosher salt

1 teaspoon sugar

1 teaspoon ground cinnamon

Mix all the ingredients and toss to combine. This will keep for a couple of weeks.

Makes about 3 tablespoons

Chile Oil

Much like acid and salt, a little bit of heat can integrate a dish and enhance the flavors already present without changing the flavor make-up. But it can be difficult to deliver heat that isn't overpowering. Adding fresh chiles is a gamble, as you are never quite sure how powerful the heat will be. So try this infused oil. It carries moderate heat and a pleasant color. Use it as a final embellishment, adding it just before serving.

1 cup extra-virgin olive oil

1 teaspoon sweet smoked paprika

1 teaspoon red chile flakes

Gently heat the olive oil in a small saucepan over low heat until it begins to shimmer. Add the paprika and the chile flakes and remove the pan from the heat. Allow the oil to cool to room temperature, then stir and pour it into an airtight storage container. Allow the mixture to sit at room temperature for 24 hours, then taste it. If it has a nice amount of heat for your taste, strain and discard the solids and reserve the oil for use; otherwise, let it sit for another few hours to develop more heat. The oil will keep, tightly covered, at room temperature for a couple of weeks.

Makes 1 cup

Citrus Oil

This is another great trick to have up your sleeve. Sure, you can squeeze a lemon wedge over a piece of fish and drizzle on some olive oil, but the flavor you get from infusing lemon zest in the oil is much softer and mellower. This oil actually combines both lemon and orange zest, resulting in a nice balance of flavors.

1 cup extra-virgin olive oil

Zest of 1 lemon, removed in strips with a peeler

Zest of 1 orange, removed in strips with a peeler

1 bay leaf

Heat the olive oil in a medium saucepan over low heat. When the oil begins to ripple from the heat, remove it from the burner and add the zests and bay leaf. Let steep overnight.

Pour the oil into an airtight container, discarding the solids. The oil will keep, tightly covered, in the refrigerator for up to 2 weeks. The oil will congeal, so remove it from the fridge 20 minutes before you intend to use it.

Makes 1 cup

Chunky Almond Oil

This is one of the most-used staples in my kitchen. It is a great sauce, as well as a flavor foundation for other dishes. I use it in a number of recipes in this book, so try a batch. It can be mixed with a little lemon juice or aged sherry vinegar to make a ten-second vinaigrette.

1 cup extra-virgin olive oil

7 ounces sliced almonds

Combine the ingredients in a small saucepan and cook over low heat, stirring occasionally, until the almonds are an even golden brown. Allow the mixture to cool to room temperature and store it in the fridge, tightly covered. The oil will congeal, so remove it from the fridge 20 minutes before you intend to use it. Will keep up to 2 weeks.

Makes about 2 cups

Anchovy Butter for Seafood

Because of the parsley, this butter has a brilliant green color, which looks beautiful melted over the top of a fish fillet. It pairs wonderfully with anything cooked on the grill—salmon, mahimahi, sardines, or, my favorite, steak. It can also be melted into freshly cooked pasta for a super-easy side dish or quick lunch, used as a garnish for soup, or spread on toasted bread. This will keep, tightly covered, in the refrigerator for up to 2 weeks and in the freezer for 4 months.

8 tablespoons butter, softened

Leaves from 1 bunch fresh flat-leaf parsley, finely chopped

Juice of 1/2 lemon

2 salt-packed (page 24) or 4 oil-packed anchovies, finely chopped

Combine all the ingredients in a small bowl and stir to mix well.

Makes about 1 cup

Anchovy Butter for Vegetables

Toss this butter with boiled, grilled, or roasted vegetables. I first had this combination when I was working in a fast-casual restaurant chain as a waiter. It was in New York City, and the clientele there was pretty tough. Food was sent back all the time for one ridiculous reason or another. But dishes with this butter never, ever got sent back. Here is my interpretation.

2 tablespoons butter, softened

2 tablespoons mayonnaise

1 tablespoon grated Parmesan cheese

1 tablespoon Worcestershire sauce

2 salt-packed anchovies (page 24) or 4 oil-packed fillets, minced into a paste

Combine all the ingredients in a small bowl and mix well. This will keep for a few days, tightly covered, in the refrigerator.

Anchovy-Dill Marinade

This is a great marinade for nearly everything, especially lamb roasts. Try it on whole fish to be cooked on the grill. For whole fish, an overnight bath in it is best, but for fillets just a few hours is enough to get great flavor. The salt and sugar act as a brine and a seasoning, so there's no need to brine the fish separately.

1 cup canola oil

1 tablespoon brown sugar

1 tablespoon kosher salt

4 cloves garlic, peeled

Fronds from 1 bunch fresh dill

4 oil-packed anchovy fillets or 2 salt-packed (see page 24) anchovies

Put all the ingredients in a blender and purée until smooth. If cooking a whole fish, score the skin with shallow incisions and pour on the marinade. Roll to coat the fish and marinate overnight. Any remaining unused marinade can be used as a room-temperature sauce if thinned out with a few teaspoons olive oil.

Blackberry-Shallot Salsa

This is a quick-to-make sauce with big impact. I love the slight crunch the shallots lend to the sweet-sour blackberries. The dash of Tabasco offers a little bite, but if you enjoy your heat, use more or add a little chopped serrano chile to the sauce.

This salsa pairs wonderfully with simple broiled fish and nearly anything that comes off the grill. Try it as a topping for grilled vegetables such as zucchini and squash or spoon it over chilled poached salmon fillets for a delicious and colorful entrée.

1 pint blackberries, sliced in half

1 shallot, finely diced

1 tablespoon chopped fresh flat-leaf parsley

Dash of Tabasco sauce

2 tablespoons extra-virgin olive oil

Pinch of kosher salt

Fresh lemon juice or honey as needed

Mix the berries, shallot, parsley, Tabasco, olive oil, and salt together in a medium bowl and gently toss to combine. Try to do this without breaking up the blackberries too much or they will turn mushy. If the blackberries are particularly sweet, add a few drops of lemon juice. If the berries are a little sour for your taste, add a few drops of honey to balance the acid. This can be made up to a half day in advance.

Makes 2 cups

Sautéed Grape and Herb Sauce

Grapes are amazing, and it seems a little silly that we don't use them for much other than table snacks. When cooking with grapes, though, they need to be paired with a savory flavor to balance their sweetness. Here I use the bite of onion and garlic. I like the taste of butter in this recipe, but olive oil is an equally good base. This sauce is a great way to dress up catfish or tilapia, and it goes really well with broiled farm-raised barramundi.

2 tablespoons butter

1 small onion, finely diced

2 cloves garlic, thinly sliced

1 cup seedless grapes, cut in half

Juice of 1 lemon

Salt

1 tablespoon chopped fresh tarragon

1 tablespoon chopped fresh flat-leaf parsley

Heat a medium sauté pan over medium heat with the butter. Add the onion and garlic once the butter has melted and cook, without stirring, until the onion is translucent, about 3 minutes. Add the grapes, toss, and cook, without stirring, until they begin to release their juices, about 3 minutes. Add the lemon juice and season to taste with salt. Toss to combine and remove from the heat.

Add the chopped herbs and continue to mix. As you toss the pan, the grapes will slightly crush and the sauce will come together. But don't mix too much or too vigorously or the sauce will turn to mush. Serve immediately.

Makes about 2 cups

Basil Pesto

I adore basil pesto and in the late summer when basil is at its best and most plentiful, you should make a stash to freeze in small quantities so you can pull it out in the darker months for an instant lift to your meal. Look around your farmers' market for a good deal on bulk quantities of basil in the late summer. The pesto freezes well and keeps up to a year. Try freezing it in ice cube trays; once frozen, wrap each block individually in plastic wrap and store them in freezer bags until ready to use. If a quart seems like too much, this recipe can easily be cut in half.

There are many different kinds of nuts you can use for this sauce; I prefer walnuts because they are usually cheaper than other types, plus they have a nice sweetness that matches well with the basil. I don't use cheese in my pesto because I prefer the clean, bright flavor of the basil to shine through. While I like pesto with cheese for pasta, I do not think that it is necessary for use with seafood.

1 cup walnuts

3 cloves garlic, peeled

1 cup canola oil (or, for added flavor, 3/4 cup canola oil plus 1/4 cup extra-virgin olive oil)

Leaves from 1 pound fresh basil

Salt

Spread the walnuts in a single layer on a baking sheet and toast in a preheated 350-degree oven for about 8 minutes. The nuts should be highly aromatic, and the thin skin should be flaky. Allow them to cool. Place the nuts in a colander and toss well with your hand to remove the flaky skin—it's bitter and doesn't purée very well, so it is best to get rid of as much as possible. After a minute of tossing, remove the cleaned nuts from the colander and discard any skin that has sloughed off.

Place the garlic and oil in a blender. Purée until the garlic is incorporated. (The garlic in the oil will help keep the basil bright green.) Add the basil leaves and purée until the mixture becomes a smooth paste. Add the walnuts and pulse until the pesto is thick. Season to taste with salt.

When storing the pesto, cover it with plastic wrap pressed against the surface of the sauce to keep air from getting to it (this will prevent discoloration). Pesto will keep refrigerated for 1 week and frozen up to 9 months.

Makes about 1 quart

266

Sun-dried Tomato Pesto

In general, I'm not a fan of dried tomatoes, but top-quality sun-dried tomatoes are the exception. This sauce is a great vehicle for them; they're simmered in wine and given a touch of sweetness by the addition of shallots. This will keep for up to a week in the fridge and for months in the freezer. It goes well with just about anything, except cereal.

When buying sun-dried tomatoes, look for a rich brick-red color; also the tomatoes should appear moist, with no discoloration. Oil packed sun-dried tomatoes also are fine for this use.

15 sun-dried tomatoes, chopped

1 shallot, finely diced

1 cup Sauvignon Blanc or Riesling

1 cup water

2 tablespoons butter

Salt

In a small saucepan, mix all the ingredients, except the salt, and place them over medium heat. Allow to simmer until most of the liquid has been absorbed, about 30 minutes.

Transfer the mixture to a food processor and pulse until it is reduced to a paste. Season to taste with salt and use at room temperature. If you make the pesto ahead of time, gently reheat it to take the chill off before serving.

Makes about 1 1/2 cups

Date and Citrus Dressing

This versatile sauce has some texture—the chewiness of the dates, as well as a little crunch from the shallots. It tastes best if it can sit for an hour after being made, but it is also great right from the get-go. Use it as a topping for broiled catfish, trout, or char, as well as a thick, slow-grilled steak—just double the lemon juice to offset the extra fat in the meat. It can be used as a salad dressing too. If you like heat, replace half the olive oil with Chile Oil (page 262).

10 dates, pitted and finely chopped

1 small shallot, finely diced

1 tablespoon whole-grain mustard

1 tablespoon chopped fresh tarragon

1 tablespoon chopped fresh flat-leaf parsley

2 tablespoons extra-virgin olive oil

Juice of 1 lemon

Salt

Combine all the ingredients in a small bowl and mix with a fork to combine. Try not to crush the dates too much, but a little mashing helps to bind the sauce. This will keep, tightly covered, in the fridge for up to 2 days before the shallots begin to spoil the flavor.

Makes about 1 cup

Pistachio Piccata

This sauce is like a chunky nut pesto. It only gets better as it sits, and is best a day after it is made. The orange and garlic are perfect flavors to accompany the sweet, rich pistachios. This is a great sauce to accompany a simply baked or grilled fillet. It is also wonderful over vegetables or mixed into a rice or quinoa pilaf.

1 cup shelled unsalted roasted pistachios

Finely grated zest of 1 orange

2 cloves garlic, finely minced or grated on a Microplane

1 tablespoon extra-virgin olive oil

Salt

Roughly chop the pistachios by crushing them with the flat blade of a knife, then chopping as you would parsley. Or you can pulse the nuts in a food processor. In a small bowl, combine the chopped pistachios with the orange zest, garlic, and olive oil, and season to taste with salt. Mix to combine and allow to sit for at least 20 minutes at room temperature. Keeps up to a week in an airtight container in the refrigerator. Serve at room temperature.

Makes about 1 cup

Minted Herb Salad

This garnish salad adds texture and a nice fresh burst of flavor that cleanses the palate. At the restaurants, I put a tuft of it alongside most entrées. If you like, double the recipe to make a side salad. This is a great way to make constant use of an herb garden—the mix can be whatever herbs you have growing.

1 small shallot, very thinly sliced

Leaves from 1/4 bunch fresh flat-leaf parsley (about 1 cup loose packed)

Leaves from 1/4 bunch fresh mint (about 1 cup loose packed)

1 tablespoon extra-virgin olive oil

Salt

Put the shallot, herbs, and olive oil in a medium bowl and toss to combine well. Season to taste with salt.

Makes 4 garnish servings

Parsley-Garlic Finishing Mix

Instead of just putting on the ubiquitous garnish of "*poof*-parsley-*bam*-confetti," chop the parsley with garlic. This brightens the fresh taste of the parsley and adds a touch of highlighting flavor to the dish. It's a particularly nice finish for roasted vegetables and other long-cooked items that might have lost their fresh taste.

1 clove garlic

Leaves from 1/4 bunch fresh flat-leaf parsley (about 1 cup loose packed)

Grated zest of 1 lemon

Finely mince the garlic, then begin to chop the parsley on top of it. The parsley will absorb the aroma of the garlic and the bits of garlic will disappear into the parsley. Finish by mixing in the lemon zest. Make this as close to serving time as possible, but, if necessary, you can prepare it a few hours ahead.

Makes about 1/4 cup

Aromatic Kitchen Potpourri

I'm regularly asked how to get rid of the smell in the house after cooking fish. My answer? Buy fresher fish. Good-quality seafood will not stink up anything, so if your house smells after cooking have a talk with your fishmonger. But this culinary potpourri is a lovely way to add a pleasant aroma to the whole experience of cooking. And if you are entertaining in the kitchen, this is an easy way to get people in the seaside mood.

1 handful rockweed (a type of seaweed that any fishmonger who sells lobster will be able to get for you if you ask in advance)

1 lemon, sliced

1 orange, sliced

2 cinnamon sticks or 1 teaspoon ground cinnamon

Put all the ingredients in a large pot and cover with cold water. Bring to a simmer, then reduce heat to low and allow to slowly steep. It will give off a wonderful fresh scent. Discard when you are done.

Sustainable Sources and Web Links

Australis Barramundi
www.thebetterfish.com
Learn all about the sustainable aquaculture practices pioneered by this company in western Massachusetts.

CleanFish Alliance
www.cleanfish.com
My good friend and mentor Tim O'Shea cofounded this visionary company that markets and distributes the finest responsibly sourced seafood from producers all over the world. While they do not sell direct to customers as of this writing, their brands are available throughout the country in grocery stores and restaurants.

EcoFish
www.ecofish.com
Henry and Lisa Lovejoy are pioneers in the world of sustainable seafood. They have been bringing great-quality products to the table for years, and they have a broad and diverse array of offerings for the home cook.

Rappahannock River Oysters and Hog Island Oysters
www.rroysters.com
www.hogislandoysters.com
While oysters are available everywhere, I think that these guys are heroes. I love what they are about, I love their oysters, and I think that they are some of the best people I have ever met. So do yourself, and the oceans, a favor and order from them.

Sunburst Trout Farms
www.sunbursttrout.com
The Eason family has been working this operation for generations, and they really know what they are doing. Sunburst has been lauded as a leader in sustainable aquaculture and their product is second to none. They have a wide variety of product available to the home cook, and the quality is equal to the very best restaurant-quality trout.

Blue Ocean Institute
http://blueocean.org/seafood/seafood-guide
Cofounded by Carl Safina, this exceptional group uses science, art, and literature to inspire a closer bond with nature, especially the sea.

Monterey Bay Aquarium Seafood Watch
www.montereybayaquarium.org/cr/seafoodwatch.aspx
Check out this great resource for the latest information on sustainable seafood solutions.

Environmental Defense Fund
www.edf.org (see also www.KidsafeSeafood.com)
In addition to a lot of other great work, the EDF produces a great wallet guide to help consumers make smart choices about seafood with regard to mercury content.

Sustainable Sushi
www.sustainablesushi.net
My friend Casson Trenor is changing the way sushi is served. Check out his site detailing the damage that can be done and the opportunities sushi restaurants have to make a change.

Acknowledgments

With gratitude to Douglas Singer, and thanks to Kirsten Bierlein, Maggie Parcells, Joan Nathan, José Andrés, Katie Stoops, Robert Egger, Jeffre and Sandy Witherly, Josh Whigham, Melanie Franks, Jason Wood, Ris Lacoste, Todd and Ellen Gray, Mike Benson, John Snellgrove, Heather Roth, Carole Greenwood, and all the chefs with whom I have had the pleasure of working.

And to the best recipe taster ever, my beautiful wife, Carrie Anne.

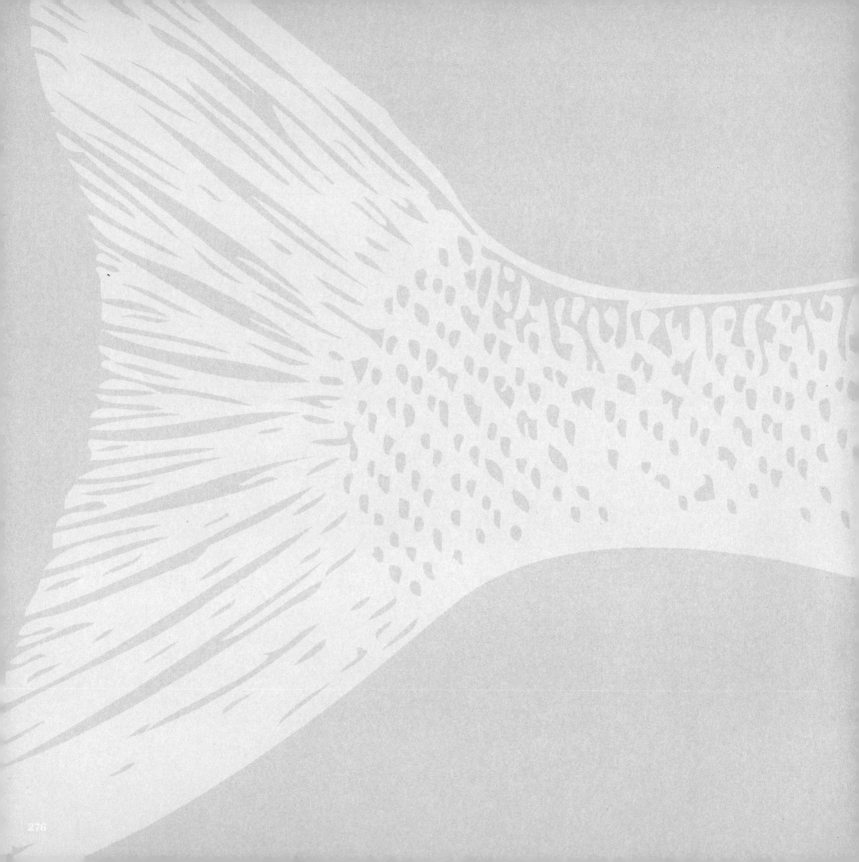